Lecture Notes in Computer Science 13268

More information about this series at https://link.springer.com/bookseries/558

Juliana Bowles · Giovanna Broccia ·
Roberto Pellungrini (Eds.)

From Data
to Models and Back

10th International Symposium, DataMod 2021
Virtual Event, December 6–7, 2021
Revised Selected Papers

Editors
Juliana Bowles 🆔
University of St Andrews
St Andrews, UK

Giovanna Broccia 🆔
ISTI-CNR
Pisa, Italy

Roberto Pellungrini 🆔
University of Pisa
Pisa, Italy

ISSN 0302-9743   ISSN 1611-3349 (electronic)
Lecture Notes in Computer Science
ISBN 978-3-031-16010-3   ISBN 978-3-031-16011-0 (eBook)
https://doi.org/10.1007/978-3-031-16011-0

This Springer imprint is published by the registered company Springer Nature Switzerland AG
The registered company address is: Gewerbestrasse 11, 6330 Cham, Switzerland

Preface

From Data to Models and Back (DataMod) is an annual, international symposium which aims to bring together practitioners, and researchers from academia, industry, and research institutions interested in the combined application of computational modeling methods with data-driven techniques from the areas of knowledge management, data mining, and machine learning. The present proceedings marks the 10th edition of the symposium.

Over the last decade, DataMod has covered a wide range of themes and topics. The modeling and analysis methodologies covered in the DataMod series include agent-based methodologies, automata-based methodologies, big data analytics, cellular automata, classification, clustering, segmentation and profiling, conformance analysis, constraint programming, data mining, differential equations, game theory, machine learning, membrane systems, network theory and analysis, ontologies, optimization modeling, petri nets, process calculi, process mining, rewriting systems, spatio-temporal data analysis/mining, statistical model checking, text mining, and topological data analysis.

The symposium welcomes applications of the above listed methodologies in a multitude of domains, such as biology, brain data and simulation, business process management, climate change, cybersecurity, ecology, education, environmental risk assessment and management, enterprise architectures, epidemiology, genetics and genomics, governance, hci and human behavior, open source software development and communities, pharmacology, resilience engineering, safety and security risk assessment, social good, social software engineering, social systems, sustainable development, threat modeling and analysis, urban ecology, smart cities, and smart lands.

Synergistic approaches may include

1. the use of modeling methods and notations in a knowledge management and discovery context, and
2. the development and use of common modeling and knowledge management/discovery frameworks to explore and understand complex systems from the application domains of interest.

This year, in its 10th edition, DataMod was held as a satellite event of the 19th International Conference on Software Engineering and Formal Methods (SEFM 2021). The symposium was held as a two-day fully virtual workshop, due to the COVID-19 pandemic. This enabled, however, the participation of a wider audience across several different time zones. All presentations and discussions were done online using the conference facilities provided and Zoom.

All contributions in the form of either regular papers (up to 18 pages) or short papers (up to 10 pages) were reviewed by three Program Committee members using a single blind peer-review process, and papers were evaluated on the basis of originality, contribution to the field, technical and presentation quality, and relevance to the symposium. EasyChair was used as an online system for both submission and review bidding and assignment. Before notifications were sent to authors, a few days were set aside for a discussion among Program Committee members to finalize the acceptance/rejection decisions.

All accepted presentations at the workshop were invited to submit a paper to be reviewed after the workshop and to be considered for the post-proceedings. From 11 submissions, this resulted in a total of 10 accepted papers, after further review from 12 experts and researchers in computer science and computational modeling.

DataMod 2021 had two invited speakers. The first invited presentation was given by Andrea Vandin on "Automated Statistical Analysis of Economic Agent-Based Models by Statistical Model Checking". The talk discussed recent work regarding a novel approach to the statistical analysis of simulation models and, especially, economical agent-based models (ABMs). In particular, Vandin presented MultiVeStA, a fully automated and model-agnostic toolkit that can be integrated with existing simulators to inspect simulations and perform counterfactual analysis. The second invited presentation was given by Antonio Cerone on "10 years of DataMod: Where to Go from Here". Cerone gave a detailed account on the ten years of activity of DataMod, summarized the scientific achievements of the symposium over the years, and addressed possible future developments for the symposium.

July 2022

Juliana Bowles
Giovanna Broccia
Roberto Pellungrini

Organization

Program Committee Chairs

Juliana Bowles	University of St Andrews, UK
Giovanna Broccia	ISTI-CNR, Italy
Roberto Pellungrini	University of Pisa, Italy

Steering Committee

Oana Andrei	University of Glasgow, UK
Antonio Cerone	Nazarbayev University, Kazakhstan
Vashti Galpin	University of Edinburgh, UK
Riccardo Guidotti	University of Pisa, Italy
Marijn Janssen	Delft University of Technology, The Netherlands
Stan Matwin	University of Ottawa, Canada
Paolo Milazzo	University of Pisa, Italy
Anna Monreale	University of Pisa, Italy
Mirco Nanni	ISTI-CNR, Italy

Program Committee

Oana Andrei	University of Glasgow, UK
Davide Basile	ISTI-CNR, Italy
Juliana Bowles	University of St Andrews, UK
Giovanna Broccia	ISTI-CNR, Italy
Marco Caminati	Lancaster University, UK
Vincenzo Ciancia	ISTI-CNR, Italy
Antonio Cerone	Nazarbayev University, Kazakhstan
Ricardo Czekster	Aston University, UK
Flavio Ferrarotti	SCCH, Austria
Vashti Galpin	University of Edinburgh, UK
Riccardo Guidotti	University of Pisa, Italy
Lars Kotthoff	University of Wyoming, USA
Giulio Masetti	ISTI-CNR, Italy
Sotiris Moschoyiannis	University of Surrey, UK
Paolo Milazzo	University of Pisa, Italy
Anna Monreale	University of Pisa, Italy
Reshma Munbodh	Brown University, USA

Mirco Nanni	ISTI-CNR, Italy
Lucia Nasti	GSSI, Italy
Roberto Pellungrini	University of Pisa, Italy
Paolo Zuliani	Newcastle University, UK

Contents

Invited Talks

MultiVeStA: Statistical Analysis of Economic Agent-Based Models by Statistical Model Checking

Andrea Vandin[1,2(✉)], Daniele Giachini[1], Francesco Lamperti[1,3], and Francesca Chiaromonte[1,4]

[1] Institute of Economics and EMbeDS, Sant'Anna School of Advanced Studies, Pisa, Italy
{a.vandin,d.giachini,f.lamperti,f.chiaromonte}@santannapisa.it
[2] DTU Technical University of Denmark, Lyngby, Denmark
[3] RFF-CMCC European Institute on Economics and the Environment, Milan, Italy
[4] Department of Statistics and Huck Institutes of the Life Sciences, Penn State University, State College, USA

Abstract. We overview our recent work on the statistical analysis of simulation models and, especially, economic agent-based models (ABMs). We present a redesign of MultiVeStA, a fully automated and model-agnostic toolkit that can be integrated with existing simulators to inspect simulations and perform counterfactual analysis. Our approach: (i) is easy-to-use by the modeler, (ii) improves reproducibility of results, (iii) optimizes running time given the modeler's machine, (iv) automatically chooses the number of required simulations and simulation steps to reach user-specified statistical confidence, and (v) automatically performs a variety of statistical tests. In particular, our framework is designed to distinguish the transient dynamics of the model from its steady-state behavior (if any), estimate properties of the model in both "phases", and provide indications on the ergodic (or non-ergodic) nature of the simulated processes – which, in turns allows one to gauge the reliability of a steady-state analysis. Estimates are equipped with statistical guarantees, allowing for robust comparisons across computational experiments. This allows us to obtain new insights from models from the literature, and to fix some erroneous conclusions on them.

Keywords: Agent-based models · Statistical model checking · Ergodicity analysis · Transient analysis · Warmup estimation · T-test and power

1 Extended Abstract

We propose a novel approach to the statistical analysis of economic agent-based models (ABMs). The analysis of ABMs is often constrained by problems of (i) computational time, (ii) correct construction of confidence bands, (iii) detection of model ergodicity, and (iv) identification of transient behaviour. All these

J. Bowles et al. (Eds.): DataMod 2021, LNCS 13268, pp. 3–6, 2022.
https://doi.org/10.1007/978-3-031-16011-0_1

issues are pivotal to the validity of a model, both when it is used for thought-experiments, and when it aims at delivering policy insights. Nevertheless, they are often overlooked [17] or solved informally without a commonly shared procedure [10].

We propose fast, easy-to-use, automated, and statistically rigorous procedures to address all these problems. We implement such procedures in Multi-VeStA, a model-agnostic statistical analyser which can be easily tool-chained with existing ABMs. Independently from the nature of the ABM at hand, the analyser performs simulations, distributing them in the cores of a machine or a network, computes statistical estimators, and implements the minimum number of simulations necessary to satisfy given conditions on confidence intervals.

The above-mentioned problems are not specific to the ABM context; they affect most simulation-based analysis approaches and were therefore tackled by many scientific communities in the past. In computer science, several automated procedures have been proposed to mitigate these problems. An example is the family of techniques known as statistical model checking (SMC) [1,18]. Roughly speaking, SMC can be seen as an automated Monte Carlo analysis guided by a property of interest given in an external property specification language. Here we focus on the statistical model checker MultiVeStA [11,16,20]. While previous versions of MultiVeStA have been successfully applied in a wide range of domains including, e.g., threat analysis models [4], highly-configurable systems [2,3,19], public transportation systems [9,11,12], robotic scenarios with planning capabilities [5,6], and crowd steering scenarios [15], it has never been employed for the analysis of ABMs. Here, we have redesigned and extended MultiVeStA to target analyses of interest for the ABM community (e.g. [13]). For example, we integrated a series of tests that allow for (i) counterfactual analysis, (ii) detection of ergodicity, and (iii) estimation of the transient period.

We demonstrate our approach in [20] using two ABMs from the literature. The first is a macro stock-flow consistent ABM from [8]. We first replicate the results from the original contribution, scaling the runtime analysis from 15 days to 15 h thanks to the automated parallelization of simulations. We also show how the statistical reliability of our approach allows us to perform meaningful counterfactual analysis.

The second ABM is a simple financial market model from [14]. This model has analytical solutions [7] which we use to assess the effectiveness of our approach. Contrarily to computational analyses reported in prior literature [14], which were biased by erroneous under-estimations of the transient period duration and of the process autocorrelation, we match the correct analytical results of the model.

In the near future, we plan to extend the number of tasks performed in an automated and user-friendly manner by our tool, e.g., including the identification of multiple stationary points. We also plan to use our tool for the analysis of other classical and novel ABMs.

The tool, models, and more information are available at: github.com/andrea-vandin/MultiVeStA/wiki.

References

1. Agha, G., Palmskog, K.: A survey of statistical model checking. ACM Trans. Model. Comp. Simul. **28**(1), 6:1–6:39 (2018)
2. ter Beek, M.H., Legay, A., Lafuente, A.L., Vandin, A.: A framework for quantitative modeling and analysis of highly (re) configurable systems. IEEE Trans. Softw. Eng. **46**(3), 321–345 (2020). http://orcid.org/10.1109/TSE.2018.2853726
3. ter Beek, M.H., Legay, A., Lluch-Lafuente, A., Vandin, A.: Quantitative analysis of probabilistic models of software product lines with statistical model checking. In: Proceedings 6th Workshop on Formal Methods and Analysis in SPL Engineering, FMSPLE@ETAPS 2015, London, UK, 11 April 2015, pp. 56–70 (2015). http://orcid.org/10.4204/EPTCS.182.5
4. ter Beek, M.H., Legay, A., Lluch-Lafuente, A., Vandin, A.: Quantitative security risk modeling and analysis with RisQFLAN. Comput. Secur. **109**, 102381 (2021). http://orcid.org/10.1016/j.cose.2021.102381
5. Belzner, L., De Nicola, R., Vandin, A., Wirsing, M.: Reasoning (on) service component ensembles in rewriting logic. In: Iida, S., Meseguer, J., Ogata, K. (eds.) Specification, Algebra, and Software. LNCS, vol. 8373, pp. 188–211. Springer, Heidelberg (2014). https://doi.org/10.1007/978-3-642-54624-2_10
6. Belzner, L., Hennicker, R., Wirsing, M.: OnPlan: a framework for simulation-based online planning. In: Braga, C., Ölveczky, P.C. (eds.) FACS 2015. LNCS, vol. 9539, pp. 1–30. Springer, Cham (2016). https://doi.org/10.1007/978-3-319-28934-2_1
7. Bottazzi, G., Giachini, D.: Far from the madding crowd: collective wisdom in prediction markets. Quant. Financ. **19**(9), 1461–1471 (2019)
8. Caiani, A., Godin, A., Caverzasi, E., Gallegati, M., Kinsella, S., Stiglitz, J.E.: Agent based-stock flow consistent macroeconomics: towards a benchmark model. J. Econ. Dyn. Control **69**, 375–408 (2016)
9. Ciancia, V., Latella, D., Massink, M., Paškauskas, R., Vandin, A.: A tool-chain for statistical spatio-temporal model checking of bike sharing systems. In: Margaria, T., Steffen, B. (eds.) ISoLA 2016. LNCS, vol. 9952, pp. 657–673. Springer, Cham (2016). https://doi.org/10.1007/978-3-319-47166-2_46
10. Fagiolo, G., Guerini, M., Lamperti, F., Moneta, A., Roventini, A.: Validation of agent-based models in economics and finance. In: Beisbart, C., Saam, N.J. (eds.) Computer Simulation Validation. SFMA, pp. 763–787. Springer, Cham (2019). https://doi.org/10.1007/978-3-319-70766-2_31
11. Gilmore, S., Reijsbergen, D., Vandin, A.: Transient and steady-state statistical analysis for discrete event simulators. In: Polikarpova, N., Schneider, S. (eds.) IFM 2017. LNCS, vol. 10510, pp. 145–160. Springer, Cham (2017). https://doi.org/10.1007/978-3-319-66845-1_10
12. Gilmore, S., Tribastone, M., Vandin, A.: An analysis pathway for the quantitative evaluation of public transport systems. In: Albert, E., Sekerinski, E. (eds.) IFM 2014. LNCS, vol. 8739, pp. 71–86. Springer, Cham (2014). https://doi.org/10.1007/978-3-319-10181-1_5
13. Grazzini, J.: Analysis of the emergent properties: stationarity and ergodicity. J. Artif. Soc. Soc. Simul. **15**(2), 7 (2012)
14. Kets, W., Pennock, D.M., Sethi, R., Shah, N.: Betting strategies, market selection, and the wisdom of crowds. In: Twenty-Eighth AAAI Conference on Artificial Intelligence (2014)

15. Pianini, D., Sebastio, S., Vandin, A.: Distributed statistical analysis of complex systems modeled through a chemical metaphor. In: International Conference on High Performance Computing and Simulation, HPCS 2014, Bologna, Italy, 21–25 July 2014, pp. 416–423 (2014). http://orcid.org/10.1109/HPCSim.2014.6903715

16. Sebastio, S., Vandin, A.: MultiVeStA: statistical model checking for discrete event simulators. In: 7th International Conference on Performance Evaluation Methodologies and Tools, ValueTools 2013, Torino, Italy, December 10–12(2013), pp. 310–315 (2013). http://orcid.org/10.4108/icst.valuetools.2013.254377

17. Secchi, D., Seri, R.: Controlling for false negatives in agent-based models: a review of power analysis in organizational research. Comput. Math. Organ. Theory. $23(1)$, 94–121 (2017). http://orcid.org/10.1007/s10588-016-9218-0

18. Sen, K., Viswanathan, M., Agha, G.: Statistical model checking of black-box probabilistic systems. In: Alur, R., Peled, D.A. (eds.) CAV 2004. LNCS, vol. 3114, pp. 202–215. Springer, Heidelberg (2004). https://doi.org/10.1007/978-3-540-27813-9_16

19. Vandin, A., ter Beek, M.H., Legay, A., Lluch Lafuente, A.: QFLan: a tool for the quantitative analysis of highly reconfigurable systems. In: Havelund, K., Peleska, J., Roscoe, B., de Vink, E. (eds.) FM 2018. LNCS, vol. 10951, pp. 329–337. Springer, Cham (2018). https://doi.org/10.1007/978-3-319-95582-7_19

20. Vandin, A., Giachini, D., Lamperti, F., Chiaromonte, F.: Automated and distributed statistical analysis of economic agent-based models. CoRR abs/2102.05405 (2021)

Ten Years of DataMod: The Synergy of Data-Driven and Model-Based Approaches

Antonio Cerone$^{(\boxtimes)}$ (iD)

Department of Computer Science, School of Engineering and Digital Sciences,
Nazarbayev University, Nur-Sultan, Kazakhstan
`antonio.cerone@nu.edu.kz`

Abstract. DataMod was founded in 2012 under the acronym of MoK-MaSD (Modelling and Knowledge Management for Sustainable Development). The original aim of the Symposium, established by the United Nations University, was to focus on modelling and analysing complex systems while using knowledge management strategies, technology and systems to address problems of sustainable development in various domain areas. The focus was soon expanded to generally addressing the complementarity of model-based and data-driven approaches and the synergetic efforts that can lead to the successful combination of these two approaches. Hence the new name of the Symposium: "From Data to Models and Back" and the new acronym, which have been used since 2016.

In this paper we will start from the origins and history of DataMod and will look into the community formed around the Symposium in order to identify some research areas that have been addressed during its first 10 years of life. In this perspective, we will try to understand to which extent the two components of the DataMod community managed to integrate and which synergies between data-driven and model-based approaches have emerged. We will also have a look at what is happening outside DataMod and we will finally discuss which research and collaboration challenges should be addressed by future editions of DataMod.

Keywords: Data-driven approached · Model-based approaches · Formal modelling · Machine learning · Process mining

1 Introduction

Although DataMod (the *International Symposium "From Data to Models and Back"*) was officially founded in 2012 under the acronym of MoKMaSD (*Modelling and Knowledge Management for Sustainable Development*), the ideas underlying the symposium developed during the previous years and found their first

Work partly funded by Project SEDS2020004 "Analysis of cognitive properties of interactive systems using model checking", Nazarbayev University, Kazakhstan (Award number: 240919FD3916).

J. Bowles et al. (Eds.): DataMod 2021, LNCS 13268, pp. 7–24, 2022.
https://doi.org/10.1007/978-3-031-16011-0_2

implementation in a special track on "Modelling for Sustainable Development" at the 9th International Conference on Software Engineering and Formal Methods (SEFM 2011). The keynote talk by Matteo Pedercini, Millennium institute, and the four accepted papers of this special track, which were included in the SEFM 2011 proceedings [7], ranged over a number of application domains: agroecosystems, policy analysis, energy consumptions, and knowledge transfer process. Such application domains were explored by using agent-based systems, system dynamics and formal methods.

This first effort, initiated through a collaboration between the International Institute for Software Technologies of the United Nations University (UNU-IIST), which was later renamed the United Nations University Institute in Macau[1], and the Millennium Institute[2], aimed at the use of mathematical/formal modelling approaches and had a strong focus on sustainable development as an umbrella for the pool of considered application domains, in line with the common objectives of the two organising institutions.

However, during the discussion at the Conference, it was recognised that mathematical/formal modelling was not enough to fully characterise the application domains addressed by the special track contributions. The large quantity and heterogeneous quality of the information involved in the modelling process could not be entirely mathematically/formally represented and manipulated, but required a multidisciplinary approach integrating a variety of knowledge management techniques. Following these considerations, it was then decided to start a symposium series with a larger scope than the one of the special track.

The rest of the paper is structured as follows. Sects. 2 and 3 go through the history of the Symposium, with Sect. 2 devoted to the MoKMaSD events (2012–2015) and Sect. 3 devoted to the DataMod events (2016–2020). Section 4 compares and discusses the approaches, extends our overview with important, synergetic work that has been carried out outside DataMod, and and explores research challenges in the context of the scope of DataMod. Finally, Sect. 5 suggests possible directions and initiatives in the ambits of the DataMod community and DataMod future events.

2   Building up an Interdisciplinary Community and Elaborating on Its Scope: MoKMaSD 2012–2015

MoKMaSD 2012, the first edition of the Symposium, was held on 2 October 2012 in Thessaloniki, Greece [23]. The aim of the symposium, as highlighted in a short position paper [22],

> was to bring together practitioners and researchers from academia, industry, government and non-government organisations to present research results and exchange experience, ideas, and solutions for modelling and analysing complex systems and using knowledge management strategies,

[1] https://cs.unu.edu.
[2] https://www.millennium-institute.org.

technology and systems in various domain areas, including economy, governance, health, biology, ecology, climate and poverty reduction, that address problems of sustainable development.

As a result of the discussion at the SEFM 2011 special track, it was decided that formal modelling could not be the exclusive focus of the new symposium. Instead, there was an explicit attempts to put together two distinct communities, the modelling community and the knowledge management community, with the initial objective of exchanging experiences, presenting ideas and solutions to each other and trying to explore possible ways of collaboration and integration of the approaches. This first edition of MoKMaSD comprised a reasonable balance of modelling and knowledge management contributions.

On the modelling side the focus was on ecosystems. Corrado Priami's invited talk [39] introduced LIME, a modelling interface featuring the intuitive modelling of plant-pollinator systems and their automatic translation into stochastic programming languages equipped with analysis support aiming at providing an assessment of the functional dynamics of ecosystems. Barbuti et al. [6] presented a formalism, inspired by concepts of membrane computing and spatiality dynamics of cellular automata, for modelling population dynamics. Bernardo and D'Alessandro [8] analysed different policies for sustainability in the energy sector, through a dynamic simulation model aiming at evaluating the dynamics of different strategies in terms of their economic impact.

On the knowledge management side there were two contributions. Bolisani et al. [11] analysed the knowledge exchange that occurs in online social networks and revisited the literature available at that time in order to identify modelling and simulation approaches that may support the analysis process. Gong and Janssen [33] defined a framework for the semantic representation of legal knowledge, aiming at the automatic creation of business processes by selecting, composing and invoking semantic web services. In particular, these two works on knowledge management tried to look at ways for combining some forms of rigorous modelling with informal knowledge management techniques, thus fully addressing MoKMaSD scope and providing important ideas for the future directions of the Symposium.

However, since MoKMaSD originated from a modelling community, mostly interested in applications to biology and ecology, and was collocated with SEFM, a formal methods conference, during the next two editions [17,27] there were stable contributions from the original modelling community, with a large predominance of the applications of formal methods to the domains of biological systems and ecosystems.

MoKMaSD 2013 [27] featured four papers on ecosystem modelling and three papers on knowledge management. Two of the latter went beyond the integration of modelling in a knowledge management setting and considered a linked data perspective to combine data from different sources and facilitate data extension and management [16,52].

MoKMaSD 2014 [17] featured three papers on ecosystem modelling (including one position paper [25]), one paper on biological modelling in a medical context [59], two papers on the application of data mining to the analysis of social networks [51] and to people's mobility flow [30], and one paper on the formal modelling of learning processes that are originated by collaboration activities within an open source software (OSS) community [47]. The application domains were expanded, with no longer an explicit focus on sustainable development. This was formalised by changing the symposium name to "Modelling and Knowledge Management applications: Systems and Domains" while preserving the acronym. The emphasis on data, which had already appeared in the 2013 symposium, was further strengthened in 2014. A *data mining* community joined the symposium contributing not only in terms of the new analysis techniques but also in terms of application domains: *social networks* [51] and *social contexts* [30,36,47]. These new injections gave the Symposium a very interdisciplinary flavour. And, actually, interdisciplinarity was explicitly recognised as a key research challenge by a contribution in the area of ecosystem modelling [25]. Moreover, a twofold role of the data in the modelling process started to appear. On the one hand, data can be used to calibrate the model, as seen in ecosystem modelling and biological modelling [59] and, on the other hand, it can contribute to the actual definition of the model itself [30,36,51].

MoKMaSD 2015 [9] represented an important milestone for the scope of the Symposium. The event programme featured two inspiring keynote talks: "Constraint Modelling and Solving for Data Mining" by Tias Guns and "Machine Learning Methods for Model Checking in Continuous Time Markov Chains" by Guido Sanguinetti. Tias Guns' talk reviewed motivations and advances in the use of constraint programming for data mining problems. In addition, in a contributed paper in the same area Grossi *et al.* presented expressive constraint programming models that support the extension of a given standard problem with further constraints, thus generating interesting variants of the problem [35]. Guido Sanguinetti's talk considered models with uncertain rates, which often occur in biology, and presented interesting ideas for using machine learning to synthesise those parameters that were to be quantified in order to run the model and use it to carry out reachability analysis and model checking.

During the discussion at the Symposium, it was explicitly recognised that modelling, even when considered in the large by incorporating formal or informal knowledge management techniques, was not enough to deal with the more and more increasing complexity of the system and size of the data. In fact, it was clear that, especially when dealing with big data, it is essential to consider real-data and compare them with the model prediction in order to validate the model and be able to use it in a practical context. As proposed in Sanguinetti's keynote talk, *machine learning* can provide a tool for making up for uncertainty and enriching incomplete models, thus, to some extent, allowing real-world data to drive the modelling process. A similar role can be played by *process mining* by extracting a descriptive process model from big data and use such a synthesised model in a number of analytical ways [19]. These synergetic aspects of modelling and data analysis paved the way for the new main scope of the Symposium.

3 Exploring Synergetic Approaches and Encouraging Interdisciplinary Collaboration: DataMod 2016–2020

DataMod 2016 [45] was the first edition using the new name of the Symposium: "From Data to Model and Back". Since then, the call for papers and the website have been clearly stating that the Symposium

> aims at bringing together practitioners and researchers from academia, industry and research institutions interested in the combined application of computational modelling methods with data-driven techniques from the areas of knowledge management, data mining and machine learning. Modelling methodologies of interest include automata, agents, Petri nets, process algebras and rewriting systems. Application domains include social systems, ecology, biology, medicine, smart cities, governance, education, software engineering, and any other field that deals with complex systems and large amounts of data. Papers can present research results in any of the themes of interest for the symposium as well as application experiences, tools and promising preliminary ideas. Papers dealing with synergistic approaches that integrate modelling and knowledge management/discovery or that exploit knowledge management/discovery to develop/synthesise system models are especially welcome.

Data mining and machine learning joined knowledge management as key areas on the data-driven side. And, most importantly, there was a new strong emphasis on synergistic approaches. Finally, as a follow-up of the Symposium, an open call for a special issue of the Journal of Intelligent Information Systems (JIIS) on "Computational modelling and data-driven techniques for systems analysis" was devoted to research results in any of the themes of interest of DataMod 2016 and the previous MoKMaSD editions [42].

The programme of DataMod 2016 started with a keynote talk titled "Mining Big (and Small) Mobile Data for Social Good", in which Mirco Musolesi explored challenges and opportunities in using big (and small) mobile data, which can be collected by means of applications running on smartphones or directly by mobile operators through their cellular infrastructure, within the modelling process and to solve systems-oriented issues. He also discussed the societal and commercial impact of this approach. Guidotti *et al.* showed that musical listening data from the large availability of rich and punctual online data sources can be exploited to create personal listening data models, which can provide higher levels of self-awareness as well as enable additional analysis and musical services both at personal and at collective level [37]. Inspired by process mining, Cerone proposed a technique, called *model mining*, to mine event logs to define a set of formal rules for generating the system behaviour. This can be achieved either by sifting an already existing *a priori* model by using the event logs to decrease the amount of non-determinism [20,21] or by inferring the rules directly from the events logs [21].

In a second keynote talk titled "The Topological Field Theory of Data: a program towards a novel strategy for data mining through data language",

Emanuela Merelli presented a topological field theory of data by making use of formal language theory in order to define the potential semantics needed to understand the emerging patterns that exist among data and that have been extracted within a mining context. Along the same lines Atienza *et al.* used *topological data analysis* to separate topological noise from topological features in high-dimensional data [3,4]. In a more practical perspective, Reijsbergen compared four approaches for generating the topology of stations in a bicycle-sharing systems and found out that a data-driven approach, in which a dataset of places of interest in the city is used to rate how attractive city areas are for station placement, outperformed the other three approaches [56].

DataMod 2017 [24] was the first two-day edition. It featured a tutorial titled "On DataMod approaches to systems analysis" by Paolo Milazzo and three keynote talks. The tutorial provided a taxonomy of approaches based on levels of knowledge of internal logic that is externalised by the system behavioral description mechanisms, ranging from purely data-driven approaches, which are essentially black boxes, to model-based, in which the internal logic is fully externalised. It then focused on approaches that combine different levels of knowledge, e.g. process mining, statistical model checking and applications of machine learning in formal verification.

Two keynote talks were on *smart cities*: "Understanding and rewiring cities using big data" by Bruno Lepri and "Exploring change planning in open, complex systems" by Siobhán Clarke". The third keynote talk was "Applications of weak behavioral metrics in probabilistic systems" by Simone Tini. Another special issue on "Computational modelling and data-driven techniques for systems analysis" was organised, this time in the Journal of Logical and Algebraic Methods in Programming (JLAMP) and restricted to revised and improved version of contributions accepted at DataMod 2017 [31].

Human cognition and *human behaviour* were interesting application areas that appeared in DataMod contributions for the first time in 2017. Broccia *et al.* proposed an algorithm for simulating the psychology of human selective attention, aiming at analysing how attention is divided during the simultaneous interaction with multiple devises, especially in the context of safety-critical systems [14]. Nasti and Milazzo took a neuroscience perspective in modelling human behaviour and proposed a hybrid automata model of the role that the dopamine system plays in addiction processes [49,50]. Finally, Carmichael and Morisset proposed the use of a methodical assessment of decision trees to predict the impact of human behaviour on the security of an organisation. In their approach, learning the behaviour from different sets of traces generated by a designed formal probabilistic model appears as an effective approach to building either a classifier from actual traces observed within the organisation or building a formal model, integrating known existing behavioural elements, which may both present high complexity, the former in selecting the best classifier and the latter in selecting the right parameters [18].

The 1st Informal Workshop on *DataMod Approaches to Systems Analysis* (**WDA 2018**), held on 5 February 2018 in Pisa, aimed at promoting the development of a research community on DataMod approaches by bringing together researchers from the computational modeling and data science communities in order to let them discuss on potential collaborations in a friendly and informal context.

DataMod 2018 [43] included various contributions on *human-computer interaction* (HCI): the keynote talk titled "Data-driven analysis of user interface software in medical devices" by Paolo Masci, two contributed papers and two presentation-only contributions. The other two keynote talks were "Safe Composition of Software Services" by Gwen Salaün and "Computational oncology: from biomedical data to models and back" by Giulio Caravagna.

The two contributed papers on HCI showed a clear synergetic flavour. Cuculo *et al.* used automatic relevance determination to classify personality gaze patterns, but with the additional, important aim of showing how machine learning-based modelling could be used for gaining explanatory insights into relevant mechanism of the studied phenomenon [28]. This form of *explainable machine learning*, which is fundamental in the synergy of model-based and data-driven approaches, will be further discussed in Sect. 4.2. Cerone and Zhexenbayeva used the CSP process algebra, to define a compositional formal model of a language learning app, a user's profile and a formal representation of data from the real usage of the application. Such a formal model is then used in a model-checking framework that supports the validation of research hypotheses relating the learner profile to the user behaviour during interaction [26]. In this synergetic approach, a formal modelling and verification method is used in a data-driven way to carry out some form of validation.

DataMod 2019 [60] featured two keynote talks: "Verification of Data in Space and Time" by Mieke Massink and "Diagrammatic physical robot models in RoboSim" by Ana Cavalcanti . Massink presented spatial and spatio-temporal logics and their use within efficient model checking methods to investigate spatial aspects of data (which may be gathered in various domains ranging from smart public transportation to medical imaging). Cavalcanti presented RoboSim, a diagrammatic tool-independent domain-specific language to model robotic platforms and their controllers and automatically generate simulations and mathematical models for proof.

The Symposium also featured a number of synergetic contributed papers. Two HCI contributions build up on previous DataMod papers. Broccia *et al.* put their previous work on modelling selective attention [14] in a synergetic context by presenting its validation against data gathered from an experimental study performed with real users involved in a "main" task perceived as safety-critical, which was performed concurrently with a series of "distractor" tasks [13]. Based on Cerone and Zhexenbayeva work [26], Aibassova *et al.* presented a language learning application equipped with instrumentation code to gather data about user behavior and use such data for testing new forms of exercises and their combination on samples of users and, after converting raw data into a formal description, also for formal verification and validation purposes [1]. Garanina *et al.* proposed an approach to automatically extracts concurrent system requirements from the technical documentation and formally verify the system design using an external or built-in verification tool. [32]. Bursic *et al.* proposed an automated approach to log anomaly detection. Their approach requires no hand-crafted features and no preprocessing of data and uses a two part unsupervised deep learning model, one applied to text for training without timestamp in order to learn a fixed dimensional embedding of the log messages, and the other applied to the text embeddings and the numerical timestamp of the message in order to detect anomalies [15].

DataMod 2020 represents an important milestone in the history of the Symposium. For the first time an LNCS volume was entirely devoted to the Symposium and titled after it [12]. This was an important step in officialising the already well-established identity of the Symposium. The keynote talk "Towards AI-driven Data Analysis and Fabrication" by Michael Vinov, IBM, presented two complementary methods for data management: a rule-based method that provides declarative language to model data logic and data rules in order to fabricate synthetic data using a constraint satisfaction programming solver, and machine-learning-based methods both for analysis of existing data and for creation of synthetic data. The latter methods themselves already match the DataMod philosophy to go "from data to model and back", but a combination with the former rule-based method could enrich machine-learning-based direction "from data to model" by adding knowledge of the behavioural logic in the spirit of explainable machine learning. In fact, a possible future combination of the two IBM approaches was discussed during the talk.

The Symposium featured 3 session: Machine Learning, Simulation-Based Approaches, and Data Mining and Processing Related Approaches. A number of approaches were presented in the area of healthcare, some of which obviously related with the COVID-19 pandemic.

Silvina *et al.* modelled and analysed the initial stage of the pathway of a cancer patient, from suspected diagnosis to confirmed diagnosis and start of a treatment (cancer waiting time). The approach is data-driven, in the sense that the structural information present in graphical data is exploited by aggregating information over connected nodes, thus allowing them to effectively capture relation information between data elements [61]. Bowles *et al.* presented an approach to evaluate the actual performance and quantify the capacity of an emergency department to support patient demand with limited resources in pre- and post-COVID-19 pandemic scenarios [?]. Milazzo considered the SIR model for spread of disease, which is based on the number of susceptible, infected and recovered individuals, and applied it to the COVID-19 pandemic to carry out stochastic analysis using the stochastic model checker PRISM. The SIR model is modified in order to include governmental restriction and prevention measures and make use of parameter estimation based on real epidemic data [44].

In addition to these simulation-based approaches, there were two more contributions in the area of healthcare. Rahman and Bowles proposed an approach to automatically infer the main components in clinical guideline sentences, using model checking to validate their correctness and combining them with the information gained from real patient data and clinical practice in order to give more suitable personalised recommendations for treating patients [53]. Munbodh *et al.* developed a framework that, for a given standardised radiation treatment planning workflow, provides real-time monitoring and visualisation and supports informed, data-driven decisions regarding clinical workflow management and the impact of changes on the existing workflow, depending on optimisation of clinical efficiency and safety and new interventions incorporated into clinical practice. [57].

Finally, Barbon Junior *et al.* studied how the performance of process mining depends on the used encoding method [5], and Nasti *et al.*, building on work first presented at DataMod 2017 [49,50], showed that the current online social networks' notifications system triggers addictive behaviors [48].

4 Looking Around and Planning for the Future: DataMod Beyond 2021

In Sects. 2 and 3 we have gone through the history of DataMod and encountered essentially two kinds of model-driven approaches to system analysis, simulation and model checking, and a number of kinds of data-driven approaches, including machine learning, deep learning and data mining. All approaches have been used within several application domains: biology, ecology, medicine, healthcare, smart cities, IoT, social networks, human/social behaviour, human cognition and HCI.

Section 4.1 compares the three fundamental kinds of approaches aiming at analysing system dynamics: formal methods (model simulation and model checking), machine learning (including deep learning) and process mining. Section 4.2 summarises the synergetic work that has currently being carried out as well as some recent results and explore research challenges in the context of the scope of DataMod.

4.1 Comparing the Approaches

In our comparison we start considering model-based approaches and, in particular formal methods, which represent the most rigorous and mathematical approach to *define* a model of a real-world system. The key word in formal approaches is *"define"* and must be intended as *formal definition* or *formal specification*, aiming not just at describing the system but, more precisely, at providing a mechanistic way to generate the system behaviour. An important aspect of this system specification process is that the resultant system model also provides an explanation of the way the system work. Although this means that we need to start from our idea and vision of the real system, which represent a sort of *a priori* explanation driving our design process, the resultant model is not just a product of our creative effort but is largely affected by the real system we observe, its behaviour, the data it receives as an input and the way such data is transformed in the output. This role of the real-world data is always present in the design process, at least implicitly, and is sometime made explicit by specific design approaches, such as iterative design, participatory design and, more in general, by all forms of agile design. However, the use of real-world data is normally an informal one and is carried out through an abstraction process. This also means that what we model is not a full representation of the real-system, but one of its possible abstract representations. Which abstraction we consider depends on what is the goal of our modelling effort, that is, on whether we aim at performing simulation and at which level of detail or we aim at proving properties and which kinds of properties.

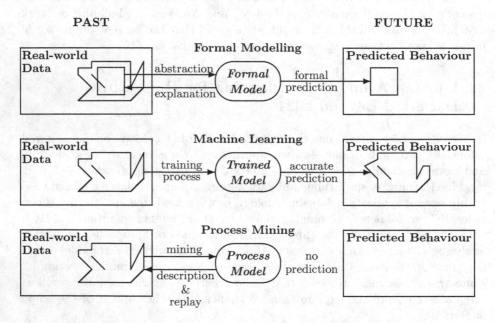

Fig. 1. Comparing Formal Modelling, Machine Learning and Process Mining

Therefore, as shown in the top part of Fig. 1, *Formal Modelling* starts from an informal use of real-world data (depicted at the top of Fig. 1 as the irregular shape on the left) to carry out an abstraction process that leads to the creation of a formal model, which provides an explanation of the relevant aspect of the past behaviour of the system (depicted at the top of Fig. 1 as the squared shape on the left) and supports the prediction of its future behaviour, still limited to the considered aspects (depicted at the top of Fig. 1 as the squared shape on the right).

As shown in the middle part of Fig. 1, *Machine Learning* processes real-world data trough a training process in order to learn the system behaviour and be able to carry out an accurate prediction of its future behaviour. The real-world data may comprise only input data (*unsupervised learning*), or also include the desired output (*supervised learning*), or may be explored in a dynamic environment trying to maximise the provided feedback, which is intended as a sort of reward (*reinforcement learning*). The training process, which is essentially a generalisation process, aims at achieving an accurate prediction of the future behaviour (depicted in the middle of Fig. 1 as the irregular shape on the right, which is very similar to the one on the left). Obviously, since the training data is finite and the future is uncertain, there is no guarantee of the performance of the training process. Therefore, it is quite common to consider probabilistic bounds in order to quantify generalisation error.

Process Mining exploits real-world data by structuring datasets in a specific way in order define a *process model* that describes the system behaviour. Here the key point is to structure the data, which is expressed in terms of *event data*, also called *event logs*. An *event* is seen as consisting of at least three components: case, activity and timestamp. An *activity* names what has happened, a *case* correlates different events under the same identifier to describe an instance of the process, and a *timestamp* is the time when the event occurs, which also provides a partial ordering of the events. There are many ways for choosing what a case, an activity and a timestamp are, while structuring the event. Different choices lead to different perspectives in describing the system. But, in general, as shown in the bottom part of Fig. 1, with respect to the considered perspective, the model is described exactly as it is observed in the real-world (depicted at the bottom of Fig. 1 as the irregular shape on the left) and can be even replayed to reproduce the exact observed behaviour. Moreover, the description is formal, typically in some variant of Petri nets, and, although a full description tends to be very complex and appears as a spaghetti-like network, it is possible to lower the detail threshold (for example by removing the least frequent process instances) to make it understandable.

Each of these three fundamental approaches have pros and cons. The *pros* can be summarised as follows.

Formal Modelling Pros. Formal Modelling allows us to both explain the past and predict the future. Moreover, having a model that explains the behaviour, we can also explicitly modify the model to carry out some form of intervention or perform control on the future behaviour. And we actually understand what we are doing.

Machine Learning Pros. Trained models may reach a very high degree of accuracy and allow us to predict the future in very fine details. We can also aim at some form of control on the system, although this is normally somehow implicitly achieved by the training algorithm in some obscure way.

Process mining Pros. Process mining supports a formal description, which is virtually a perfect description of the past. Moreover, looking at the mainstream behaviour allows us to explain the past and identify deviations and bottlenecks.

The *cons* can be summarised as follows.

Formal Modelling Cons. A first problem is that by working on an abstract representation we have only a partial description of the real-world system that focuses on specific aspects but it is not accurate. A second problem is the complexity of the analysis algorithms, which may cause state-space explosion or require too long a computational time.

Machine Learning Cons. Trained models are not in general explainable and this has two negative consequences. First, there are a number of contexts in which it is necessary to explain to customers and/or users how the prediction is attained. This is the case for safety critical systems, which require to prove that the used training algorithms are correct and the prediction accuracy covers the most critical cases, as well as for informing the customer on how the system carries out its tasks. Second, it is not possible to explicitly modify the model in order to carry out a deliberate intervention, since changes to the model can only implicitly occur through learning.

Process Mining Cons. Process models are descriptive, but in general not predictive. The full description is too large and complex to be understandable and usable and the mainstream behaviour is normally not sufficiently detailed to attain a correct prediction.

4.2 Current Research on Synergetic Approaches

In Sect. 3 we have seen a number of synergetic approaches presented and/or discussed at DataMod. Guido Sanguinetti's keynote talk at MokMaSD 2015 showed how to use machine learning to synthesise parameters that are needed to carry out reachability analysis and model checking, paving the way to the general use of machine learning for making up for uncertainty and enriching incomplete models. Then, starting with Mirco Musolesi's DataMod 2016 keynote talk, we have seen attempts to use real-world data to synthesise a formal model [18,21] and to enrich [53], improve [1,20] or validate [13] an existing system model. We have seen that data from documentation may be used to extract system requirements, which can then be fed to a formal verification tool [32]. And we have also seen that real-world data may be combined with a formal model in order to support the validation of research hypotheses [26].

As Milazzo discussed in the tutorial he presented at DataMod 2017, data-driven approaches are essentially black boxes whose internal logics is not visible. As we mentioned in Sect. 4.1, normally this is also the case for machine learning. However, among the several works on machine learning presented at DataMod events, Cuculo *et al.* showed how machine learning-based modelling could be used for gaining explanatory insights into relevant mechanisms of the studied phenomenon [28].

Explainable machine learning may be seen as an implementation of the *right to explanation* [29], whereby the user or the customer acquires knowledge about the internal logic of the system. Domain knowledge is a necessary prerequisite for effectively using machine learning to get scientific results but is not suffi-cient in order to understand how a specific model operates and the underlying reasons for the decisions made by the model. In fact, three further elements are necessary in order to gain scientific insights and discoveries from a machine learning algorithm: *transparency, interpretability* and *explainability* [58]. Trans-parency is achieved if the processes that extracts model parameters from training data and generates labels from testing data can be described and motivated by the approach designer (what has been used and why). Interpretability refers to presentation of properties of the trained model making their meanings understandable to a human, that is, mapping the abstract concepts that define the meanings to the domain knowledge of the human (how we understand the training model). The concept of explainability, however, still belongs to a gray area, due to its intrinsic vagueness, especially in terms of completeness and degree of causality. Although a recent work [46] partitions explanatory questions into three classes, what-questions (e.g., What event happened?), how-questions, (e.g., How did that event happen?) and why-questions (e.g., Why did that event happen?), it is the actual machine-learning user's goal that must drive the choice of the appropriate questions. This means that even if transparency and interpretability are met, they can only lead to a satisfactory explanation if we ask the appropriate questions.

Therefore, the lack of a joint concept of explainability has resulted in the development of several alternative explainability techniques, each of them with a different emphasis and different advantages and disadvantages. Islam *et al.* carried out a survey of 137 recently published papers in the area of explainable artificial intelligence (another name for 'explainable machine learning') finding that most of the work is in the safety-critical domains worldwide, deep learning and ensemble models are the most exploited models, visual explanations are preferred by end-users and robust evaluation metrics are being developed to assess the quality of explanations [38]. However, there is a lack of work that aims at exploiting synergies between machine-learning-based and model-based approaches. One of the few exceptions is the work by Liao and Poggio, who suggested to convert a neural network to a symbolic description to gain interpretability and explainability [41]. They propose to use "objects/symbols" as a basic representational atom instead of the N-dimensional tensors traditionally used in "feature-oriented" deep learning. This supports the explicit representation of symbolic concepts thus achieving a form of "symbolic disentanglement" that makes properties interpretable. Although little explored so far, Liao and Poggio's proposal appears as a promising direction towards a higher explainability of machine learning models. In Sect. 3 we discussed another proposal along these lines: in his keynote talk at DataMod 2020, Michael Vinov presented IBM ideas for combining their complementary methods for data management, i.e., a rule-based method and a machine-learning-based method.

In general, we can say that the DataMod community represents the ideal ensemble to pursue the objective of exploiting synergies between machine-learning-based and model-based approaches. Working together towards this objective should be set as a priority goal for the future DataMod events and initiatives.

Finally, we would like to consider the large amount of open data made available in OSS repositories. These data repositories not only include code but also documentation, emails and other forms of communication, test cases, bug reports, feature proposals, etc. Traditional data mining techniques as well as process mining have been used to analyse various aspects of OSS communities, project and the processes involving them, such as contribution patterns, learning and skill acquisition [19]. Machine learning and deep learning techniques have also been used for probabilistic learning of large code bases (called *big code*) from OSS repositories [2]. Here the objective is the exploitation of the information extracted from such existing code bases in order to provide statistically likely solutions to problems that are hard to solve with traditional formal analysis techniques (*statistical code modelling*). Examples of such problems are: program synthesis [40,55], code property prediction [54] and code deobfuscation [10]. The dual of statistical code modelling is *probabilistic programming*, which aims at deploying programming language concepts to facilitate the programming of new machine-learning algorithms [34]. Exploiting the big code available on OSS repositories through process mining and machine learning could be another objective on which the DataMod community should join forces and focus in the future.

5   Conclusion and Future Initiatives

We have gone through the history of the DataMod symposium since its beginning in 2012 under the acronym MoKMaSD. We have highlighted some important works that have been contributed during these ten years of life of DataMod. In particular, we have considered those contributions that addressed synergies between data-driven and model-based approaches. We have also compared different approaches to modelling and put DataMod contributions in the context of the current research. Finally, we have identified two priority areas in which the heterogenous DataMod community has the potential to work successfully: explainable machine learning and the application of data-driven approaches to big code. We have proposed these areas as common objectives on which the DataMod community should join forces and focus in the future.

We would like to conclude that putting this proposals into practice requires the commitment of the DataMod community to invest time and resources into their concrete implementation. In particular, organisational and collaborative efforts are needed to create motivations and the appropriate context to enable us to productively work together. Time seems to be mature for a second informal workshop with a similar scope as WDA 2018, possibly with a more flexible, hybrid format (physical and virtual), which would encourage extensive participation. A number of further initiatives could be used to foster and focus collaboration, including the creation of working groups on specific research topics/challenges and/or addressing specific objectives, the preparation of one or more joint position paper(s) and the inclusion of talks from experts in the considered priority areas within the programme of the next WDA workshop.

Acknowledgments. We would like to thank the Program Co-chairs of DataMod and Paolo Milazzo for their comments during the presentation of this work at DataMod 2021. Paolo also provided important materials and pointers to further information, which were essential in the preparation of both the presentation and this paper.

References

1. Aibassova, A., Cerone, A., Tashkenbayev, M.: An instrumented mobile language learning application for the analysis of usability and learning. In: Sekerinski, E., et al. (eds.) FM 2019. LNCS, vol. 12232, pp. 170–185. Springer, Cham (2020). https://doi.org/10.1007/978-3-030-54994-7_13
2. Allamanis, M., Barr, E.T., Devanbu, P., Sutton, C.: A survey of machine learning for big code and naturalness. ACM Comput. Surv. (CSUR) **51**(4), 81 (2018)
3. Atienza, N., Gonzalez-Diaz, R., Rucco, M.: Separating topological noise from features using persistent entropy. In: Milazzo, P., Varró, D., Wimmer, M. (eds.) STAF 2016. LNCS, vol. 9946, pp. 3–12. Springer, Cham (2016). https://doi.org/10.1007/978-3-319-50230-4_1
4. Atienza, N., Gonzalez-Diaz, R., Rucco, M.: Persistent entropy for separating topological features from noise in vietoris-rips complexes. J. Intell. Inf. Syst. **52**(3), 637–655 (2017). https://doi.org/10.1007/s10844-017-0473-4
5. Barbon Junior, S., Ceravolo, P., Damiani, E., Marques Tavares, G.: Evaluating trace encoding methods in process mining. In: Bowles, J., Broccia, G., Nanni, M. (eds.) DataMod 2020. LNCS, vol. 12611, pp. 174–189. Springer, Cham (2021). https://doi.org/10.1007/978-3-030-70650-0_11
6. Barbuti, R., Cerone, A., Maggiolo-Schettini, A., Milazzo, P., Setiawan, S.: Modelling population dynamics using grid systems. In: Cerone, A., et al. (eds.) SEFM 2012. LNCS, vol. 7991, pp. 172–189. Springer, Heidelberg (2014). https://doi.org/10.1007/978-3-642-54338-8_14
7. Barthe, G., Pardo, A., Schneider, G. (eds.): SEFM 2011. LNCS, vol. 7041. Springer, Heidelberg (2011). https://doi.org/10.1007/978-3-642-24690-6
8. Bernardo, G., D'Alessandro, S.: Transition to sustainability: Italian scenarios towards a low-carbon economy. In: Cerone, A., et al. (eds.) SEFM 2012. LNCS, vol. 7991, pp. 190–197. Springer, Heidelberg (2014). https://doi.org/10.1007/978-3-642-54338-8_15
9. Bianculli, D., Calinescu, R., Rumpe, B. (eds.): SEFM 2015. LNCS, vol. 9509. Springer, Heidelberg (2015). https://doi.org/10.1007/978-3-662-49224-6
10. Bichsel, B., Raychev, V., Tsankov, P., Vechev, M.: Statistical deobfuscation of android applications. In: Proceedings of the 2016 ACM SIGSAC Conference on Computer and Communications Security. ACM (2016)
11. Bernardo, G., D'Alessandro, S.: Transition to sustainability: Italian scenarios towards a low-carbon economy. In: Cerone, A., et al. (eds.) SEFM 2012. LNCS, vol. 7991, pp. 190–197. Springer, Heidelberg (2014). https://doi.org/10.1007/978-3-642-54338-8_15
12. Bowles, J., Broccia, G., Nanni, M. (eds.): DataMod 2020. LNCS, vol. 12611. Springer, Cham (2021). https://doi.org/10.1007/978-3-030-70650-0
13. Broccia, G., Milazzo, P., Belviso, C., Montiel, C.B.: Validation of a simulation algorithm for safety-critical human multitasking. In: Sekerinski, E., et al. (eds.) FM 2019. LNCS, vol. 12232, pp. 99–113. Springer, Cham (2020). https://doi.org/10.1007/978-3-030-54994-7_8
14. Broccia, G., Milazzo, P., Ölveczky, P.C.: An algorithm for simulating human selective attention. In: Cerone, A., Roveri, M. (eds.) SEFM 2017. LNCS, vol. 10729, pp. 48–55. Springer, Cham (2018). https://doi.org/10.1007/978-3-319-74781-1_4
15. Bursic, S., Cuculo, V., D'Amelio, A.: Anomaly detection from log files using unsupervised deep learning. In: Sekerinski, E., et al. (eds.) FM 2019. LNCS, vol. 12232, pp. 200–207. Springer, Cham (2020). https://doi.org/10.1007/978-3-030-54994-7_15

16. Cáceres, P., Cuesta, C.E., Cavero, J.M., Vela, B., Sierra-Alonso, A.: Towards knowledge modeling for sustainable transport. In: Counsell, S., Núñez, M. (eds.) SEFM 2013. LNCS, vol. 8368, pp. 271–287. Springer, Cham (2014). https://doi.org/10.1007/978-3-319-05032-4_20

17. Cimatti, A., Sirjani, M. (eds.): SEFM 2017. LNCS, vol. 10469. Springer, Cham (2017). https://doi.org/10.1007/978-3-319-66197-1

18. Carmichael, P., Morisset, C.: Learning decision trees from synthetic data models for human security behaviour. In: Cerone, A., Roveri, M. (eds.) SEFM 2017. LNCS, vol. 10729, pp. 56–71. Springer, Cham (2018). https://doi.org/10.1007/978-3-319-74781-1_5

19. Cerone, A.: Process mining as a modelling tool: beyond the domain of business process management. In: Bianculli, D., Calinescu, R., Rumpe, B. (eds.) SEFM 2015. LNCS, vol. 9509, pp. 139–144. Springer, Heidelberg (2015). https://doi.org/10.1007/978-3-662-49224-6_12

20. Cerone, A.: Refinement mining: using data to sift plausible models. In: Milazzo, P., Varró, D., Wimmer, M. (eds.) STAF 2016. LNCS, vol. 9946, pp. 26–41. Springer, Cham (2016). https://doi.org/10.1007/978-3-319-50230-4_3

21. Cerone, A.: Model mining. J. Intell. Inf. Syst. **52**(3), 501–532 (2017). https://doi.org/10.1007/s10844-017-0474-3

22. Cerone, A., Garcia-Perez, A.: Modelling and knowledge management for sustainable development. In: Cerone, A., et al. (eds.) SEFM 2012. LNCS, vol. 7991, pp. 149–153. Springer, Heidelberg (2014). https://doi.org/10.1007/978-3-642-54338-8_12

23. Cerone, A., et al. (eds.): SEFM 2012. LNCS, vol. 7991. Springer, Heidelberg (2014). https://doi.org/10.1007/978-3-642-54338-8

24. Cerone, A., Roveri, M. (eds.): SEFM 2017. LNCS, vol. 10729. Springer, Cham (2018). https://doi.org/10.1007/978-3-319-74781-1

25. Cerone, A., Scotti, M.: Research challenges in modelling ecosystems. In: Canal, C., Idani, A. (eds.) SEFM 2014. LNCS, vol. 8938, pp. 276–293. Springer, Cham (2015). https://doi.org/10.1007/978-3-319-15201-1_18

26. Cerone, A., Zhexenbayeva, A.: Using formal methods to validate research hypotheses: the Duolingo case study. In: Mazzara, M., Ober, I., Salaün, G. (eds.) STAF 2018. LNCS, vol. 11176, pp. 163–170. Springer, Cham (2018). https://doi.org/10.1007/978-3-030-04771-9_13

27. Counsell, S., Núñez, M. (eds.): SEFM 2013. LNCS, vol. 8368. Springer, Cham (2014). https://doi.org/10.1007/978-3-319-05032-4

28. Cuculo, V., D'Amelio, A., Lanzarotti, R., Boccignone, G.: Personality gaze patterns unveiled via automatic relevance determination. In: Mazzara, M., Ober, I., Salaün, G. (eds.) STAF 2018. LNCS, vol. 11176, pp. 171–184. Springer, Cham (2018). https://doi.org/10.1007/978-3-030-04771-9_14

29. Edwards, L., Veale, M.: Slave to the algorithm? why a 'right to an explanation' is probably not the remedy you are looking for. Duke Law Technol. Rev. **16**(1), 18–84 (2017)

30. Gabrielli, L., Furletti, B., Giannotti, F., Nanni, M., Rinzivillo, S.: Use of mobile phone data to estimate visitors mobility flows. In: Canal, C., Idani, A. (eds.) SEFM 2014. LNCS, vol. 8938, pp. 214–226. Springer, Cham (2015). https://doi.org/10.1007/978-3-319-15201-1_14

31. Galpin, V., Milazzo, P., Monreale, A.: Guest editors' foreword. J. Logic. Algebraic Methods Program. **109**, 1–2 (2019)

32. Garanina, N., Anureev, I., Sidorova, E., Koznov, D., Zyubin, V., Gorlatch, S.: An ontology-based approach to support formal verification of concurrent systems. In: Sekerinski, E., et al. (eds.) FM 2019. LNCS, vol. 12232, pp. 114–130. Springer, Cham (2020). https://doi.org/10.1007/978-3-030-54994-7_9

33. Gong, Y., Janssen, M.: A framework for translating legal knowledge into administrative processes: dynamic adaption of business processes. In: Cerone, A., et al. (eds.) SEFM 2012. LNCS, vol. 7991, pp. 204–211. Springer, Heidelberg (2014). https://doi.org/10.1007/978-3-642-54338-8_17

34. Gordon, A.D., Henzinger, T.A., Nori, A.V., Rajamani, S.K.: Probabilistic programming. In: FOSE 2014: Future of Software Engineering Proceedings, pp. 167–181. ACM (2014)

35. Grossi, V., Monreale, A., Nanni, M., Pedreschi, D., Turini, F.: Clustering formulation using constraint optimization. In: Bianculli, D., Calinescu, R., Rumpe, B. (eds.) SEFM 2015. LNCS, vol. 9509, pp. 93–107. Springer, Heidelberg (2015). https://doi.org/10.1007/978-3-662-49224-6_9

36. Guidotti, R., Monreale, A., Rinzivillo, S., Pedreschi, D., Giannotti, F.: Retrieving points of interest from human systematic movements. In: Canal, C., Idani, A. (eds.) SEFM 2014. LNCS, vol. 8938, pp. 294–308. Springer, Cham (2015). https://doi.org/10.1007/978-3-319-15201-1_19

37. Guidotti, R., Rossetti, G., Pedreschi, D.: AUDIO ERGO SUM. In: Milazzo, P., Varró, D., Wimmer, M. (eds.) STAF 2016. LNCS, vol. 9946, pp. 51–66. Springer, Cham (2016). https://doi.org/10.1007/978-3-319-50230-4_5

38. Islam, M.R., Ahmed, M.U., Barua, S., Begum, S.: A systematic review of explainable artificial intelligence in terms of different application domains and tasks. Appl. Sci. **12**(3), 1353–1391 (2022)

39. Kahramanoğulları, O., Lynch, J.F., Priami, C.: Algorithmic systems ecology: experiments on multiple interaction types and patches. In: Cerone, A., et al. (eds.) SEFM 2012. LNCS, vol. 7991, pp. 154–171. Springer, Heidelberg (2014). https://doi.org/10.1007/978-3-642-54338-8_13

40. Liang, P., Jordan, M.I.: Learning programs: A hierarchical Bayesian approach. In: Proceedings of the 27th International Conference on Machine Learning (ICML 2010), pp. 639–646. ACM (2010)

41. Liao, Q., Poggio, T.: Object-oriented deep learning. CBMM Memo No. 70, Center for Brains, Minds, and Machines, McGovern Institute for Brain Research, MIT. (2017)

42. Matwin, S., Tesei, L., Trasarti, R.: Computational modelling and data-driven techniques for systems analysis. J. Intell. Inf. Syst. **52**(3), 473–475 (2019). https://doi.org/10.1007/s10844-019-00554-z

43. Mazzara, M., Ober, I., Salaün, G. (eds.): STAF 2018. LNCS, vol. 11176. Springer, Cham (2018). https://doi.org/10.1007/978-3-030-04771-9

44. Milazzo, P.: Analysis of COVID-19 Data with PRISM: parameter estimation and SIR modelling. In: Bowles, J., Broccia, G., Nanni, M. (eds.) DataMod 2020. LNCS, vol. 12611, pp. 123–133. Springer, Cham (2021). https://doi.org/10.1007/978-3-030-70650-0_8

45. Milazzo, P., Varró, D., Wimmer, M. (eds.): STAF 2016. LNCS, vol. 9946. Springer, Cham (2016). https://doi.org/10.1007/978-3-319-50230-4

46. Miller, T.: Explanation in artificial intelligence: insights from the social sciences. Artif. Intell. **267**, 1–38 (2019)

47. Mukala, P., Cerone, A., Turini, F.: An abstract state machine (ASM) representation of learning process in FLOSS communities. In: Canal, C., Idani, A. (eds.) SEFM

2014. LNCS, vol. 8938, pp. 227–242. Springer, Cham (2015). https://doi.org/10.1007/978-3-319-15201-1_15

48. Nasti, L., Michienzi, A., Guidi, B.: Discovering the impact of notifications on social network addiction. In: Bowles, J., Broccia, G., Nanni, M. (eds.) DataMod 2020. LNCS, vol. 12611, pp. 72–86. Springer, Cham (2021). https://doi.org/10.1007/978-3-030-70650-0_5

49. Nasti, L., Milazzo, P.: A computational model of internet addiction phenomena in social networks. In: Cerone, A., Roveri, M. (eds.) SEFM 2017. LNCS, vol. 10729, pp. 86–100. Springer, Cham (2018). https://doi.org/10.1007/978-3-319-74781-1_7

50. Nasti, L., Milazzo, P.: A hybrid automata model of social networking addiction. J. Logic. Algebraic Methods Program. **100**, 215–229 (2018)

51. Nozza, D., Maccagnola, D., Guigue, V., Messina, E., Gallinari, P.: A latent representation model for sentiment analysis in heterogeneous social networks. In: Canal, C., Idani, A. (eds.) SEFM 2014. LNCS, vol. 8938, pp. 201–213. Springer, Cham (2015). https://doi.org/10.1007/978-3-319-15201-1_13

52. Perez, A., Larrinaga, F., Curry, E.: The role of linked data and semantic-technologies for sustainability idea management. In: Counsell, S., Núñez, M. (eds.) SEFM 2013. LNCS, vol. 8368, pp. 306–312. Springer, Cham (2014). https://doi.org/10.1007/978-3-319-05032-4_22

53. Rahman, F., Bowles, J.: Semantic annotations in clinical guidelines. In: Bowles, J., Broccia, G., Nanni, M. (eds.) DataMod 2020. LNCS, vol. 12611, pp. 190–205. Springer, Cham (2021). https://doi.org/10.1007/978-3-030-70650-0_12

54. Raychev, V., Vechev, M., Krause, A.: Predicting program properties from "big code". In: Proceedings of the 42nd ACM SIGPLAN-SIGACT Symposium on Principles of Programming Languages (POPL 2015). ACM (2015)

55. Raychev, V., Vechev, M., Yahav, E.: Code completion with statistical language models. In: Proc. of the 35th ACM SIGPLAN Conference on Programming Language Design and Implementation, pp. 419–428. ACM (2014)

56. Reijsbergen, D.: Probabilistic modelling of station locations in bicycle-sharing systems. In: Milazzo, P., Varró, D., Wimmer, M. (eds.) STAF 2016. LNCS, vol. 9946, pp. 83–97. Springer, Cham (2016). https://doi.org/10.1007/978-3-319-50230-4_7

57. Munbodh, R., Leonard, K.L., Klein, E.E.: Deriving performance measures of workflow in radiation therapy from real-time data. In: Bowles, J., Broccia, G., Nanni, M. (eds.) DataMod 2020. LNCS, vol. 12611, pp. 206–216. Springer, Cham (2021). https://doi.org/10.1007/978-3-030-70650-0_13

58. Roscher, R., Bohn, B., Duarte, M.F., Garcke, J.: Explainable machine learning for scientific insights and discoveries. IEEE Access **8**, 42200–42216 (2020)

59. Sameen, S., Barbuti, R., Milazzo, P., Cerone, A.: A mathematical model for assessing KRAS mutation effect on monoclonal antibody treatment of colorectal cancer. In: Canal, C., Idani, A. (eds.) SEFM 2014. LNCS, vol. 8938, pp. 243–258. Springer, Cham (2015). https://doi.org/10.1007/978-3-319-15201-1_16

60. Sekerinski, E., et al. (eds.): FM 2019. LNCS, vol. 12232. Springer, Cham (2020). https://doi.org/10.1007/978-3-030-54994-7

61. Silvina, A., Redeker, G., Webber, T., Bowles, J.: A simulation-based approach for the behavioural analysis of cancer pathways. In: Bowles, J., Broccia, G., Nanni, M. (eds.) DataMod 2020. LNCS, vol. 12611, pp. 57–71. Springer, Cham (2021). https://doi.org/10.1007/978-3-030-70650-0_4

Model Verification

Analysis and Verification of Robustness Properties in Becker-Döring Model

Lucia Nasti[✉][iD], Roberta Gori[iD], and Paolo Milazzo[iD]

Department of Computer Science, University of Pisa, Largo Bruno Pontecorvo, 3,
56127 Pisa, Italy
{lucia.nasti,gori,milazzo}@di.unipi.it

Abstract. Many biochemical processes in living cells involve clusters
of particles. Such processes include protein aggregation and the development of intracellular concentration gradients. To study these mechanisms, we can apply coagulation-fragmentation models describing populations of interacting components. In this context, the Becker-Döring
equations - theorized in 1935 - provide the simplest kinetic model to
describe condensations phenomena. Experimental works on this model
reveal that it exhibits robustness, defined as the system's capability to
preserve its features despite noise and fluctuations. Here, we verify the
robustness of the BD model, applying our notions of initial concentration robustness (α-robustness and β-robustness), which are related to the
influence of the perturbation of the initial concentration of one species
(i.e., the input) on the concentration of another species (i.e., the output)
at the steady state. Then, we conclude that a new definition of robustness, namely the asymptotic robustness, is necessary to describe more
accurately the model's behavior.

Keywords: Becker-Döring equations · Robustness · Modeling ·
Simulation

1 Introduction

Many biochemical processes in living systems are combined with the formation
of clusters of particles, such as protein aggregation [23], polymerization [14,15],
and formation of intracellular concentration gradients [13]. These biological phenomena have been studied through the application of coagulation-fragmentation
models that describe populations of interacting components [12,17].

In this context, one of the most common models is based on the Becker-
Döring equations (BD), which were theorized for the first time in 1935, by the
two authors who gave the name of the model [6]. They proposed an infinite
system of ordinary differential equations as a model for the time evolution of the
distribution of cluster sizes for a system [3,8].

In parallel with experimental work [23], it has been observed that
coagulation-fragmentation models can show *robustness* with respect to perturbations: changing parameters (such as the particles' concentration) does not
change the cluster distribution.

© Springer Nature Switzerland AG 2022
J. Bowles et al. (Eds.): DataMod 2021, LNCS 13268, pp. 27–43, 2022.
https://doi.org/10.1007/978-3-031-16011-0_3

Indeed, at various frequencies and timescales, internal and external fluctuations can alter specific functions or traits of biological systems, causing genetic mutations, loss of structural integrity, diseases, and so on. Nevertheless, many biological networks can maintain their functionalities despite perturbations: this distinct property is known as *robustness* [16]. Robust traits are pervasive in biology: they involve various structural levels, such as gene expression, protein folding, metabolic flux, species persistence. For this reason, the study of robustness is essential for biologists, whose aim is to understand the functioning of a biological system.

In general, investigating biological systems is extremely challenging because they are characterized by non-linearity and non-intuitive behaviors. They can be studied by performing wet-lab (*in vitro*) experiments, or through mathematical or computational (*in silico*) methods on pathway models [4]. Unfortunately, the applicability of these approaches is often hampered by the complexity of the models to be analyzed (often expressed in terms of *ordinary differential equations* (ODEs) or Markov chains). An alternative way is to infer a specific property from the system [5], such as monotonicity [1,10,21] and steady-state reachability [9], by looking only at the structure of the system, without the need of studying or simulating its dynamics. Establishing such properties, indeed, provides information on the Chemical Reaction Network (CRN) dynamics without the need of performing several numerical simulations [19]. Unfortunately, the applicability of these structural approaches is often limited to rather specific classes of CRNs.

We proceed by verifying the robustness of the Becker-Döring model applying different approaches. We first apply the *sufficient condition* proposed by Shinar and Feinberg in [24,25], which allows robustness to be derived directly from a syntactical property of the pathway, without the need of studying or simulating its dynamics. In particular, they investigate the specific notion of the *absolute concentration robustness*, for which a system is robust if there is at least one chemical species that has – at the equilibrium – the same identical concentration even in presence of perturbations. We show that the definition given by Shinar and Feinberg is particularly limiting in the description of the BD model's behavior. Then, we proceed applying our definition of α-robustness [20], which can help us to quantify the influence that the initial concentrations of a species has on the steady state of the system. In this context, a system is α-robust with respect to a given set of initial concentration intervals if the concentration of a chosen output molecule at the steady state varies within an interval of values $[k - \frac{\alpha}{2}, k + \frac{\alpha}{2}]$ for some $k \in \mathbb{R}$. In addition, we can apply the relative notion of β-robustness, which can be obtained easily by dividing α by k, to study which perturbation influences more the distribution of the clusters and in which way.

By using this approach, we find that by increasing the initial concentration of the input in Becker-Döring system, the α value decreases continuously. Thus, in order to describe more accurately the model's behaviour, we introduce the notion of the *asymptotic robustness*. In addition, to support our result obtained by simulations, in this case we are able to study analytically the steady state of the BD system. Note that, as already mentioned, this analysis is possible only in particular cases because of the complexity of the biological systems.

This work is organized as follows. Before introducing in detail the mathematical properties of Becker-Döring equations in Sect. 2.2, in Sect. 2.1 we present some notions that will be assumed in the rest of the paper about the representation of chemical reactions. In Sect. 3 we verify the robustness of the BD model, we define the new notion of the asymptotic robustness, and we present the analytical study of the steady state. Finally, in Sect. 4 we draw our conclusions and discuss future work.

2   Background

We introduce some notions that will be assumed in the rest of the paper. In the first part, we focus on the representation of chemical reactions, considering one of the main methods that we can use to describe them: the *deterministic approach*. In the second part, we illustrate the characteristics of the BD model, focusing on its mathematical aspects.

2.1   Chemical Reaction

A chemical reaction is a transformation that involves one or more chemical species, in a specific situation of volume and temperature.

We call *reactants* the chemical species that are transformed, while those that are the result of the transformation are called *products*. We can represent a chemical reaction as an equation, showing all the species involved in the process.

A simple example of chemical reaction is the following elementary reaction:

$$a\mathrm{A} + b\mathrm{B} \underset{k_{-1}}{\overset{k_1}{\rightleftharpoons}} c\mathrm{C} + d\mathrm{D} \tag{1}$$

In this case, A, B, C, D are the species involved in the process: A and B are the reactants, C and D are the products. The parameters a, b, c, d are called *stoichiometric coefficients* and represent the number of reactants and products participating in the reaction. The arrow is used to indicate the direction in which a chemical reaction takes place. In the example, the double arrow means that the reaction is *reversible* (it can take place in both ways). When we have only one arrow, it means that the reaction is *irreversible*, that is it is not possible to have the opposite transformation. The two reaction rates constant k_1 and k_{-1} quantify the rate and direction of a chemical reaction, where the rate is the speed at which a chemical reaction takes place. To describe the dynamical behaviour of the chemical reaction network, we can use the *law of mass action*, which states that the rate of a reaction is proportional to the product of the reactants. Applying the *law of mass action* to the system, we obtain, for each chemical species, a differential equation describing the production and the consumption of the considered species. Considering the generic chemical Eq. 1, we obtain:

$$\frac{d[A]}{dt} = \overbrace{-ak_1[A]^a[B]^b}^{\substack{\text{direct reaction} \\ \text{term}}} \overbrace{+ak_{-1}[C]^c[D]^d}^{\substack{\text{inverse reaction} \\ \text{term}}}$$

$$\frac{d[B]}{dt} = -bk_1[A]^a[B]^b + bk_{-1}[C]^c[D]^d$$

$$\frac{d[C]}{dt} = +ck_1[A]^a[B]^b - ck_{-1}[C]^c[D]^d$$

$$\frac{d[D]}{dt} = +dk_1[A]^a[B]^b - dk_{-1}[C]^c[D]^d.$$

where, in each equation, we isolated the term describing the direct reaction from the one describing the inverse reaction. With these two terms, we implicitly considered, for each element, the processes of consumption and production.

We can abstract the dynamics of the CRN using the *stoichiometric matrix* $\Gamma = \{n_{ij}\}$, where each row corresponds to a substance S_i and each column to a reaction R_j. The matrix entries n_{ij} are determined considering how the substance is involved in each reaction of the system. If the substance is a reactant or a product of the reaction, the entry is the stoichiometric coefficient of the species, otherwise, the entry is 0. The sign of the stoichiometric coefficient is conventionally assigned as *positive* if the species is a product and *negative* if it is a reactant. The stoichiometric matrix of the CRN (1) is:

$$\Gamma = \begin{array}{c} \\ A \\ B \\ C \\ D \end{array} \begin{array}{c} \mathcal{R}_1 \quad \mathcal{R}_{-1} \\ \begin{pmatrix} -a & +a \\ -b & +b \\ +c & -c \\ +d & -d \end{pmatrix} \end{array}.$$

2.2 The Becker-Döring equations

The Becker-Döring equations (BD) describe two principal phenomena, namely the *coagulation* and the *fragmentation* of clusters of particles, based on two processes:

1. a *monomer* (or *elementary particle*) is a cluster characterized by a size i equal to 1. Hitting a cluster of size $i \geq 1$, it gives rise to a coagulation phenomenon, producing a cluster of dimension $i + 1$;
2. a cluster of size $i \geq 2$ can be subjected to a spontaneous fragmentation, splitting itself in a cluster of size $i - 1$ and a monomer.

BD equations can be described by a CRN that, for each $i \in \mathbb{N}$, includes the reaction

$$C_1 + C_i \underset{b_{i+1}}{\overset{a_i}{\rightleftharpoons}} C_{i+1} \tag{2}$$

where C_i denotes a cluster of i particles, while kinetic coefficients a_i and $b_i + 1$ stand for the rate of aggregation and fragmentation, respectively. Coefficients a_i and $b_i + 1$ may depend on i, but for the moment we assume them to be constant values (denoted a and b).

By applying the *law of mass action* to the BD model we obtain a differential equation for each cluster size i, which can be generalized by the following recursive definition:

$$\begin{cases} \frac{d[C_1]}{dt} = -J_1 - \sum_{k \geq 1}^{C_1(0)} J_k \\ \frac{d[C_i]}{dt} = J_{i-1} - J_i \end{cases} \tag{3}$$

for every $i \geq 2$, where J_i is the flux:

$$J_i = a[C_1][C_i] - b[C_{i+1}]. \tag{4}$$

In Formula (4), it is possible to recognize the generic process of coagulation, as a second order reaction, and the generic process of fragmentation, as a first order linear reaction.

At the basis of this model there are three fundamental assumptions:

- only a monomer coalesces to give rise a cluster;
- a cluster can release spontaneously a (single) monomer;
- at the initial stage of the system, only $C_1(0)$, namely the initial concentration of monomers, is different from 0, hence all the clusters, with size $i \geq 2$, develop successively.

From the last assumption, it follows that the initial concentration of C_1 determines the mass of the system, hence the largest dimension of the cluster that can be formed. Indeed, if we add 5 molecules in an ideal closed pot, the maximum cluster will have size 5, and the only possible clusters will be C_2, C_3, C_4, and C_5. Then, in a model with the initial concentration of monomers $C_1(0) = 5$, we will actually only have 4 enable reversible reactions (so, the size of the CRN is actually finite) as follows:

$$\begin{aligned} C_1 + C_1 &\underset{b}{\overset{a}{\rightleftharpoons}} C_2 \\ C_1 + C_2 &\underset{b}{\overset{a}{\rightleftharpoons}} C_3 \\ C_1 + C_3 &\underset{b}{\overset{a}{\rightleftharpoons}} C_4 \\ C_1 + C_4 &\underset{b}{\overset{a}{\rightleftharpoons}} C_5 \end{aligned} \tag{5}$$

Then, we obtain the following equations:

$$\begin{cases} \frac{d[C_1]}{dt} = -2a[C_1]^2 + 2b[C_2] - a[C_1][C_2] + b[C_3] - a[C_1][C_3] + b[C_4] - a[C_1][C_4] + b[C_5] \\ \frac{d[C_2]}{dt} = +a[C_1]^2 - b[C_2] - a[C_1][C_2] + b[C_3] \\ \frac{d[C_3]}{dt} = +a[C_1][C_2] - b[C_3] - a[C_1][C_3] + b[C_4] \\ \frac{d[C_4]}{dt} = +a[C_1][C_3] - b[C_4] - a[C_1][C_4] + b[C_5] \\ \frac{d[C_5]}{dt} = +a[C_1][C_4] - b[C_5]. \end{cases}$$

We notice that the expression for the biggest cluster is different from the others. In the previous example, indeed, the biggest cluster is C_5, which can only participate in fragmentation, otherwise other interactions it would create cluster bigger than 5, which is the total mass of the system. This is evident, also considering the fluxes.

Considering again a system with $C_1(0) = 5$, there are 4 fluxes, as follows:

$$
\begin{aligned}
J_1 &= a[C_1]^2 - b[C_2] \\
J_2 &= a[C_1][C_2] - b[C_3] \\
J_3 &= a[C_1][C_3] - b[C_4] \\
J_4 &= a[C_1][C_4] - b[C_5].
\end{aligned}
\tag{6}
$$

There is not a flux J_5 because the cluster of dimension 5 can be only involved in a spontaneous fragmentation because of the mass conservation.

The mass of the system (ρ) is conserved, hence the considered system has neither sinks nor sources. From the generic Formula (3) of differential equations we can deduce that the mass of system depends on the initial condition of the system and has the following form:

$$
\sum_{i \geq 1} iC_i(t) = \rho
\tag{7}
$$

3   Verification of Robustness Properties in Becker-Döring model

The Becker-Döring equations can be used to study different biological phenomena, as the formation of gradient concentrations, which we can define as the measurement of the variation of quantity of molecules from one area to another in the same system. This phenomenon is experimentally observable in unicellular and multicellular organisms, and it is involved in various processes, such as cellular differentiation, as described in [23,27].

In [23], the authors develop a theoretical model describing cluster aggregation-fragmentation in subcellular systems, based on the Becker-Döring equations, and show that, in particular conditions, the concentration gradient can be robust to relevant biological fluctuations. Therefore, we proceed to verify formally the robustness of the system based on Becker-Döring equations, applying different approaches that we can summarize as follows:

- *Application of Feinberg's Deficiency Theorems*;
- *Application of α-robustness and β-robustness*;
- *Analytical study of the steady state solution.*

3.1   Application of Deficiency Theorems

Biological properties are challenging to study because they require the observation of the system behavior, considering all the possible initial states.

For example, regarding the robustness evaluation of a signaling pathway, all the combinations of initial concentrations of chemical species need to be examined, and this requires many simulations with different hypotheses. For this reason, in literature, numerous papers introduce methods and approaches that assess this property by avoiding simulating the entire system. In particular, the study of how network structure/topology affects its dynamics, known as Chemical Reaction Network Theory (CRNT), has introduced concepts, such as the *deficiency*, and gives conditions for the existence, uniqueness, multiplicity, and stability of equilibrium points on networks endowed with different kinetics (e.g. mass action) [11]. In this context, the work done by Shinar and Feinberg provides a clear example of CRNT's application and lays the foundations to prove how the structure of a CRN characterizes its behavior. In [9], the *Deficiency One Theorem* and *Deficiency Zero Theorem* are presented, and both of them give crucial information about the steady state of the system, using only linear algebra and without any simulation.

In [24,25] the authors identify simple yet subtle structural attributes that impart concentration robustness to a mass action network that owns them. In their framework a biological system shows *absolute concentration robustness* (ACR) for an active molecular species if the concentration of such species is identical in every positive steady state the system admits. To describe their result, we need to introduce some terminology from CRNT. Consider the following mass action toy system, consisting of two species (A, B) and two reactions (R_1, R_2):

$$A + B \xrightarrow{k_1} 2B$$
$$B \xrightarrow{k_2} A,$$

(Example 1)

where (k_1, k_2) are commonly referred to as *kinetic* or *rate constants*.

The authors represent the system above as a directed graph, using the Standard Reaction Diagram (SRD), shown in Fig. 1. Each node of the graph is a *complex* of the network, defined as the group of reactants/products that are linked by

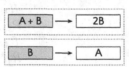

Fig. 1. SRD representation of our toy model

arrows. In this case, there are 4 nodes (A+B, 2B, B, A), represented in the solid boxes. A complex is called *terminal*, if it lies always at the tail of reaction arrows, otherwise it is *non-terminal*. In the example, there are two non-terminal nodes (A+B, B), in grey, and two terminal nodes (2B, A), in white. The groups in which the network is divided are its *linkage classes*; here, there are two linkage classes, in the dashed boxes. Finally, we introduce the *deficiency* δ of the network, a non-negative integer index representing the amount of *linear independence* among the reactions of the network and it is calculated as $\delta = n - l - r$, where n and l are the numbers of nodes and linkage classes, respectively, r is the rank of the stoichiometric matrix Γ. The deficiency of the network is equal to 1 ($\delta = 4 - 2 - 1$).

Shinar and Feinberg prove that a mass action system, which admits a positive steady state and is characterized by $\delta = 1$, shows absolute concentration robustness if it has two non-terminal complexes that differ only in one species [24]. In our example, complexes "A+B" and "B" differ in species "A".

On the contrary, if the deficiency is equal to zero, no matter what values the rate constants take, there is no species relative to which the system exhibits absolute concentration robustness, as proved in [25].

Application of the Deficiency One Theorem on BD Model. In order to verify the robustness of the Becker-Döring model, as first step we proceed calculating its deficiency. We consider the set of reactions of Example 5.

As for Example 1, to calculate the deficiency δ, we need to define the number of nodes and the linkage classes, and the rank of the matrix stoichiometric matrix, Γ. In this case, we consider as a species each possible cluster C_i.

- *Nodes* (n) are one or more chemical species involved in forward and backward reaction. We have 8 nodes: $C_1 + C_1$, C_2, $C_1 + C_2$, C_3, $C_1 + C_3$, C_4, $C_1 + C_4$, C_5;
- *linkage classes* (l) are the "groups" of reactions which compose the network, then we have 4 linkage classes;
- Considering the following matrix $r \times N$ (which is the transpose of the stoichiometric matrix Γ), we obtain that the *rank* (r) is 4.

$$
\begin{array}{c}
\phantom{R_{1b}} \\
R_1 \\
R_{1b} \\
R_2 \\
R_{2b} \\
R_3 \\
R_{3b} \\
R_4 \\
R_{4b}
\end{array}
\begin{array}{c}
C_1\ C_2\ C_3\ C_4\ C_5 \\
\left[\begin{array}{rrrrr}
-2 & +1 & 0 & 0 & 0 \\
+2 & -1 & 0 & 0 & 0 \\
-1 & -1 & +1 & 0 & 0 \\
+1 & +1 & -1 & 0 & 0 \\
-1 & 0 & -1 & +1 & 0 \\
+1 & 0 & +1 & -1 & 0 \\
-1 & 0 & 0 & -1 & +1 \\
+1 & 0 & 0 & +1 & -1
\end{array}\right]
\end{array}
$$

Then, the deficiency $\delta = n - l - r$ is equal to $\delta = 8 - 4 - 4 = 0$. Therefore, as described in [25] each of the clusters involved in the system cannot be considered robust according to the definition given by Shinar and Feinberg. Therefore, we proceed applying our definition of the *initial concentration robustness*, which extends the definition given in [25].

3.2 Application of α-robustness and β-robustness

As already described in [20], we want to focus on the evaluation of the initial concentration robustness. We want to vary the concentration of at least one chemical species (namely the *input*) and to verify, at the equilibrium, if the concentration of another species (namely the *output*) is included in an interval of possible values. In order to do that, we recall the definition of the initial concentration robustness, that are formalized by continuous Petri nets. Petri nets has the advantage to provide a graphical support that abstracts away from technical details in the system description. As demonstrated by many biologists, in fact, graphical representations of qualitative trends are often useful to provide intuitions on the network main features [7].

Definition 1 (Continuous Petri net). A *continuous Petri net* N can be defined as a quintuple $\langle P, T, F, W, m_0 \rangle$ where:

- P is the set of continuous *places*, conceptually one for each considered kind of system resource;
- T is the set of continuous *transitions* that consume and produce resources;
- $F \subseteq (P \times T) \bigcup (T \times P) \to \mathbb{R}_{\geq 0}$ represents the set of arcs in terms of a function giving the weight of the arc as result: a weight equal to 0 means that the arc is not present;
- $W : F \to \mathbb{R}_{\geq 0}$ is a function, which associates each transition with a *rate*;
- m_0 is the *initial marking*, that is the initial distribution of *tokens* (representing resource instances) among places. A marking is defined formally as $m : P \to \mathbb{R}_{\geq 0}$. The domain of all markings is M.

Tokens are movable objects, assigned to places, that are consumed by transitions in the input places and produced in the output places. Graphically, a Petri net is drawn as a graph with nodes representing places and transitions. Circles are used for places and rectangles for transitions. Tokens are drawn as black dots inside places. Graph edges represent arcs and are labeled with their weights. To faithfully model biochemical networks, the marking of a place is not an integer (the number of tokens) but a positive real number (called *token value* representing the concentration of a chemical species. Each transition is associated with a kinetic constant, that determines the rate of (continuous) flow of tokens from the input to the output places of the transition.

In order to give the definition, we recall some notions introduced by Nasti et al. in [20]. The initial marking is defined as an assignment of a fixed value to each place p. Now, it is possible to generalize the idea of initial marking by considering a marking as an assignment of a *interval of values* to each place p of the Petri net.

We first recall the definition of the domain of intervals.

Definition 2 (Intervals). The interval domain is defined as

$$\mathcal{I} = \{[min, max] \mid min, max \in \mathbb{R}_{\geq 0} \cup \{+\infty\} \text{ and } min \leq max\}.$$

An interval $[min, max] \in \mathcal{I}$ is *trivial* iff $min = max$. Moreover, $x \in [min, max]$ iff $min \leq x \leq max$.

We now define interval markings.

Definition 3 (Interval marking). Given a set of places P, an *interval marking* is a function $m_{[\,]} : P \to \mathcal{I}$. The domain of all interval markings is $M_{[\,]}$.

An interval marking in which at least one interval is non-trivial represents an infinite set of markings, one for each possible combination of values of the non-trivial intervals. Therefore, given an interval marking, we relate it with the markings as in the original Petri nets formalism in the following way:

Given $m \in M$ and $m_{[\ ]} \in M_{[\ ]}$, $m \in m_{[\ ]}$ iff $\forall p \in P$, $m(p) \in m_{[\ ]}(p)$.

In a Petri net we assume that there exists *at least one* input place and *exactly one* output place representing input and output species of the modeled biochemical network, respectively. Under this assumption, we can give the formal definition of robustness.

Definition 4 (α-Robustness). A Petri net N with output place O is *α-robust with respect to a given interval marking* $m_{[\ ]}$ iff $\exists k \in \mathbb{R}$ such that $\forall m \in m_{[\ ]}$, the marking m' corresponding to the concentrations at the steady state reachable from m, is such that

$$m'(O) \in [k - \frac{\alpha}{2}, k + \frac{\alpha}{2}].$$

To compare the α-robustness of different systems or the α-robustness of the same system with different perturbations, we have to introduce another notion: the *relative β-robustness*. First of all, we introduce the concept of normalization of α-robustness defined as:

Definition 5 (Normalized α-robustness). Let N, α ans k be as in Definition 4. The normalized α-robustness of the output O, denoted n_O, is defined as $\frac{\alpha}{k}$.

Definition 6 (Normalized Input). Let N and α be as in Definition 4. Let $[min, max]$ with $min \neq max$ be the interval marking of the input I, defining its initial conditions, and k_I be its midpoint. The normalized input n_I, is defined as $\frac{max - min}{k_I}$.

Therefore, we can state the definition of relative initial concentration robustness as follows:

Definition 7 (Relative β-robustness). Let N be as in Definition 4. The relative initial concentration robustness, denoted as β-robustness, is defined as: $\frac{n_O}{n_I}$, where n_O and n_I are respectively the normalized α-robustness and the normalized input I.

Application α-robustness and β-robustness on BD Model. In order to apply our definition 4, we need to build the Petri net of the BD model, as represented in Fig. 2. We associate to each cluster a place, represented by a circle, and to each reaction a transition, represented by a square. We connect places and transitions by arrows that are defined by the reactions. We identify as input and output of the network the concentration of monomer C_1, in agreement with the assumptions we mentioned in Sect. 2.2. Indeed, C_1 is the only cluster present at the initial state of the system, and it is the cluster involved in every aggregation

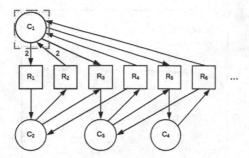

Fig. 2. The Petri net for the BD model. C_1 is both the input and the output of the network. The encountered problems are that the Petri net is potentially infinite and, by changing the initial conditions of the network, we obtain different Petri nets

and fragmentation process. We notice that the Petri net is potentially infinite, because every time we change the initial concentration of the system we change the set of differential equations, describing the system.

We change the mass of the system, in a wide range of values, to study the concentration of monomers at the steady state. As we can notice in Fig. 3, we find out that, assuming as constant the coefficient rates $a = 1$ and $b = 1$, the concentration of C_1 tends to 1 at the steady state, even with very different initial conditions: we change the initial concentration of C_1 in the range [5, 1500].

Then, we proceed applying the definition of β-robustness (Definition 7). Considering as initial conditions the interval $C_1 = [100, 300]$. By looking at the simulation results, we find that at the steady state, the concentration of C_1 is within the interval and [0.91, 0.95].

We calculate the normalized α-robustness (Definition 5), obtaining:

$$n_O = \frac{\alpha}{k} = \frac{0.04}{0.93} = 0.04.$$

The normalized input values is calculated as follows:

$$n_I = \frac{m_I}{k_I} = \frac{[300 - 100]}{\frac{[300+100]}{2}} = 1.$$

Then, the relative β-robustness is trivially calculated as follows:

$$\beta - robustness = \frac{n_O}{n_I} = 0.04.$$

In Table 1, we summarize the initial concentration of C_1, its concentrations at the steady state, the α and the β-robustness. We notice that increasing the initial concentration of the input, we obtain that the α-robustness of the model tends to 0. This result leads us to formalize a new notion of robustness, namely the *asymptotic robustness*.

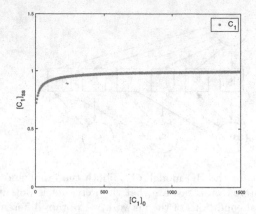

Fig. 3. Simulations result of Becker-Döring model. We plot on the horizontal axis the initial concentration of C_1, in a range $[5, 1500]$, and on the vertical axis the concentration of C_1 at the steady state. We assume the coefficient rates a and b are constant and equal to 1

Definition 8 (Asymptotic Robustness). Let N, α and k be as in Definition 4. A Petri net N with output place O is *asymptotically robust* iff as $k \to \infty$, $\alpha \to 0$.

Table 1. The intervals, the concentrations of monomer reached at the steady state, and the value of the α and β-robustness

Intervals	Steady state concentration	α-robustness	β-robustness
$[100, 300]$	$[0.91, 0.95]$	0.03	0.04
$[300, 500]$	$[0.95, 0.97]$	0.02	0.04
$[500, 700]$	$[0.97, 0.98]$	0.01	0.03
$[700, 900]$	$[0.9806, 0.985]$	0.005	0.004

The simulations about the asymptotic robustness persuade us to analytically study the solution of the steady state formula because we want to verify this particular systems behaviour formally. However, this approach cannot be applied indistinctly because of the biological systems' complexity. Indeed, in most cases, it is not possible to derive analytically the steady state formula.

3.3 Analysis of the Steady State

In the simulation result shown in Fig. 3, the concentration of monomer C_1 appears to be robust at the steady state. Indeed, we change, in a wide range of values, the input of the system (C_1) and we notice that the output (C_1) tends to 1 at the steady state, considering the coefficient rates a and b constant and equal to 1.

Then, in line with the other works presented in literature [3,18,22], our main result in the analytical study of steady state is the following:

Theorem 1 (Monomers Steady State). *Let a and b be the coefficient rates of coagulation and fragmentation process in the Becker-Döring system, ρ the mass of the system and $[C_1]_{ss}$ the concentration of monomers at the steady state. Then, as $\rho \to \infty$, $[C_1]_{ss} \to \frac{b}{a}$.*

Proof As described in Sect. 2.2, the crucial assumption of the Becker-Döring model is mass conservation, which therefore depends on the initial concentration of monomers, hence the mass ρ at the initial state will remain the same at the steady state, that is the sum of the fluxes of the species goes to zero. Then, recalling Formula 7, we can write:

$$\rho(0) = \rho(\infty) = \sum_{i=1}^{k} i \cdot C_i, \qquad (8)$$

where k is the maximum number of molecules in the system, hence it is $k = \rho$. Generalizing the fluxes formulas, as in example 6, we deduce the general steady state formula for a cluster of dimension i, as follows:

$$[C_i]_{ss} = \left(\frac{a}{b}\right)^{i-1} [C_1]_{ss}^i. \qquad (9)$$

Replacing (9) in (8), we obtain:

$$\begin{aligned} \rho &= \sum_{i=1}^{k} i \left(\frac{a}{b}\right)^{i-1} [C_1]_{ss}^i \\ &= \frac{b}{a} \sum_{i=1}^{k} i \left(\frac{a}{b}[C_1]_{ss}\right)^i \\ &= \frac{b}{a} \frac{k(\frac{a}{b}C_1)^{k+2} - (k+1)(\frac{a}{b}C_1)^{k+1} + (\frac{a}{b}C_1)}{(1 - \frac{a}{b}C_1)^2}. \end{aligned} \qquad (10)$$

We want to study the asymptotic behaviour of C_1, then we define:

$$\lim_{t \to \infty} C_1(t) := x_k.$$

Equating (10) with its general form, we get:

$$k = x + \frac{a}{b}2x^2 + \ldots + \frac{a^{k-1}}{b^{k-1}}kx^k = \frac{b}{a} \cdot \frac{k \cdot \frac{a}{b}x^{(k+2)} - (k+1) \cdot \frac{a}{b}x^{(k+1)} + \frac{a}{b}x}{(1 - \frac{a}{b}x)^2}.$$

We can rearrange the previous expression as follows:

$$1 = \frac{x}{k} + \frac{a}{b}\frac{2}{k}x^2 + \dots + \frac{a^{k-1}}{b^{k-1}}x^k = \frac{b}{a} \cdot \frac{k \cdot \frac{a}{b}x^{(k+2)} - (k+1) \cdot \frac{a}{b}x^{(k+1)} + \frac{a}{b}x}{k \cdot (1 - \frac{a}{b}x)^2}, \quad (11)$$

and we define:

$$g_k(x) = \frac{x}{k} + \frac{a}{b}\frac{2}{k}x^2 + \dots + \frac{a^{k-1}}{b^{k-1}}x^k,$$

$$= \frac{b}{a} \cdot \frac{k \cdot \frac{a}{b}x^{(k+2)} - (k+1) \cdot \frac{a}{b}x^{(k+1)} + \frac{a}{b}x}{k \cdot (1 - \frac{a}{b}x)^2}.$$

We will need both expressions because they make it simpler to observe different properties.

– $g_k(x)$ is an increasing function of x
– with simple algebraic manipulation, we get:

$$g_k(x) = \frac{1}{k} \cdot \frac{b}{a}\left(\frac{a}{b}x + \frac{a^2}{b^2}2x^2 + \dots + k\frac{a^k}{b^k}x^k\right)$$

from which it is easy to see that:

$$g_k\left(\frac{b}{a}\right) = \frac{1}{k} \cdot \frac{b}{a}(1 + 2 + \dots + k) = \frac{b}{a} \cdot \frac{k+1}{2}.$$

– Following the first two items, we notice that there is one and only one solution for the equation $g_k(x) = 1, \forall k$, in the range $\left[0, \frac{b}{a}\right]$.
– Looking at the other expression for the function $g_k(x)$, we find that

$$\lim_{k \to \infty} g_k(x) = 0, \quad \forall x \in \left[0, \frac{b}{a}\right).$$

– Because of the previous limit, if we now take a generic $x^* < \frac{b}{a}$, then, for k large enough we will have $g_k(x^*) < g_k(x_k) \equiv 1$ Since the function is increasing and monotonic with respect to x, then:

$$\frac{g_k(x_k) - g_k(x^*)}{x_k - x^*} > 0 \Rightarrow x_k > x^*.$$

This shows that, for k large enough, $x_k > x^*, \forall x^* < \frac{b}{a}$. Therefore $x_k \geq \frac{b}{a}$.

For an intuitive visualization of what just said, in Fig. 4 we show a plot of the $g_k(x)$ in the particular case where $a = b$.

Our result is shown also in Fig. 3, where we consider as rates of the system $a = b$.

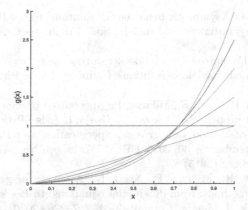

Fig. 4. The plot of the function $g(x)$. Graphically, we see that the curves of function $g(x)$ will be closer to zero, increasing the value of k

4   Conclusion and Future Work

In this paper we focused on the study of robustness of Becker-Döring equations [2], a model that describes condensations phenomena at different pressures. First, we show that the definition given by Shinar and Feinberg is particularly limiting in the description of the BD model's behavior. Then, by applying our definitions of α and β robustness, we show how the BD model is robust with respect to the perturbation on the initial concentration of monomers.

Concerning this, we prove that the concentration of monomer tends to the ratio of coefficients at the steady state and we show this result by simulations. This result leads us to introduce a new notion of robustness, namely the asymptotic robustness. This new notion intends to describe how a system becomes more robust increasing the initial concentration of the input. In order to support our result, in this case, we studied analytically the solution of the steady state formula. Note that, as remarked in the text, it is not always possible to solve the differential equations system.

We have analysed so far the Becker-Döring equations assuming that the coefficient rates of agglomeration and fragmentation are constant real values. We could improve this analysis introducing some physical aspects of the model. As described in [3,22,26], the size and the shape of clusters involved in the reactions influence the dynamical properties of the system. The next step of this preliminary research will be to simulate this system using real rates from specific application domains, useful to describe biological phenomena such as protein aggregation in neurodegenerative diseases.

References

1. Angeli, D., De Leenheer, P., Sontag, E.D.: On the structural monotonicity of chemical reaction networks. In: 2006 45th IEEE Conference on Decision and Control, pp. 7–12. IEEE (2006)

2. Ball, J.M., Carr, J.: Asymptotic behaviour of solutions to the Becker-döring equations for arbitrary initial data. Proc. R. Soc. Edinb. Sect. A Math. **108**(1–2), 109–116 (1988)

3. Ball, J.M., Carr, J., Penrose, O.: The Becker-döring cluster equations: basic properties and asymptotic behaviour of solutions. Commun. Math. Phys. **104**(4), 657–692 (1986)

4. Barbuti, R., Gori, R., Levi, F., Milazzo, P.: Specialized predictor for reaction systems with context properties. In: Suraj, Z., Czaja, L. (eds.) Proceedings of the 24th International Workshop on Concurrency, Specification and Programming, Rzeszow, Poland, September 28–30, 2015. CEUR Workshop Proceedings, vol. 1492, pp. 31–43. CEUR-WS.org (2015)

5. Barbuti, R., Gori, R., Milazzo, P., Nasti, L.: A survey of gene regulatory networks modelling methods: from differential equations, to Boolean and qualitative bioinspired models. J. Membr. Comput. **2**(3), 207–226 (2020)

6. Becker, R., Döring, W.: Kinetische behandlung der keimbildung in übersättigten dämpfen. Ann. Phys. **416**(8), 719–752 (1935)

7. Blanchini, F., Franco, E.: Structurally robust biological networks. BMC Syst. Biol. **5**(1), 74 (2011)

8. Burton, J.: Nucleation theory. In: Berne, B.J. (eds.) Statistical Mechanics. Modern Theoretical Chemistry, vol. 5, pp. 195–234. Springer, Boston, MA (1977). https://doi.org/10.1007/978-1-4684-2553-6_6

9. Feinberg, M.: Chemical reaction network structure and the stability of complex isothermal reactors-i. the deficiency zero and deficiency one theorems. Chem. Eng. Sci. **42**(10), 2229–2268 (1987)

10. Gori, R., Milazzo, P., Nasti, L.: Towards an efficient verification method for monotonicity properties of chemical reaction networks. In: Bioinformatics, pp. 250–257 (2019)

11. Gunawardena, J.: Chemical reaction network theory for in-silico biologists. Notes (2003). http://vcp.med.harvard.edu/papers/crnt.pdf

12. Hingant, E., Yvinec, R.: Deterministic and stochastic Becker–döring equations: past and recent mathematical developments. In: Holcman, D. (ed.) Stochastic Processes, Multiscale Modeling, and Numerical Methods for Computational Cellular Biology, pp. 175–204. Springer, Cham (2017). https://doi.org/10.1007/978-3-319-62627-7_9

13. Hoze, N., Holcman, D.: Coagulation-fragmentation for a finite number of particles and application to telomere clustering in the yeast nucleus. Phys. Lett. A **376**(6–7), 845–849 (2012)

14. Hozé, N., Holcman, D.: Modeling capsid kinetics assembly from the steady state distribution of multi-sizes aggregates. Phys. Lett. A **378**(5–6), 531–534 (2014)

15. Hoze, N., Holcman, D.: Kinetics of aggregation with a finite number of particles and application to viral capsid assembly. J. Math. Biol. **70**(7), 1685–1705 (2014). https://doi.org/10.1007/s00285-014-0819-2

16. Kitano, H.: Biological robustness. Nat. Rev. Genet. **5**(11), 826–837 (2004)

17. Krapivsky, P.L., Redner, S., Ben-Naim, E.: A Kinetic View of Statistical Physics. Cambridge University Press, Cambridge (2010)

18. Kreer, M.: Classical Becker-döring cluster equations: rigorous results on metastability and long-time behaviour. Ann. Phys. **505**(4), 398–417 (1993)

19. Nasti, L.: Verification of Robustness Property in Chemical Reaction Networks. Ph.D. thesis, Universitità di Pisa, Dipartimento di Informatica (2020)

20. Nasti, L., Gori, R., Milazzo, P.: Formalizing a notion of concentration robustness for biochemical networks. In: Mazzara, M., Ober, I., Salaün, G. (eds.) STAF 2018. LNCS, vol. 11176, pp. 81–97. Springer, Cham (2018). https://doi.org/10.1007/978-3-030-04771-9_8
21. Nasti, L., Gori, R., Milazzo, P., Poloni, F.: Efficient analysis of chemical reaction networks dynamics based on input-output monotonicity. arXiv preprint arXiv:2107.00289 (2021)
22. Penrose, O.: Metastable states for the Becker-döring cluster equations. Commun. Math. Phys. **124**(4), 515–541 (1989)
23. Saunders, T.E.: Aggregation-fragmentation model of robust concentration gradient formation. Phys. Rev. E **91**(2), 022704 (2015)
24. Shinar, G., Feinberg, M.: Structural sources of robustness in biochemical reaction networks. Science **327**(5971), 1389–1391 (2010)
25. Shinar, G., Feinberg, M.: Design principles for robust biochemical reaction networks: what works, what cannot work, and what might almost work. Math. Biosci. **231**(1), 39–48 (2011)
26. Slemrod, M.: The becker-döring equations. In:Bellomo, N., Pulvirenti, M. (eds.) Modeling and Simulation in Science, Engineering and Technology, pp. 149–171. Springer, Boston (2000). https://doi.org/10.1007/978-1-4612-0513-5_5
27. Wolpert, L.: Positional information and the spatial pattern of cellular differentiation. J. Theor. Biol. **25**(1), 1–47 (1969)

A Secure User-Centred Healthcare System: Design and Verification

Eduard Baranov[1](✉) ⓘ, Juliana Bowles[2] ⓘ, Thomas Given-Wilson[1] ⓘ,
Axel Legay[1] ⓘ, and Thais Webber[2] ⓘ

[1] Computer Science and Engineering Department, Université Catholique de Louvain,
Louvain-la-Neuve, Belgium
{eduard.baranov,thomas.given-wilson,axel.legay}@uclouvain.be
[2] School of Computer Science, University of St Andrews, St Andrews KY16 9SX, UK
{jkfb,tcwds}@st-andrews.ac.uk

Abstract. With ever increasing amounts of travel, it is essential to
have access to a patient's medical data from different sources including
many jurisdictions. The Serums project addresses this goal by creating
a healthcare sharing system that places privacy and security aspects at
the center. This raises significant challenges to both maintain privacy
and security of medical data and to allow for sharing and access. To
address these strict requirements the Serums system design is supported
by formal methods where design decisions are modelled and checked to
meet safety and security properties. We report an experience in support
of the system design with formal modelling with the UPPAAL tool and
analysis with exhaustive and statistical model checking. Results show
that statistical model checking being a simulation-based technique can
significantly improve feasibility of analysis while providing support for
design decisions to ensure privacy and security.

Keywords: Healthcare · Data sharing · Privacy · Security · Design
verification · Formal modelling

1 Introduction

Improving patient care has become a priority across European healthcare
providers and government establishments [19]. There is an increasing movement
towards fulfilling patients' rights to securely access and share their health data
across borders [27]. For example, when traveling abroad a patient may require a
specialist to follow up their ongoing treatment; the patient may even experience
some kind of medical emergency. Such data sharing can help healthcare professionals and organisations to improve their care services to patients in terms of
efficiency, effectiveness, and enhanced decision making [10]. However, a healthcare data sharing system must ensure data protection and security and be in
line with the European General Data Protection Regulation[1] (GDPR).

---

[1] Information on GDPR can be found at https://gdpr-info.eu/.

J. Bowles et al. (Eds.): DataMod 2021, LNCS 13268, pp. 44–60, 2022.
https://doi.org/10.1007/978-3-031-16011-0_4

The EU Horizon 2020 research project Serums[2] aims to increase healthcare provision in Europe through the proposal of a secure and transparent data sharing platform able to ensure privacy when accessing patient data [23]. Serums is grounded in two major pillars. First, the application of innovative techniques and emergent technologies like Blockchain and Data Lake to increase reliability and resilience against cyber-attacks. Second, to promote user trust in the safe and secure operation of the system in hospitals and clinics. The literature points out that Blockchain and smart contracts have great potential for enabling secure medical data access to healthcare parties [30, 35].

The core of the Serums Smart Health Central System (SHCS), which is the focus of this paper, involves several software components interacting with each other to provide fine-grained access control with audit trail to the patients' medical information stored in multiple data vaults.

A mechanism to customise access control over medical records is put in place between Blockchain and Data Lake technologies to allow authorised users to access medical data on demand, following data access rules predetermined by patients and healthcare organisations within the system. The data exchange format provided by Data Lake in Serums is the Smart Patient Health Record (SPHR), which provides metadata information linking the patients to subsets of medical data distributed across different hospital databases. Access rules to the SPHR are part of the smart contracts that can be customised by users in the Blockchain.

Serums provides the means in which patients can create access rules over personal records to healthcare professionals as well as healthcare organisations (i.e., administrators) can manage its users and specific rules to establish the boundaries for accessing patient data. For instance, the system allows authorised users to define *who* and *when* exactly *what* parts of medical records can be accessed. The Serums SHCS aims to maintain the system's security with reduced likelihood of privacy breaches. Due to the sensitive area that concerns Serums, verifying its platform is an important step in the system development cycle of the project [23]. Especially, one must prove that the architecture design choices ensure meeting strict privacy and security requirements. Such validation shall be done at design time as per request of the GDPR.

In this paper, we focus on this validation objective using formal methods, i.e., by applying approaches that work on a formal representation of both the system and the requirements under validation. Such representation is language agnostic which allows us to concentrate on the requirements to be verified. Another advantage of formal representation is that this naturally offers a clear semantics, which are particularly useful to improve the system in case of bug detection. Formal methods have been used in multiple projects to support the analysis of systems and their design, e.g. [8, 13, 21, 24, 26]. One of the commonly used representations for systems is transition systems [4] where system behaviour is modelled with a set of states and a relation between them describing how the system can change states. In formal methods, requirements are represented with temporal logic [5].

---

[2] For more information refer to https://www.serums-h2020.org.

Such logic is a temporal extension of the classical Boolean logic that permits the validation of a hypothesis on sequences of transitions.

Among existing formal methods that can be applied to transition systems and temporal logic, there is *Model checking* (MC) [14,32]. MC offers an exhaustive exploration of the state space of the system. Contrary to software testing, MC guarantees that any behaviour of the model satisfies the property. Unfortunately, albeit the approach has been widely deployed, it is still subject to the so-called state space explosion problem: state space of non-trivial systems can be extremely large making exhaustive exploration infeasible. To avoid these issues, several authors have proposed *Statistical Model Checking* (SMC) [22,28,29,34] as a compromise between testing and MC. The core idea of SMC is to run many simulations on which a property is checked and to use a statistical algorithm to decide the probability of the property to be satisfied with a selected degree of confidence. SMC has been broadly applied in different areas and projects including [6,7,18,25,36,38].

The contribution of the paper is to provide a formal representation of the Serums platform and to validate Serums requirements on the formal representation. The SMC approach has been implemented in a wide range of tools (a comparison can be found in [3]), among which we have selected the UPPAAL toolset [1,9,16] that includes an SMC engine. UPPAAL supports both MC and SMC, is efficient, and has been used in many projects, e.g. [20,31,33]. The Serums platform in UPPAAL is represented with stochastic timed automata, i.e., transition systems equipped with both timed and stochastic information [17]. The timing constraints are currently not being used, though the tool support offers a possibility to extend the model and to consider time-dependent properties in the future. Our model is parametrisable, scalable, and modular in such a way that we offer a library of automata to represent and hence duplicate at will each piece of the system. This aspect allows easy incorporation of any conceptual change that may occur in the project and simulation of real-life situations.

We first verified a set of safety and reachability properties on increasing model size (obtained by increasing the number of users of the model). This allowed us to show that the system behaves correctly in non-trivial instantiations with many users. While MC can only be applied to a significantly simplified model, SMC can verify the full model. In a second step, we proposed a transition-system based representation of an attacker, i.e., a malicious user that would try to have access to Serums Data Lake without going through the central system. In case of success, such attacker could get access to private data of others which would compromise the security of the entire design. With our model we were able to show that the first version of the platform integration was indeed subject to such attack. By using UPPAAL, we were able to correct our model and hence the corresponding concrete design.

The structure of the paper is as follows. Section 2 introduces UPPAAL tool and related concepts. Section 3 overviews the Serums platform architecture detail specifying components and interactions in the form of a workflow. Section 4 presents the model created with the UPPAAL tool that is used for the evaluation of the Serums platform design. Subsection 4.1 demonstrates the model checking process considering reachability and safety properties and providing a comparison between MC and SMC approaches. Section 5 introduces a security aspect to the verification process exploring the resilience of the design to attacks and the necessity of security consideration at design stage. Section 6 highlights the applicability and the need for SMC in cases like Serums to ensure the system reaches the expected behaviour providing privacy and security to end-users.

2   Background

Systems in UPPAAL are modelled as a set of timed automata interacting with each other via channels controlling the synchronisation of transitions of several automata and shared variables. UPPAAL also provides a mechanism to model multiple automata with identical behaviour - a template that can have parameters and be instantiated any number of times for the simulation. Templates provide means to analyse different scenarios with various number of automata.

For the properties, UPPAAL provides a query language based on a simplified version of Timed Computation Tree Logic (TCTL). Temporal operators require a property to hold in either all execution paths, denoted with A, or in at least one execution path, denoted with E. In addition, operators have different modalities quantifying over specific paths. For example, $A\Box p$ requires proposition p to hold in all states of all execution paths and $E\Diamond p$ requires p to hold in at least one state of at least one execution path. Note that UPPAAL does not allow nesting of formulas involving temporal operators, i.e. temporal operator can only be the outermost operator in the formula, therefore formulas like $E\Diamond p$ && $E\Diamond q$ shall be separated into 2 queries for p and q respectively.

Contrary to MC exhaustively exploring the state space, SMC is based on the idea of performing large number of system executions and monitoring the desired property on the executions. For non-deterministic systems, each execution would be different, thus multiple executions would explore various parts of the system behaviour. Being a simulation-based approach, SMC is known to be less time and memory consuming than MC. UPPAAL SMC [16] is an extension of UPPAAL to perform Statistical Model Checking. The extension works with stochastic timed automata, adds probabilistic choice between enabled transitions and probability distribution for time delays. For the interaction between automata only broadcast channels are allowed to be used to ensure components be non-blocking.

For the queries, UPPAAL SMC uses an extension of Metric Interval Temporal Logic (MITL). Note that property check with SMC engine is performed on finite traces unlike in original UPPAAL tool, therefore linear time is considered instead of branching. Basic temporal operators in UPPAAL SMC are $\Box p$ and $\Diamond p$ checking that p holds in all or at least one state of the trace respectively. There are different types of SMC queries supported by UPPAAL, the following ones are used further in the paper. The first type computes a probability of a property to be satisfied and is specified with $Pr[\# \leq N]\ F$, where F is a property specified

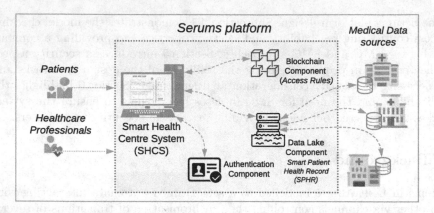

Fig. 1. An instance of the Serums platform with local Blockchain, Data Lake, and Authentication Components.

with MITL, N is the maximal trace length and $\#$ indicates that we consider number of transitions in the trace length instead of time. The result of such query would be an interval $[x - \epsilon, x + \epsilon]$ with a confidence α, where ϵ and α are selected parameters. Another query type checks a hypothesis that probability of a property to be satisfied is above a given threshold: $Pr[\# \leq N]\ F \geq p_0$, where F and N are defined as above. For each query UPPAAL SMC builds a monitor that can check the property during the simulation, thus avoiding creation of a full simulation trace if the property can be decided on the first few steps. For the details of the monitoring, we address the reader to [12].

3 Serums System Design

The Serums project [23] addresses the need to securely share medical data to allow healthcare provision across different healthcare providers. For a patient visiting a new hospital, e.g., after the relocation to a different city or country, there shall be a simple way to access the patient's medical history as it is essential to provide effective healthcare. In contention with data sharing, the GDPR requires that the data shall be under the control of the patient: a patient's consent and approval are necessary for data access. The project goal is to create a platform for accessing and transferring these medical records in a secure and privacy-preserving manner among parties [23] that also meet regulatory requirements.

The overall architecture of the proposed platform is shown in Fig. 1. Serums platform architecture consists of several components interacting with a Smart Health Centre System (SHCS) [37]. The SHCS is a front-end that interacts with users (patients and professionals) and it is connected directly to other architectural components [11]. The Authentication component, which is central to check users' credentials, enables users' requests placed to other core components, like

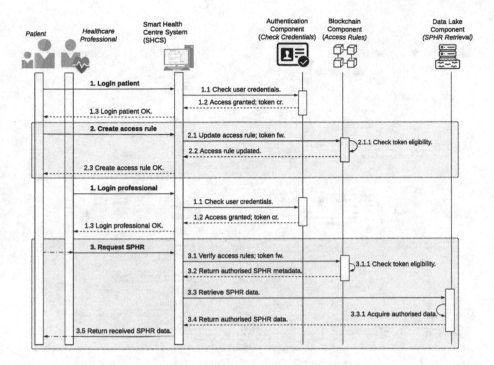

Fig. 2. Serums sequence diagram design showing the workflow for the main functionalities in the system.

Blockchain and Data Lake. The Data Lake component is responsible for performing on-demand data acquisition and data processing: it can retrieve data from different sources and create a Smart Patient Health Record (SPHR) [10] structuring medical data as metadata. Upon request a patient's data can be securely retrieved and visualised by a given authorised healthcare professional.

Patients can control the data sharing with fine-grained access rules stored in smart contracts in the Blockchain component. The smart contracts contain access rules defining the access granted or denied to individuals, to parts of the patient's record, and for a given period of time. For example, a patient can make general information such as *name* and *blood type* be available to all medical personnel while specific *test results* shall be visible to the treating doctor only.

The main workflow of the Serums system is shown in Fig. 2. At first step (1) a patient tries to connect to the Serums SHCS and the request (1.1) is processed by the Authentication component. Authentication is done via JSON Web Token (JWT): a user after successful login receives a token that identifies him in all subsequent requests. At the next step (2) the patient can create a data access rule, for example, allowing a given healthcare professional to see his treatment history. This rule is added to the Blockchain (2.1), which first checks the forwarded access token for eligibility (2.1.1). At any further time, a healthcare professional can login (similarly via authentication component) and

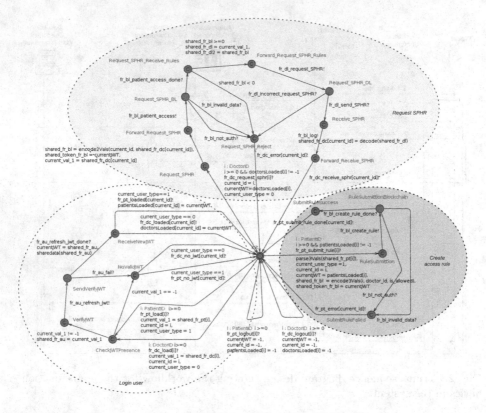

Fig. 3. SHCS component model.

choose to request patient's record (3). The request is sent to Blockchain (3.1) which confirms the access token eligibility (3.1.1) and afterwards returns to the SHCS the authorised metadata (3.2) that can be retrieved to the user according to the current rules in place for him. The SHCS then requests the medical data retrieval to the Data Lake component (3.3), which acquires data from varied data sources (3.3.1) and return the SPHR data to the requester in the front-end (3.4).

4 Serums System Modelling and Verification

Formal model being developed during design time can vastly improve safety and security of the resulted system. Building models of well-defined design decisions is straightforward and these models can then be analysed or verified using techniques such as MC and SMC. Given such a set of requirements, MC and SMC can provide insight on which decisions provide more guarantees.

For the verification of the Serums system design we are building a model within the UPPAAL tool and using it to check properties and to test different design options. In the figures automata are represented with a graph where

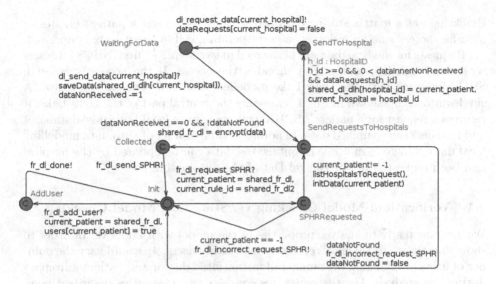

Fig. 4. Data Lake component model.

nodes are states of the system (their names are labelled with maroon) and edges are transitions defining how the system change states. Transitions have optional labels: tan label defines local variables to be used in other labels; green label is a guard controlling transition availability; turquoise label specifies synchronisation channel; blue label describe variables updates. Committed states marked with symbol C provide an additional control over system execution: if at least one automaton is in committed state then next transition shall be from one of such states. Detailed description of UPPAAL models can be found in [9].

The model follows the Serums platform (Fig. 1) design and involves one or several automata for each component. The SHCS automaton shown in Fig. 3 is the central component interacting with users and other Serums components. Automata modelling patients and healthcare professionals are quite similar: they first can try to login to the Serums SHCS which includes interaction with the front-end Authentication automaton and then send one of the requests depicted in the sequence diagram in Fig. 2. In the model and properties, the term *doctor* is used in place of healthcare professional.

Login requests are initialised by users via interaction with SHCS that transfers them to the Authentication component modelled with two automata. The first automaton interacts with users during login and sign-up procedures and the second serves as a back-end simply responding to requests. Upon successful login, the back-end automaton generates an abstracted JWT that is shared with the user. The JWT is included in all subsequent user requests.

To create and modify access rules, user interacts with SHCS which forwards the request to the Blockchain automaton. Currently, we do not check properties of the Blockchain technology or smart contracts. Therefore, we abstract the

Blockchain as a matrix storing data access rules. Whenever a patient creates or modifies access rule for a doctor, a corresponding cell of the matrix is updated.

Requests for medical data are performed in two steps. At first, SHCS interacts with the Blockchain automaton checking the access. If the access is granted, SHCS interacts with the Data Lake modelled with two types of automata. A single automaton shown in Fig. 4 represents the central part of the Data Lake: it receives a request for a patient's SPHR, collects it from local hospitals' databases and transfers the combined data. In addition, there is a set of automata modelling local data storage in multiple hospitals; the data can be updated by the hospital and been requested by the central Data Lake automaton.

4.1 Verification: Model Checking vs. Statistical Model Checking

We are now ready to analyse properties of the model with UPPAAL. In order to show that the system behaves correctly with many users, we would vary the number of users by changing the number of instantiated doctor and patient automata during the analysis. For the paper, we consider two properties described hereafter.

1. Reachability property: doctors are able to receive an SPHR, in particular for any doctor there exists an execution path where the doctor can receive an SPHR of some patient.
2. Safety property: a doctor receives a patient's SPHR only if there is an access rule allowing the doctor to do so at the moment of request.

UPPAAL encoding of the reachability property consists of a set of queries; each query concerns a single doctor. The queries are $E\Diamond(d_i.\texttt{SPHRReceived})$, where d_i is the ith doctor and $\texttt{SPHRReceived}$ is a state of doctor's automaton in which SPHR is received. We consider a property satisfied if all queries are satisfied, the property checking time is computed as a sum of query times, and the memory consumption is the maximal consumption among all queries. Note that in the query we check presence of at least one execution path reaching $\texttt{SPHRReceived}$ state rather than all paths; indeed one potential execution is all patients blocking some doctor forever.

Committed states in the model forbid parallel execution of SPHR requests and access rule modifications ensuring that no rule can be added or modified during SPHR request. Therefore, the safety property can be checked by the presence of [rules in the blockchain allowing access to the doctor at the state where the doctor receives SPHR. It must hold for any doctor at any point of time. The property is specified with the formula $A\Box\,\forall d\!:\!Doctor\ (d.\texttt{SPHRReceived} \implies blockchain.rules[d][sphr.patient] = \texttt{ALLOW})$.

In our experiments we are interested in a verification result as well as in time and memory required to perform them. Properties have been checked on a laptop with i7-8650U CPU and 16 Gb of RAM.

Exhaustive MC is known to be afflicted by state space explosion [15]. On our model, MC quickly runs out of available RAM. One option to perform MC is to

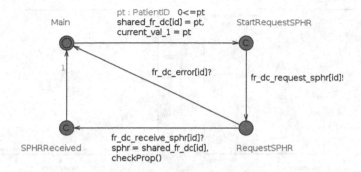

Fig. 5. Simplified automaton of a doctor.

simplify the model: we only keep automata and transitions directly related to request SPHR routine (cf. Fig. 2) and remove everything else. In particular, we keep:

1. automata for doctors, assuming them to be logged in and having an access token (i.e. all transitions related to login and to sign up are removed) shown in Fig. 5;
2. SHCS keeping only top part of the Fig. 3 (Request SPHR area);
3. Blockchain processing a single request to check access rules with assumption that rules are already created by patients and cannot be changed ensuring that for each doctor there is at least 1 patient providing access to the data;
4. Data Lake with an assumption that all patients' data in the model is accessible directly from central automaton without requesting storage at the hospitals.

The model checking results are shown in Fig. 6. Reachability property queries are evaluated within milliseconds: there are only a few available execution paths, and the desired state is reachable in less than 20 transitions. The safety property requires checking all the states of the model and, since the number of states grows exponentially with the number of doctors, there was not enough RAM to check the model with 8 doctors[3].

SMC provides an alternative to the exhaustive method since the simulation does not require computation of full state space while high confidence can be achieved without large time expenses [22,28]. Memory consumption is also low since states that are not visited during the simulation are not generated. Encoding of properties is adapted as follows. For the reachability property we compute the probability of the state to be reached on traces of bounded length. In the original property we were checking the existence of at least one path, therefore for SMC we consider the property to be satisfied if the resulting probability is not close to 0. Note that the results of the SMC query provide more information: it also provides an estimation of the number of paths visiting the state.

---

[3] It is possible to simplify the property by checking it separately for each doctor, however the simplification doesn't affect RAM consumption while single doctor check takes almost the same time as the check for all doctors.

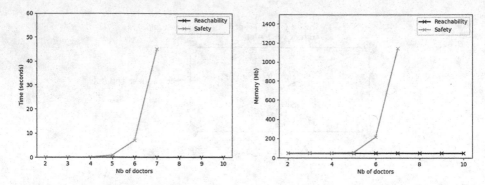

Fig. 6. Model checking time and memory with respect to the number of doctors on the simplified model. Safety property for 8 doctors runs out of RAM after 10 min execution without providing the result.

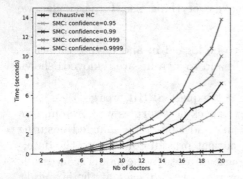

Fig. 7. SMC time on a simplified model for the reachability property with different confidence levels.

Fig. 8. SMC time on a simplified model for the safety property with different confidence levels.

The safety property has been checked with a hypothesis testing: H0 states that the property is satisfied with a probability above a selected threshold θ and H1 that the probability is below. An indifference region around θ covers the cases when it is not possible to select one of the hypotheses.

To compare results with the exhaustive model checking we used the same model and the following parameters for the SMC: traces are bounded with 1,000 transitions, ϵ value for approximation interval for reachability property is 0.01, threshold for safety hypothesis is 0.99 with indifference region [0.985, 0.995], confidence levels are 0.95, 0.99, 0.999, and 0.9999. The SMC engine is also able to estimate the number of data requests done within traces of given length, for 1,000 transitions the expected value is 75.

The results of SMC evaluation are shown on Fig. 7 and Fig. 8. Reachability property is computed slower than with exhaustive model checking due to fact that evaluation is not stopped after finding a single trace reaching the desired state but exploring multiple traces until the probability is computed with the

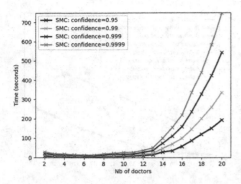 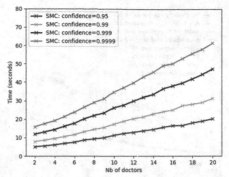

Fig. 9. SMC time on a complete Serums model for the reachability property. **Fig. 10.** SMC time on a complete Serums model for the safety property.

desired confidence. Confidence level 0.95 requires almost 200 simulations and level 0.9999 requires more than 500 simulations. Safety property can be validated with SMC within 3 s even with 20 doctors, while the exhaustive method requires more than 40 s for 7 doctors and 1 Gb of RAM. All SMC checks required just 50 Mb of RAM.

While MC fails to check properties on a complete Serums model, SMC due to low memory requirements can provide results on the complete model. It involves patients modifying access rules at runtime; therefore, doctors could have access to the data during a limited interval of time and there is no guarantees that a doctor would have any access granted. Since the complete model is much larger, we raised the trace length to 10, 000; and expected number of SPHR requests to 450.

The plots presented in Fig. 9 and Fig. 10 show the computation times for both properties. Again, 50 Mb of RAM was sufficient to calculate the results. Safety property can be evaluated within 1 min even for a 0.9999 confidence. For the reachability property, we report time for a single query for one doctor. This property requires a large number of simulations to provide the satisfaction probability interval with the desired confidence due to high randomness of the system (the SPHR can be received only after a patient creates a rule allowing that). For 20 doctors, the confidence level of 0.9999 requires more than 20, 000 simulations, thus taking about 12 min.

Figure 11 and Fig. 12 show the average time needed for a single simulation on simplified and complete models respectively computed as a total verification time divided by the number of simulations. Unsurprisingly, simulation time is independent from the desired level of confidence. Simulations for the reachability property are on average faster than for safety: the former ones can often be decided after few simulation steps while the latter ones (in case of being satisfied) requires simulating steps until the trace length bound. Note that the complexity of the model does not have a big impact on the simulation time: switching from a simplified model to a much more complex complete model and raising trace length by a factor of 10 affects the simulation time by a factor of 20.

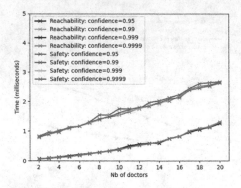 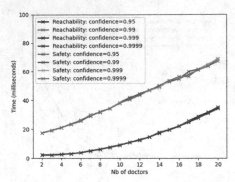

Fig. 11. SMC average time per simulation on a simplified model.

Fig. 12. SMC average time per simulation on a complete model.

5   Adding Security Requirements

Systems working in the real world should consider not only reachability and safety properties but security properties as well. Security properties shall check correctness of system behaviour in the presence of attackers. One cannot expect that users would follow the behaviour expected by the developers and the system must prevent all threatening interactions. Consideration of security properties shall be done at the design stage since vulnerabilities can be introduced there. In this section we show a simple attack vector and illustrate how formal modelling can help with detection of vulnerabilities.

The modular structure of the Serums system enables a distributed setup. In this case the components' API becomes available to the attackers. A problem arises with API of the Data Lake component. Considering an SPHR retrieval request (step 3.3 in Fig. 2), the only information received by the Data Lake is metadata about which part of patient's data shall be collected. The information of the original requester is not provided.

The existence of the Serums formal model allows us to validate whether this decision and the presence of an attacker can violate some of the properties. The modifications applied to the model are the following. Firstly, we model an attacker that imitates a doctor, but sending a request to the Data Lake instead of SHCS system. Metadata is not taken from the Blockchain rule but generated by an attacker. Secondly, we add a transition to the Data Lake automaton to receive request from the attacker (like receiving request from SHCS) and a transition to send the reply back. The modification has been done on both complete Serums model and its simplified version.

Exhaustive MC performed on the modified simplified model shows that the safety property defined in Subsect. 4.1 is violated. There is a possibility to receive patient data without the stored rule allowing this. Indeed, an attacker can fabricate metadata granting unrestricted access to the patient's record and request all the data allowed by this fabricated metadata. SMC performed on both versions of the modified model rejects the hypothesis that the property is satisfied

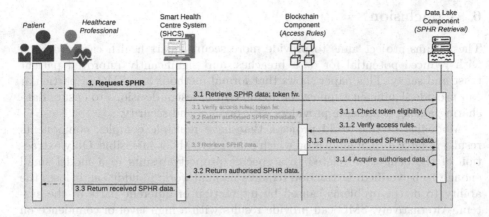

Fig. 13. Sequence diagram with alternate design for the SPHR data request functionality in the system.

with probability above 0.99, i.e., there exist simulations on which the property is violated. This conclusion was drawn in less than 10 simulations.

The presence of this attack required us to modify the design of the system. The second proposed version of this functionality has a different behaviour and is illustrated with bold arrows in Fig. 13. Arrows depicted in light grey represent the previous interactions among components to make clear the system changes towards increased security. In this new version, the SHCS component directly sends all information to the Data Lake (3.1) and it is the Data Lake's responsibility to interact with the Blockchain and collect the data access rules (3.1.2). The Data Lake receives a patient id, a doctor id, and a doctor's access token and checks that the data is requested for the owner of the access token.

The Serums model has been updated to respect the new design flow. An attacker in this model can try to send any patient and any doctor id, however we assume that attacker cannot steal or forge someone else's access token. Verification of the properties with both exhaustive and statistical model checking showed that the properties are satisfied even with the presence of an attacker. The reachability property shows that the attacker can still receive some patient's data, however the safety property guarantees that the access to such data has been granted. Thus, we can conclude that the new design prevents the considered attack and covers the vulnerability.

Under the assumption that components' API is available from the outside world and that the request source cannot be identified, the model checking shows that the first version of the design has a vulnerability breaching the data confidentiality. For the second design the considered attack vector does not work. Thorough exploration of the design with the formal modelling allows us to find issues at the design time.

6   Conclusion

The Serums project aims to provide more secure smart health care provision with reduced potential for data breaches, and significantly improved patient trust and safety. This paper shows that formal methods and SMC in particular can provide significant support for architectural design decisions to ensure data sharing among healthcare providers with privacy and security.

Modelling of real-world projects that have multiple complex components results in large formal models on which exhaustive MC is infeasible. Only extraction of the behaviour related to a specific property results in a model small enough to be verified. Extraction requires manual work; in addition, it loses the ability to detect problems caused by interaction of different parts of the system. Alternatively, SMC can provide results with a high level of confidence on a complete model, exploring interactions between different functionalities and is capable of finding design flaws.

Future work includes two main directions. Verification of the Serums design to satisfy the remaining requirements and resilience against other attack vectors, including modelling and verification of smart contracts used in the blockchain model based on the approach from [2]. The other is the evaluation of the effectiveness of this proposed design on real-world healthcare environments provided by the Use Case partners in the project.

Acknowledgements. This research is funded by the EU H2020 project SERUMS (grant 826278). We thank Matthew Banton from the University of St Andrews for comments that greatly improved the platform security properties and Serums partners from Accenture and Sopra Steria for their help on the architectural diagrams design.

References

1. Uppaal. https://www.uppaal.org
2. Abdellatif, T., Brousmiche, K.L.: Formal verification of smart contracts based on users and blockchain behaviors models. In: 2018 9th IFIP International Conference on New Technologies, Mobility and Security (NTMS), pp. 1–5. IEEE (2018)
3. Agha, G., Palmskog, K.: A survey of statistical model checking. ACM Trans. Model. Comput. Simul. (TOMACS) 28(1), 1–39 (2018)
4. Arnold, A.: Finite Transition Systems - Semantics of Communicating Systems. Prentice Hall International Series in Computer Science, Prentice Hall (1994)
5. Baier, C., Katoen, J.P.: Principles of Model Checking. MIT press, Cambridge (2008)
6. Baranov, E., Given-Wilson, T., Legay, A.: Improving Secure and Robust Patient Service Delivery. In: Margaria, T., Steffen, B. (eds.) ISoLA 2020. LNCS, vol. 12476, pp. 404–418. Springer, Cham (2020). https://doi.org/10.1007/978-3-030-61362-4_23
7. Basu, A., Bensalem, S., Bozga, M., Delahaye, B., Legay, A.: Statistical abstraction and model-checking of large heterogeneous systems. Int. J. Softw. Tools Technol. Transfer 14(1), 53–72 (2012)

8. ter Beek, M.H., et al.: Adopting formal methods in an industrial setting: the railways case. In: ter Beek, M.H., McIver, A., Oliveira, J.N. (eds.) FM 2019. LNCS, vol. 11800, pp. 762–772. Springer, Cham (2019). https://doi.org/10.1007/978-3-030-30942-8_46

9. Behrmann, G., David, A., Larsen, K.G.: A tutorial on UPPAAL. In: Formal Methods for the Design of Real-Time Systems, pp. 200–236. Springer (2004). https://doi.org/10.1007/978-3-540-30080-9_7

10. Bowles, J., Mendoza-Santana, J., Vermeulen, A.F., Webber, T., Blackledge, E.: Integrating healthcare data for enhanced citizen-centred care and analytics. Stud. Health Tech. Inf. **275**, 17–21 (2020)

11. Bowles, J., Mendoza-Santana, J., Webber, T.: Interacting with next-generation smart patient-centric healthcare systems. In: UMAP'20 Adjunct: Adjunct Publication of the 28th ACM Conference on User Modeling, Adaptation and Personalization, pp. 192–193, July 2020

12. Bulychev, P., et al.: Monitor-based statistical model checking for weighted metric temporal logic. In: International Conference on Logic for Programming Artificial Intelligence and Reasoning, pp. 168–182. Springer (2012). https://doi.org/10.1007/978-3-642-28717-6_15

13. Cerone, A., Elbegbayan, N.: Model-checking driven design of interactive systems. Electron. Notes Theor. Comput. Sci. **183**, 3–20 (2007)

14. Clarke, E.M., Emerson, E.A.: Design and synthesis of synchronization skeletons using branching time temporal logic. In: Kozen, D. (ed.) Logic of Programs 1981. LNCS, vol. 131, pp. 52–71. Springer, Heidelberg (1982). https://doi.org/10.1007/BFb0025774

15. Clarke, E.M., Klieber, W., Nováček, M., Zuliani, P.: Model checking and the state explosion problem. In: Meyer, B., Nordio, M. (eds.) LASER 2011. LNCS, vol. 7682, pp. 1–30. Springer, Heidelberg (2012). https://doi.org/10.1007/978-3-642-35746-6_1

16. David, A., Larsen, K.G., Legay, A., Mikučionis, M., Poulsen, D.B.: Uppaal SMC tutorial. Int. J. Softw. Tools Technol. Transfer **17**(4), 397–415 (2015)

17. David, A., et al.: Statistical model checking for networks of priced timed automata. In: Fahrenberg, U., Tripakis, S. (eds.) FORMATS 2011. LNCS, vol. 6919, pp. 80–96. Springer, Heidelberg (2011). https://doi.org/10.1007/978-3-642-24310-3

18. Ellen, C., Gerwinn, S., Fränzle, M.: Statistical model checking for stochastic hybrid systems involving nondeterminism over continuous domains. Int. J. Softw. Tools Technol. Transfer **17**(4), 485–504 (2014). https://doi.org/10.1007/s10009-014-0329-y

19. Gavrilov, G., Vlahu-Gjorgievska, E., Trajkovik, V.: Healthcare data warehouse system supporting cross-border interoperability. Health Informat. J. **26**(2), 1321–1332 (2020)

20. Gu, R., Enoiu, E., Seceleanu, C.: TAMAA: Uppaal-based mission planning for autonomous agents. In: Proceedings of the 35th Annual ACM Symposium on Applied Computing, pp. 1624–1633 (2020)

21. Harrison, M.D., Masci, P., Campos, J.C.: Formal modelling as a component of user centred design. In: Mazzara, M., Ober, I., Salaün, G. (eds.) STAF 2018. LNCS, vol. 11176, pp. 274–289. Springer, Cham (2018). https://doi.org/10.1007/978-3-030-04771-9_21

22. Hérault, T., Lassaigne, R., Magniette, F., Peyronnet, S.: Approximate probabilistic model checking. In: Steffen, B., Levi, G. (eds.) VMCAI 2004. LNCS, vol. 2937, pp. 73–84. Springer, Heidelberg (2004). https://doi.org/10.1007/978-3-540-24622-0_8

23. Janjic, V., Bowles, J., Vermeulen, A., et al.: The serums tool-chain: ensuring security and privacy of medical data in smart patient-centric healthcare systems. In: 2019 IEEE International Conference on Big Data, pp. 2726–2735, December 2019
24. Jetley, R., Iyer, S.P., Jones, P.: A formal methods approach to medical device review. Computer **39**(4), 61–67 (2006)
25. Kalajdzic, K., et al.: Feedback control for statistical model checking of cyber-physical systems. In: Margaria, T., Steffen, B. (eds.) ISoLA 2016. LNCS, vol. 9952, pp. 46–61. Springer, Cham (2016). https://doi.org/10.1007/978-3-319-47166-2_4
26. Kwiatkowska, M., Lea-Banks, H., Mereacre, A., Paoletti, N.: Formal modelling and validation of rate-adaptive pacemakers. In: 2014 IEEE International Conference on Healthcare Informatics, pp. 23–32. IEEE (2014)
27. Larrucea, X., Moffie, M., Asaf, S., Santamaria, I.: Towards a GDPR compliant way to secure European cross border healthcare industry 4.0. Comput. Stand. Interf. **69**, 103408 (2020)
28. Legay, A., Delahaye, B., Bensalem, S.: Statistical model checking: an overview. In: International Conference on Runtime Verification, pp. 122–135. Springer (2010). https://doi.org/10.1007/978-3-642-16612-9_11
29. Legay, A., Lukina, A., Traonouez, L.M., Yang, J., Smolka, S.A., Grosu, R.: Statistical model checking. In: Computing and Software Science, pp. 478–504. Springer (2019). https://doi.org/10.1007/978-3-319-91908-9_23
30. McGhin, T., Choo, K.K.R., Liu, C.Z., He, D.: Blockchain in healthcare applications: research challenges and opportunities. J. Netw. Comput. Appl. **135**, 62–75 (2019)
31. Mercaldo, F., Martinelli, F., Santone, A.: Real-time SCADA attack detection by means of formal methods. In: 2019 IEEE 28th International Conference on Enabling Technologies: Infrastructure for Collaborative Enterprises (WETICE), pp. 231–236. IEEE (2019)
32. Queille, J.P., Sifakis, J.: Specification and verification of concurrent systems in CESAR. In: International Symposium on Programming. pp. 337–351. Springer (1982). https://doi.org/10.1007/3-540-11494-7_22
33. Ravn, A.P., Srba, J., Vighio, S.: Modelling and verification of web services business activity protocol. In: Abdulla, P.A., Leino, K.R.M. (eds.) TACAS 2011. LNCS, vol. 6605, pp. 357–371. Springer, Heidelberg (2011). https://doi.org/10.1007/978-3-642-19835-9_32
34. Sen, K., Viswanathan, M., Agha, G.: On statistical model checking of stochastic systems. In: Etessami, K., Rajamani, S.K. (eds.) CAV 2005. LNCS, vol. 3576, pp. 266–280. Springer, Heidelberg (2005). https://doi.org/10.1007/11513988_26
35. Tanwar, S., Parekh, K., Evans, R.: Blockchain-based electronic healthcare record system for healthcare 4.0 applications. J. Inf. Secur. Appl. **50**, 102407 (2020)
36. Ter Beek, M.H., Legay, A., Lafuente, A.L., Vandin, A.: A framework for quantitative modeling and analysis of highly (re) configurable systems. IEEE Trans. Software Eng. **46**(3), 321–345 (2018)
37. Webber, T., Santana, J.M., Vermeulen, A.F., Bowles, J.K.F.: Designing a patient-centric system for secure exchanges of medical data. In: Gervasi, O., et al. (eds.) ICCSA 2020. LNCS, vol. 12254, pp. 598–614. Springer, Cham (2020). https://doi.org/10.1007/978-3-030-58817-5_44
38. Zuliani, P.: Statistical model checking for biological applications. Int. J. Softw. Tools Technol. Transfer **17**(4), 527–536 (2014). https://doi.org/10.1007/s10009-014-0343-0

Model-Based Security Assessment on the Design of a Patient-Centric Data Sharing Platform

Matthew Banton[ID], Thais Webber[ID], Agastya Silvina[ID],
and Juliana Bowles[✉][ID]

School of Computer Science, University of St Andrews, St Andrews KY16 9SX, UK
{tcwds,jkfb}@st-andrews.ac.uk

Abstract. The architectural design of a healthcare data sharing system must cope with security requirements especially when the system integrates different data sources and patient-centric features. The design choices come with different risks, where vulnerabilities and threats highly depend on how the system components interact and depend on each other to operate as well as how it handles the external connections. This paper focuses on security aspects arising early in the design phase of a patient-centric system. The system presents a blend of emergent technologies such as novel authentication methods, blockchain for access control, and a data lake for patient metadata storage and retrieval based on access rules. We exploit a model-based approach to tackle security assessment using attack-defense trees (ADtrees) formalism and other support diagrams altogether as a way to model and analyse potential attack paths to the system and its countermeasures. The modelling approach helps creating a framework to support the attack vectors analysis and the proposal of appropriate defense mechanisms within the system architecture.

Keywords: Healthcare systems · Patient-centric system · Data sharing · Security assessment · Attack-defense trees

1 Introduction

With data breaches on the rise especially after the Covid-19 pandemic [25], the design of robust healthcare platforms leveraging patient-centric features is crucial to allow vital health data to be securely shared among professionals and organisations without leaking patients' private confidential information to any unauthorised user [6].

The research in this paper was supported by the EU H2020 project SERUMS: Securing Medical Data in Smart Patient-Centric Healthcare Systems (grant code 826278).

J. Bowles et al. (Eds.): DataMod 2021, LNCS 13268, pp. 61–77, 2022.
https://doi.org/10.1007/978-3-031-16011-0_5

The EU project Serums[1] [5,6,13,37] proposes a secure patient-centric architectural model integrating modern technologies for user authentication [4,8], granular access to medical records through personalised access rules stored on a blockchain [1], and a data lake for patients' metadata storage and retrieval [37], among other goals. Both blockchain and data lake in the platform are essential components for the access control over medical records, where the former authorises users' data requests in real-time and on-demand, and the later subsequently retrieves only to authorised users the agreed medical data to be shared, running an underlying fine-grained authorisation scheme [6,7].

Serums platform propose features that allow patients full control over their data, which can be stored in different locations, under different data protection regulations and formats [6,18], however, it also opens opportunities for malicious actors to exploit the vulnerabilities to access the system and exfiltrate confidential data or even compromise patient safety [2,22,36]. Attacks in this sense may vary from threatening patients' privacy and data confidentiality, for example, targeting specifically the system authentication module to gain access to sensitive data through social engineering (e.g., phishing attacks), to sniffing the network to intercept traffic using ample techniques and resources, which could also threaten data integrity and availability [31,36].

Model-based security assessments [27] are a viable and visual way of understanding and mapping most likely threats and vulnerabilities of a system. It increases situational awareness and assists modellers in addressing the set of attack vectors (and pathways) at the same time ensuring security controls in place are addressing potential issues that may arise. Several cyber security databases provide information and knowledge on threats, vulnerabilities, tactics and techniques based on real-world observations. MITRE Adversarial Tactics, Techniques, and Common Knowledge (ATT&CK) [24] is a framework that contains information on adversary behaviour (tactics and techniques), providing a structured view on attack lifecycles and target platforms, helping analysts to prioritise the threats to organisations and systems. Vulnerabilities databases across the world (e.g., CVSS, CVE) map and provide a common interface for security analysts when addressing such shortcomings [23,28].

Among different formalisms to reason and describe security aspects [27], Attack-Defense trees (ADtrees) [12] are an approach that extends the Attack Trees formalism [38], including not only the actions of an attacker, but also possible counteractions of the defender. Its strength is that it provides a broad visualisation of discovering attack vectors and defenses to system architectural designers and developers [12]. ADtrees are also capable of providing quantitative evaluation when the model reaches a reasonable state of maturity and refinement, e.g., calculating a set of measures like probability, cost and time, through a bottom-up procedure implemented in the ADTool software [15].

Focusing more on software architecture, Mal-activity diagrams (MAD), which are a form of UML activity diagram, could be complementary to the ADtree

---

[1] For more information on Serums project please refer to https://www.serums-h2020.org.

approach since they allow modelling the progression of malicious activities and actors within the system while including information on how the system could defend against these activities [20]. The strength of MAD is the flexibility to detail the model with internal system processes and components interactions. We can therefore use an ADtree to gather an overview of possible attacks and countermeasures, particularly related to adversaries trying to gain access to sensitive data like credentials information through social engineering, then escalating their attack to make use of system features. Using MAD [19] we can show how these attacks and countermeasures would work in practice.

While ADtrees and MAD have been proposed to work together in the past [19], few papers have discussed how to link them, or the process that should be involved in doing so. In this paper, we apply a process that starts with building an ADTree based upon a well-known cyber-adversary behaviour and taxonomy knowledge database (i.e., MITRE [24]) and conclude with a MAD model based upon a threat identified in an initial security assessment [2]. These models are part of an overall security analysis of Serums, which includes formal verification methods [27] and broad security assessment through models [10].

This paper is structured as follows. Section 2 brings background information and related work on the formal modelling of systems focusing on security aspects, especially using ADtrees and MAD. Section 3 presents a brief description on the Serums system design (Subsect. 3.1) and a description of the Serum security assessment using ADTrees (Subsect. 3.2). Section 4 expands the ADtrees scope, modelling MAD to include a more visual description on the system pathways whilst under attack highlighting architectural aspects and mechanisms to mitigate the risk of these attacks. Section 5 presents considerations on the way that modelling activities can demonstrate aspects of security within Serums system, and how they can evolve to serve as basis to quantitative evaluations in future.

2   Background and Related Work

Cyber-security assessment is essential in healthcare systems to keep confidential data safe, especially with the increase in threats during the recent pandemic and the financial impact on the health sector [3,21,25]. Moreover, patients have legal rights in regard to the way healthcare organisations and systems store, access, process, transmit and share their private information [18]. Thus, when designing patient-centric systems for data sharing it is important not only to include security practices and comply with regulations related to data protection such as GDPR, but also conduct different assessments on the system vulnerabilities, threats and security controls enabled by the chosen technologies [31,35].

Being able to combine the above-mentioned requirements (that the system be dependable and secure [27] whilst providing patients full lawful access to their data) requires the data sharing system to be evaluated from both a theoretical and practical level. From the theoretical viewpoint, the system must be able to mitigate common security vulnerabilities and threats. This can be analysed with different security assessment methodologies, using frameworks and widely recognised security knowledge databases [23,24] but also with diverse modelling practices for security inspections [16,19,27,34]. Typically, multiple complementary modelling approaches together can provide a richer, more comprehensive cyber security assessment on the system under study [26,27].

Several studies using mostly tree-based format [19,26,30,38] have been proposed to model and inspect security aspects in systems, e.g., identifying security threats such as attempts to gain unauthorised access, unsafe system pathways leading to confidential data, among other related security risk analysis [35]. Fault Tree Analysis (FTA) [27] is a traditional method of evaluating the reliability of safety critical systems. The advantages of FTA include being able to identify potential failures deductively, creating a graphical aid for system analysis, and being able to highlight important elements of a system related to the failure. Research on applied FTA for enhanced design of security-critical systems include requirements identification and analysis for an intrusion detection system (IDS) [11] and more recently security failure analysis of smart homes [39].

However, fault tree analysis is both complex, and not suited to security specific situations, i.e., understanding an attackers specific capabilities, or what the life cycle of an attack might include. Further, Attack Trees (AT) [33] introduce a methodical way of describing systems based on the attacks they may encounter. AT provide a method to formally reason about the security of a system, and to capture and reuse the security expertise within the system. They focus more on the mapping of security breaches as system failures, thus modelling possible attacks against the system [26]. They are particularly useful for plotting the progression of possible threats and how to deal with them. The AT root node is the attacker's goal (e.g., information disclosure), and each leaf node is a potential subgoal (or step) the attacker can exploit to reach the root, which means the attack is complete. In the literature, recent applications of AT formalism to assess healthcare systems security include the analysis of IoT devices and their interconnections, just to name a few [14,40].

Attack-Defense Trees (ADtrees) [16] extended AT formalism adding countermeasures to the tree, using green squares for defenses as opposed to the red circles representing attackers. This allows for an intuitive and visual representation of the interaction between possible attacks and defensive measures. The ADTree modelling allows refinement of nodes into sub-goals nodes. These refinements can be either disjunctive (the goal of a node is achieved when at least one of its sub-goals is achieved) or conjuctive (the goal of a node is achieved when all of its sub-goals are achieved; graphically this includes an arc joining sub-goals nodes of a node). Moreover, ADtrees can be also extended to analyse quantitatively attack-defense scenarios and rank possible attacks for given attribute domains using the Attack-Defense Tree Tool (ADTool) [15]. However, this attack-centric view of the system limits the precision defensive strategies can be analysed with, as it does not account for existing defensive strategies within the system. It also does not allow for the visualisation of the evolution of a system's security, since that evolution can only be understood in view of both the attackers and defenders' actions in the tree [16].

Alternatively, from a software design perspective, Misuse Cases [29, 34] were applied to encourage the system developer (or software architect) to think like an attacker and represent the requirements of (malicious) users in comprehensible models applying UML-based graphical format. The approach facilitates the communication of system requirements among developers and stakeholders and may lead to the development of a system with decreased cyber security risks. However, such models are not well suited to expand the view on the lifecycle of an attack, thus Guttorm [19, 34] proposed Mal-activity diagrams (MAD). MAD provide a way to view the lifecycle of an attack, and the various actions one or more attacks may perform to realise an attack, as well as a way to view these internal interactions. They provide elements to represent the actions performed by users (attackers) to realise an attack within a system, also depicting the existent interactions among components.

Finally, modelling security aspects of systems through different formalisms is an invaluable way to comprehensively study security issues, detecting system's weaknesses and vulnerabilities [27]. We can assume that multiple modelling techniques are helpful in different ways, and that they can be complimentary [9, 19, 38]. Therefore, it is recommended to use different models and frameworks to assess system security during its design phase [27].

3   Assessment of Attack Scenarios

In this paper we model a high-level cyber security scenario in which we assess the kinds of attacks a particular data sharing system may come under, as well as offer countermeasures. We then expand on this high-level scenario by drilling down into one type of attack (through social engineering) that has been highlighted in a previous research paper [2], with description of four potential threat scenarios concerning both confidentiality and availability aspects of the data sharing system. In this paper, we discuss a threat mostly related to confidentiality, specifically phishing attack scenarios.

3.1   Serums System Design Overview

Serums proof-of-concept (POC) system [13] integrates different software components and technologies to provide a confidential, secure and transparent medical cross-country data sharing platform to users in the healthcare domain. Users are mainly patients and healthcare professionals. Administrators in organisations also make part of the system, contributing to access control over confidential medical records (management of access rules) and creation of new Serums' users. The system should allow organisations to follow laws and regulations (such as GDPR), in a similar manner to how they already do [6].

Figure 1 depicts a high-level overview of the system as a deployment diagram. Serums POC system is a web-based application containing both a front-end and a backend. The front-end consists of both the Serums API, and the SHCS (Smart Health Centre System). The SHCS allows patients users to securely login in the platform, retrieve own records that are stored in multiple locations (organised by a data lake) through secure data transfers along a blockchain network. They can also create their individual set of access rules, which either enable or deny selected professionals from accessing their confidential medical records. The Serums API alternatively integrates the SHCS with the various technologies being used by Serums in the backend (i.e., the blockchain, data lake and authentication module).

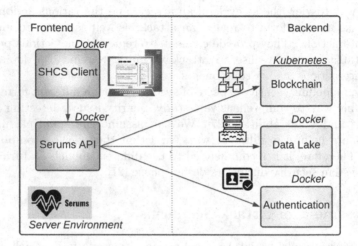

Fig. 1. Serums POC system deployment diagram.

Healthcare professionals, once authenticated in the system (within the SHCS), can search for patients, and retrieve medical records according to their set of access rules provided by patients and administrators. A Serums ID and successful authentication are important requirements to start performing activities in the system. Professionals can also create requests for medical data access to patients, especially to refer to historical data on this patient (i.e., records stored in different locations that are not originally granted access) or current/new collected medical data (e.g., health tracking devices, other health monitoring systems). Patients can promptly accept (or reject) these access requests in the system once they are successfully authenticated in the system.

Internally, the backend is composed of loosely coupled software components in order to fulfil the above-mentioned requirements and provide enhanced security in transactions performed within the system [37]. The authentication module [8] contains novel methods and pictorial passwords, along with traditional textual passwords and other security techniques, to ensure different levels of security checks in this first layer of system access [4]. After it releases a secure access token, functionalities related to medical records retrieval invoke the Serums data lake to process the requests and build a Smart Patient Health Record (SPHR) [5] to the user. SPHR contains authorised health metadata from different sources (locations), provided the user has conflict-free access rules in place. These rules establish which professional (considering location and authorisation) can have access to what (granular medical data selected by the patient) and when (validity of the rule) [1]. The blockchain component stores and manages the patients' access rules, providing secure authorisation process for data retrievals requested by users (patients and professionals) based on stored access rules [7] with audit trail. Serums POC system aims to demonstrate the interoperability among technologies but also evaluate the public trust and security perception on the proposed solution for healthcare provision.

3.2   Serum Security Assessment Using ADtrees

Serums POC system design presents modern technologies integrated to mitigate several modern cyber threats. During its design, we choose ADtrees [12] as a threat modelling methodology to visualise and analyse potential attacks to the Serums system. ADtrees provide useful construct set capabilities to model the exploit of attack vectors and to propose countermeasures considering top level components of the system architecture.

Our initial assessment published in [2] has provided insights into the possible attacks to Serums system related to malicious users gaining access to confidential medical records. The scenario we are dealing with involves applying phishing technique, which is a known Initial Access tactic employed by adversaries aiming to get into the system [24].

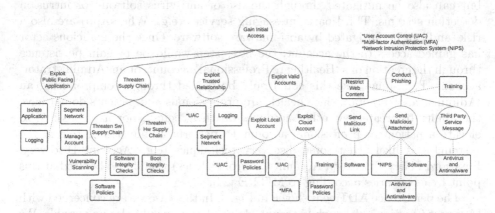

Fig. 2. ADtree for initial access based on MITRE ATT&CK.

The MITRE ATT&CK framework [24] presents a comprehensive list of attack vectors and threat actors in such a well-structured way that enables to integrate the knowledge on unique tactics, techniques, and procedures (TTPs) into the ADtrees. Figure 2 shows an ADTree interpretation of the Initial Access tactic unfolding its techniques and countermeasures.

We have identified possible attack vectors and established which malicious actions (i.e., red circles in the ADtree are adversaries' goals and respective sub-goals) could be performed by their means like exploitation of a public facing application, supply chain, trusted relationships, valid accounts, or Spearphishing. The sub-goals nodes in the ADtree are disjuctive, which means at least one of them, when reached, make the goal achieved. Potential countermeasures (i.e., green squares), especially for phishing, include 'Restricting web-based content', 'Training', 'Software', 'Anti-malware' and 'NIPS' (i.e., Network Intrusion Protection System) to mitigate different types of phishing attempts. It can be seen that, for example, "Threaten Supply Chain" is refined into two potential actions (sub-goals), either hardware (e.g., ensure hardware is distributed with built in vulnerabilities the attacker can access) or software (e.g., create a software update for software used in the system that gives the attacker access to the systems it is installed on). These actions have the potential mitigation applying 'Vulnerability Scanning', 'Software Policies', and 'Integrity Checks'. 'Vulnerability Scanning' helps to ensure that software updates are free from known vulnerabilities, even if distributed by a trusted source, whereas 'Software Policies' can help limit the impact of a successful attack through methods such as 'Sandboxing'.

Meanwhile, integrity checks can help ensure that the software (or hardware) being installed does come from a legitimate source and has been approved by the manufacturer. Primarily we are interested in the phishing technique, which has malicious link, attachment or via third party messages as vectors. Links can be mitigated through software disabling links, and through restricting access to potentially malicious sites as well as training users. Attachments are similar but can also be mitigated through the use of anti-virus software or intrusion detection systems. Third party messaging services (e.g., WhatsApp) are also a risk, and can be mitigated by anti-malware software. Once the malicious actor has gained access to the account, the next step would be to gain persistence through the creation of a 'Healthcare Professional' account, or an 'Administrator' account. Persistence like this could only be gained through compromising an 'Administrator' account, since healthcare professionals and patients do not have the ability to create new other accounts on their behalf, nor it is possible to elevate a patient or professional account to perform administrator role in the system. It is likely that some discovery techniques (e.g., Account Discovery, Password Policy Discovery, Account Control Policies) would also be used at this point by adversaries according to MITRE [24].

The persistence ADTree is shown in Fig. 3. In this case we are concerned with 'Account Creation', although 'Account Manipulation' would also be possible. We can identify promising mitigation being Multi-factor Authentication ('MFA') and 'Account Management'. It would make sense to employ both countermeasures, potentially having MFA second check when a new professional account is created (as this should only happen when a new medical professional starts working at an organisation), as well as having automated tools to track new employees being created, and ways to link them to external data to ensure the employee is real (e.g., using an employee ID). Once the actor has access to a medical professional account, they would need to employ more Spearphishing attempts, this time defined under Lateral movement (Fig. 4), and internal Spearphishing specifically. This would take the form of asking patients to give the malicious actors account permission to access their medical records.

Internal Spearphishing is difficult to mitigate, since it is based on abuse of system features. As such, training is listed as the main mitigation. It would be important to ensure that patients are informed of who may be expected to access their data and are informed of any requests ahead of time so that unsolicited access requests are unusual and could raise a patients suspicions. Financial institutions often advise their customers on possible fraud and threats by ensuring their correspondence contains phrases such as "We will never call and ask you to provide your bank details."

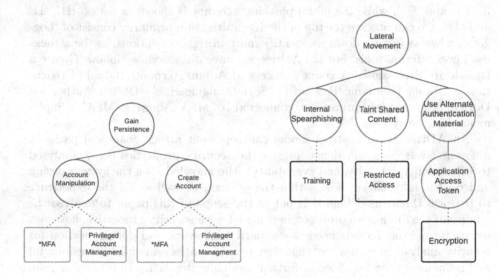

Fig. 3. ADtree for credential access.   **Fig. 4.** ADtree for lateral movement.

However, with a healthcare organisation and systems having potentially thousands of users, it is likely that some patients would allow their data to be viewed. Detection is therefore the next best mitigation approach, requiring both network and application logging. In Serums case, the logs could be stored on the blockchain, ensuring that they are not deleted or edited, and that the account making the requests can be identified and any rules created can be undone quickly, or the request removed if the patient has not replied. It is likely the logged information would also feed into a Security Information and Event Management system (or SIEM).

Once patients have given access to the malicious medical account, the actor would need to collect and then exfiltrate the data. The malicious actor would assume the medical account will be identified eventually, and the data will need to be sent to a location the actor can access it independently of the Serums. This would likely take the form of automated collection, for instance, a script that automatically attempt to access records of any patients a request has been sent to, and if successful, save the data to an external file by reading the archive files (WAR) xml. Again, this activity is difficult to mitigate, since the data is supposed to be accessible by anyone that has been given permission. However, information requests are logged on the blockchain (even if successful or not) and would likely be a part of a SIEM as security measure.

When aggregating these trees together, we obtain the ADtree in Fig. 5. The aggregation is performed by connecting the afore-mentioned trees in the order of the attack, with the goal ('Accessing patient data') being at the top. Requesting patient data (i.e., exfiltrating) is next, followed by the Spearphishing attempt to receive permission to access the data ('D1' and 'E1'). Persistence is gained in 'F1' and 'G1', while the initial phishing attempt is shown in nodes 'H1', 'I1' and 'J1'. We can observe the top of the tree mitigation primarily consist of 'Logging', whereas further down we identify more mitigation options, as the attacks use fewer internal tools. For the ADtree we have discussed, we follow 'Create a Healthcare Professional Account', 'Access to Admin Account', 'Obtain Credentials', 'Obtain Username/Password', 'Social Engineering'. 'Obtain Authorised Device' is a secondary protection, connected to 'MFA', showing 'MFA' is implemented in the system.

An ADtree as an abstract model can represent attack goals and paths in different levels of detail, depending on the security properties being analysed (confidentiality, integrity, and availability), the knowledge on the system design and on the information flow within the system, as well as on the experience to perform threat modeling. It is out of the scope of this paper to analyse the quality of the models we proposed in contrast with security properties, however, we supported our models using a standard framework and documentation for security analysis in such a way that they provide paths semantically meaningful and refinements can be added in further modeling iterations. In future, we plan to quantitatively assess these attack-defense scenarios for Serums, particularly in terms of time, detectability, and impact, seeking to determine a satisfiability attribute (the probability of the scenario succeeding) [15,17].

4   UML-Based Mal-Activity Diagrams

We have expanded the ADTrees into a process, detailing where and how the mitigation's can play a role in diminishing the attack. As stated in Sect. 1 and Sect. 2, Mal-activity diagrams (MAD) are an intuitive way to visualise this process based on UML activity diagram principles [32]. They allow us to observe what vulnerabilities occur in the functional system with coded defenses. The ADTrees in Sect. 3 set the outline for the MAD, with each red circle being an action the attacker performs, and each green square being a potential countermeasure. All that remains is to build the process and insert what the reactions of the system would be, assuming a successful attack at each stage.

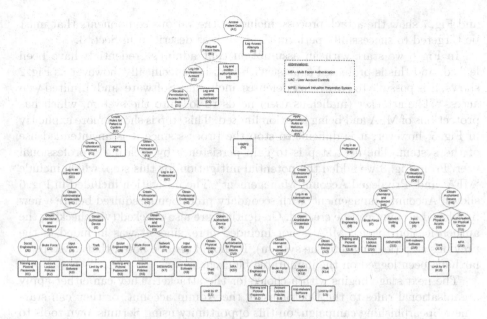

Fig. 5. Integrated ADtree based on MITRE ATT&CK for the 'access of patient data' threat scenario. Nodes containing arcs represent conjunctive sub-goals nodes to achieve a goal node in the tree.

4.1 Mal-Activity Modelling Process

The ADtree provides a broader overview of possible vectors but is not tied to specific attacks (refer to Sect. 2). Thus, extending it to a MAD, we approach a specific attack followed by its vector. As we are tackling the Scenario 2 identified in [2], the vector being followed is one where the malicious user gains control over an 'Administrator' account and uses it to create a 'Professional' account and assign several patients access rules to it. This means following the branch on the left, starting at node 'I1' in Fig. 5. The red circles proceeding up the tree, create a path from 'I1' (then up to 'H1', 'G1', 'F1', and so on), which will then be interpreted as the malicious actions within the MAD. However, some of the paths derived from the ADtree (Fig. 5) are not actions that would be included in the MAD simply because the MAD is more specifically referring to a single attack vector. Of note is node 'H1' ('Obtain Administrator Credentials'), which would also assume the theft of an authorised device mentioned in the MAD (i.e., this would warrant its own diagram). Without this action being shown, nodes 'G1' and 'H1' are essentially the same node. Additionally, not all mitigation strategies are appropriate for the system, and the attacker behaviour modelled in some of the ADtree branches will not need to be replicated in the MAD. Within the ADtree, the mitigation nodes are generic responses, not suited to a design view of the system itself. Within the MAD, we can design where and when specific mitigation strategies are implemented and integrated into the system. Figure 6 and Fig. 7 show the attack process, including the various components that must be targeted to successfully perform the attack as described in Sect. 3.

In Fig. 6 we start with an assumption that admin's credentials have been leaked, and this is protected against with training specifically, however as Fig. 2 shows, it is possible to have other defenses, including 'Software' and 'Limited web access'. The attacker (malicious user) needs to log into the system, which has protections of MFA and being location limited. This step is shown more explicitly in Fig. 5, however, it is difficult to stop the process since it is an intended use of the system. The next step is to gain persistence by creating a professional user. From Fig. 3 we added the potential mitigation for this step, which include 'MFA' and 'Privileged Account Management'. The mitigation included in Fig. 6 shows 'Account Management' with secondary proof being required before a new privileged account can be created. Credentials are also checked (via checking the authentication token). MFA is not included here, since it was included in the previous step (logging into the system). It should also be noted that all steps so far have been logged on the immutable blockchain.

The next stage begins with a choice for the attacker. They can either apply organisational rules to the Doctor using the Admin account, or they can start a new Spearphishing campaign, on this opportunity using Serums' own tools to get users to give the attacker access to their data. In both cases the new rules are logged. In Sect. 3 we discuss the route of requesting access from users using Serums own tools. The potential protection includes ensuring that patients are aware of when they should and should not be expecting requests for access to their data (which is included in Fig. 7). This is connected to Fig. 4, however

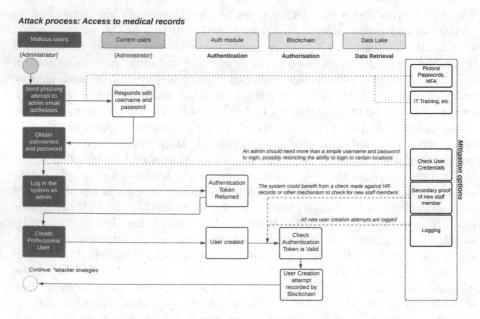

Fig. 6. Mal-activity diagram based on the ADtree on Fig. 5.

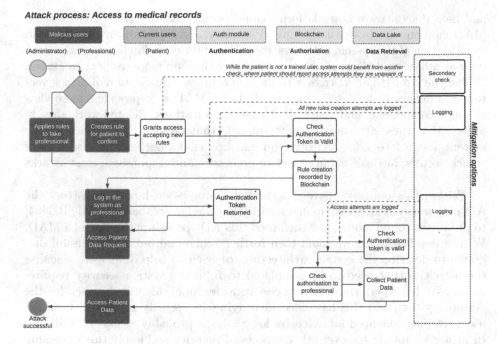

Fig. 7. Mal-activity diagram based on the ADtree on Fig. 5 (cont.).

as mentioned in Sect. 3.2, this would be difficult to mitigate since it is hard to differentiate from normal system use and the steps of an attack, unless a mass campaign was launched that could be detected by a SIEM. Another action difficult to detect would be data collation. The attacker would only need to log into Serums as the professional user and access the data, potentially using external browser-based tools to automatically collate it.

We can now observe the proposed countermeasures, and how they fit into the system overall. For every action the attacker performs, there is a log or a secondary check to attempt to ensure the action is legitimate. We can also see the process maps well from the ADtree (Fig. 5). For example, on creating a new user, the countermeasure listed is to have a secondary check to ensure new users are legitimate. In Fig. 6 we reinforce this with the countermeasure 'Secondary proof of new user'. From the combination of these models, we can observe broadly (using the ADtree) that the attack processes should be discoverable, and from the MAD we can review how these checks would work in practice.

5 Conclusion

Model-based approaches such as ADtrees and other rich diagrams like MAD together can be a way to model and analyse potential attack paths and its countermeasures within systems. They surely expand the knowledge on vulnerabilities and help demonstrate how platforms could reduce security risks. ADtrees and MAD can support in expanding initial security assessments providing a broad visualisation of the system pathways, its vulnerabilities and defenses, and can be used as a base to design software architectures that are more resilient to attack. Where the strength of ADtrees is to provide a broad visualisation of attack vectors and defenses, the descriptive potential of a MAD is to provide a close view of single components and system flow when under attack. Related work already argued that these are complimentary models that provide holistic view of the system design leveraging security requirements, enabling the early discovery of attack vectors, intrinsic detail of system processes, and responses against attacks [20].

Within this paper we have practised the process on how to construct the ADtree for a system, based upon a security knowledge database like MITRE [24] to produce a sound model, and then used this ADtree as input to model a MAD. With a detailed MAD we could then further refine and build other useful diagrams to describe the system architecture, or even to help developers visualise the activities that need to be completed to fulfil the system security requirements. We have performed this process considering an identified attack for the Serums system, and this has aided identifying its security measures (focus on users training, the need for extensive log analysis, probably as part of a SIEM). In future we intend to cover other aspects of security and apply this modelling process to other attack types. At present we have only shown one attack type and vector, and it would be beneficial to show the process has broad applicability. Finally, we would like to include a quantitative evaluation of the ADtrees especially to prioritise the required MAD. Quantitative evaluations of ADtrees have been discussed by [17], and we believe that such an evaluation would give further inputs to build secure systems.

References

1. Banton, M., Bowles, J., Silvina, A., Webber, T.: Conflict-free access rules for sharing smart patient health records. In: Proceedings of the 5th International Joint Conference on Rules and Reasoning (RuleML+RR 2021). LNCS, vol. 12851, pp. 1–15. Springer (2021). https://doi.org/10.1007/978-3-030-91167-6
2. Banton, M., Bowles, J., Silvina, A., Webber, T.: On the benefits and security risks of a user-centric data sharing platform for healthcare provision. In: UMAP 2021 Adjunct: Publication of the 29th ACM Conference on User Modeling, Adaptation and Personalization, pp. 351–356 (2021). https://doi.org/10.1145/3450614.3464473
3. BBC, O.: Cyber attack 'most significant on Irish state' (2021). https://www.bbc.co.uk/news/world-europe-57111615. Accessed 16 Feb 2022
4. Belk, M., Fidas, C., Pitsillides, A.: FlexPass: symbiosis of seamless user authentication schemes in IoT. In: Extended Abstracts of the 2019 CHI Conference on Human Factors in Computing Systems. ACM, New York, NY, USA (2019). http://orcid.org/10.1145/3290607.3312951
5. Bowles, J., Mendoza-Santana, J., Vermeulen, A.F., Webber, T., Blackledge, E.: Integrating healthcare data for enhanced citizen-centred care and analytics. Stud. Health Technol. Inform. **275**, 17–21 (2020). https://doi.org/10.3233/SHTI200686

6. Bowles, J., Mendoza-Santana, J., Webber, T.: Interacting with next-generation smart patient-centric healthcare systems. In: UMAP 2020 Adjunct: Adjunct Publication of the 28th ACM Conference on User Modeling, Adaptation and Personalization, pp. 192–193, July 2020. https://doi.org/10.1145/3386392.3399561
7. Bowles, J., Webber, T., Blackledge, E., Vermeulen, A.: A blockchain-based healthcare platform for secure personalised data sharing. Stud. Health Technol. Inform. Public Health Informat. **281**, 208–212 (2021). https://doi.org/10.3233/SHTI210150
8. Constantinides, A., Belk, M., Fidas, C., Pitsillides, A.: Design and development of the Serums patient-centric user authentication system. In: UMAP 2020 Adjunct: Adjunct Publication of the 28th ACM Conference on User Modeling, Adaptation and Personalization, pp. 201–203, July 2020. https://doi.org/10.1145/3386392.3399564
9. Fraile, M., Ford, M., Gadyatskaya, O., Kumar, R., Stoelinga, M., Trujillo-Rasua, R.: Using attack-defense trees to analyze threats and countermeasures in an ATM: a case study. In: IFIP Working Conference on The Practice of Enterprise Modeling, pp. 326–334. Springer (2016). https://doi.org/10.1007/978-3-319-48393-1
10. Given-Wilson, T., Legay, A.: Formalising fault injection and countermeasures. In: Proceedings of the 15th International Conference on Availability, Reliability and Security. ARES 2020. ACM, New York, NY, USA (2020). https://doi.org/10.1145/3407023.3407049
11. Helmer, G., Wong, J., Slagell, M., Honavar, V., Miller, L., Lutz, R.: A software fault tree approach to requirements analysis of an intrusion detection system. Requirements Eng. **7**(4), 207–220 (2002). https://doi.org/10.1007/s007660200016
12. Hermanns, H., Krämer, J., Krčál, J., Stoelinga, M.: The value of attack-defence diagrams. In: International Conference on Principles of Security and Trust, pp. 163–185. Springer (2016). https://doi.org/10.1007/978-3-662-49635-0
13. Janjic, V., et al.: The serums tool-chain: ensuring security and privacy of medical data in smart patient-centric healthcare systems. In: 2019 IEEE International Conference on Big Data, pp. 2726–2735. IEEE, Los Angeles, CA, USA, December 2019. https://doi.org/10.1109/BigData47090.2019.9005600
14. Kammüller, F.: Combining secure system design with risk assessment for IoT healthcare systems. In: 2019 IEEE International Conference on Pervasive Computing and Communications Workshops (PerCom Workshops), pp. 961–966. IEEE (2019). https://doi.org/10.1109/PERCOMW.2019.8730776
15. Kordy, B., Kordy, P., Mauw, S., Schweitzer, P.: ADTool: security analysis with attack-defense trees. In: International Conference on Quantitative Evaluation of Systems (QEST), pp. 173–176. Springer (2013). https://doi.org/10.1007/978-3-642-40196-1
16. Kordy, B., Mauw, S., Radomirović, S., Schweitzer, P.: Foundations of attack-defense trees. In: Degano, P., Etalle, S., Guttman, J. (eds.) Formal Aspects of Security and Trust. FAST 2010. LNCS, vol. 6561, pp. 80–95. Springer, Berlin, Heidelberg (2011). https://doi.org/10.1007/978-3-642-19751-2
17. Kordy, B., Mauw, S., Schweitzer, P.: Quantitative questions on attack-defense trees. In: International Conference on Information Security and Cryptology, pp. 49–64. Springer (2012). https://doi.org/10.1007/978-3-642-37682-5
18. Larrucea, X., Moffie, M., Asaf, S., Santamaria, I.: Towards a GDPR compliant way to secure European cross border healthcare industry 4.0. Comput. Stand. Interf. **69**, 103408 (2020). https://doi.org/10.1016/j.csi.2019.103408

19. Löhner, B.: Attack-defense-trees and other security modeling tools. In: Niedermayer, H. (ed.) Network Architectures and Services, Seminar Future Internet, pp. 97–103 (2018). https://doi.org/10.2313/NET-2018-11-1
20. Mai, P.X., Goknil, A., Shar, L.K., Pastore, F., Briand, L.C., Shaame, S.: Modeling security and privacy requirements: a use case-driven approach. Inf. Softw. Technol. **100**, 165–182 (2018). https://doi.org/10.1016/j.infsof.2018.04.007
21. McKeon, J.: KY Hospital Systems Still Down 1 Week After Cybersecurity Incident, Health IT Security, xtelligent Healthcare Media (2022). https://www.healthitsecurity.com/news/ky-hospital-systems-still-down-1-week-after-cybersecurity-incident. Accessed 16 Feb 2022
22. Meingast, M., Roosta, T., Sastry, S.: Security and privacy issues with health care information technology. In: 2006 International Conference of the IEEE Engineering in Medicine and Biology Society, pp. 5453–5458. IEEE (2006). https://doi.org/10.1109/IEMBS.2006.260060
23. MITRE Corporation: Common vulnerability and exposures, https://cve.mitre.org/. Accessed 16 Feb 2022
24. MITRE Corporation: MITRE ATT&CK, https://www.attack.mitre.org/. Accessed 16 Feb 2022
25. Muthuppalaniappan, M., Stevenson, K.: Healthcare cyber-attacks and the COVID-19 pandemic: an urgent threat to global health. Int. J. Qual. Health Care **33**(1), mzaa117 (2021). https://doi.org/10.1093/intqhc/mzaa117
26. Nagaraju, V., Fiondella, L., Wandji, T.: A survey of fault and attack tree modeling and analysis for cyber risk management. In: 2017 IEEE International Symposium on Technologies for Homeland Security (HST), pp. 1–6. IEEE (2017). https://doi.org/10.1109/THS.2017.7943455
27. Nicol, D., Sanders, W., Trivedi, K.: Model-based evaluation: from dependability to security. IEEE Trans. Depend. Secure Comput. **1**(1), 48–65 (2004). https://doi.org/10.1109/TDSC.2004.11
28. NIST Information Technology Laboratory: National vulnerability database (nvd), https://www.nvd.nist.gov/vuln. Accessed 16 Feb 2022
29. Opdahl, A.L., Sindre, G.: Experimental comparison of attack trees and misuse cases for security threat identification. Inf. Softw. Technol. **51**(5), 916–932 (2009). https://doi.org/10.1016/j.infsof.2008.05.013
30. Piètre-Cambacédès, L., Bouissou, M.: Beyond attack trees: dynamic security modeling with Boolean logic driven Markov processes (BDMP). In: 2010 European Dependable Computing Conference, pp. 199–208. IEEE (2010). https://doi.org/10.1109/EDCC.2010.32
31. Priya, R., Sivasankaran, S., Ravisasthiri, P., Sivachandiran, S.: A survey on security attacks in electronic healthcare systems. In: 2017 International Conference on Communication and Signal Processing (ICCSP), pp. 691–694. IEEE (2017). https://doi.org/10.1109/ICCSP.2017.8286448
32. Rumbaugh, J., Jacobson, I., Booch, G.: Unified Modeling Language Reference Manual, The (2nd Edition). Pearson Higher Education (2004)
33. Schneier, B.: Attack trees. Dr Dobb's J.-Softw. Tools. Profess. Programm. **24**(12), 21–31 (1999). https://www.cse.sc.edu/zeng1/csce790-f21/papers/attacktrees.pdf
34. Sindre, G.: Mal-activity diagrams for capturing attacks on business processes. In: Sawyer, P., Paech, B., Heymans, P. (eds.) Requirements Engineering: Foundation for Software Quality, pp. 355–366. Springer, Heidelberg (2007). https://doi.org/10.1007/978-3-540-73031-6

35. Souppaya, M., Scarfone, K.: Guide to data-centric system threat modeling. Technical report. Draft NIST Special Publication 800–154, National Institute of Standards and Technology (2016). https://www.csrc.nist.gov/publications/detail/sp/800-154/draft

36. Ullah, F., Edwards, M., Ramdhany, R., Chitchyan, R., Babar, M.A., Rashid, A.: Data exfiltration: a review of external attack vectors and countermeasures. J. Netw. Comput. Appl. **101**, 18–54 (2018). https://doi.org/10.1016/j.jnca.2017.10.016

37. Webber, T., Santana, J.M., Vermeulen, A.F., Bowles, J.K.F.: Designing a patient-centric system for secure exchanges of medical data. In: Gervasi, O., et al. (eds.) ICCSA 2020. LNCS, vol. 12254, pp. 598–614. Springer, Cham (2020). https://doi.org/10.1007/978-3-030-58817-5_44

38. Wideł, W., Audinot, M., Fila, B., Pinchinat, S.: Beyond 2014: formal methods for attack tree-based security modeling. ACM Comput. Surv. **52**(4), 1–36 (2019). https://doi.org/10.1145/3331524

39. Wongvises, C., Khurat, A., Fall, D., Kashihara, S.: Fault tree analysis-based risk quantification of smart homes. In: 2017 2nd International Conference on Information Technology (INCIT), pp. 1–6 (2017). https://doi.org/10.1109/INCIT.2017.8257865

40. Xu, J., Venkatasubramanian, K.K., Sfyrla, V.: A methodology for systematic attack trees generation for interoperable medical devices. In: 2016 Annual IEEE Systems Conference (SysCon), pp. 1–7. IEEE (2016). https://doi.org/10.1109/SYSCON.2016.7490632

Towards Model Checking Video Streams Using VoxLogicA on GPUs

Laura Bussi[1,2](✉) [iD], Vincenzo Ciancia[2] [iD], Fabio Gadducci[1] [iD],
Diego Latella[2] [iD], and Mieke Massink[2] [iD]

[1] Dipartimento di Informatica, Università di Pisa, Pisa, Italy
laura.bussi@phd.unipi.it, fabio.gadducci@unipi.it
[2] Istituto di Scienza e Tecnologie dell'Informazione "A. Faedo", Consiglio Nazionale delle Ricerche, Rome, Italy
{l.bussi,v.ciancia,d.latella,m.massink}@isti.cnr.it

Abstract. We present a feasibility study on the use of spatial logic model checking for real-time analysis of high-resolution video streams with the tool `VoxLogicA`. `VoxLogicA` is a voxel-based image analyser based on the Spatial Logic for Closure Spaces, a logic catered to deal with properties of spatial structures such as topological spaces, graphs and polyhedra. The underlying language includes operators to model proximity and reachability. We demonstrate, via the analysis of a series of video frames from a well-known video game, that it is possible to analyse high-resolution videos in real-time by exploiting the speed-up of `VoxLogicA-GPU`, a recently developed GPU-based version of the tool, which is 1–2 orders of magnitude faster than its previous iteration. Potential applications of real-time video analysis include medical imaging applications such as ultrasound exams, and other video-based diagnostic techniques. More broadly speaking, this work can be the first step towards novel information retrieval methods suitable to find information in a declarative way, in possibly large collections of video streams.

1 Introduction

The topological approach to Spatial Model Checking, introduced in [8,9], provides tools and techniques, typical of the Formal Methods community, for the analysis of graph-based spatial data. Some early, prominent applications of the technique can be found in the area of Smart Cities and Smart Transportation (see [12,13], and also the more recent work in [15]). The spatial model checking approach of `VoxLogicA`[1] (see [4] and the tutorial [11]) aims at encoding Expert Knowledge in executable form in the domain of Medical Imaging. The focus is

---

[1] `VoxLogicA` is Free and Open Source Software. Source code and binaries are available at https://github.com/vincenzoml/VoxLogicA.

Research partially supported by the MIUR Project PRIN 2017FTXR7S IT-MaTTerS".
The authors are listed in alphabetical order, as they equally contributed to this work.

J. Bowles et al. (Eds.): DataMod 2021, LNCS 13268, pp. 78–90, 2022.
https://doi.org/10.1007/978-3-031-16011-0_6

on procedures that are intelligible by domain experts and not solely by pro-grammers. By design, this idea can operate in conjunction with other forms of analysis; for instance, a VoxLogicA procedure could be used to delimit a larger area within which a Machine Learning procedure can be used to provide a more detailed analysis. This would give rise to a form of Hybrid Artificial Intelligence. Such larger areas could reflect specific domain oriented guidelines or analysis protocols, for example to make sure that the Machine Learning procedure focuses on the right region of interest to reduce the number of false positives. The spatial model checker VoxLogicA automatically computes the result of ImgQL (Image Query Language) queries on (possibly large) image datasets.

In [4], a ten-lines-long ImgQL specification was used for the segmentation of Glioblastoma, a common form of brain tumour, in circa 200 cases from the 2017 "Brain Tumour Segmentation (BraTS) challenge" dataset. Spatial Model Checking is fast, and specifications are intelligible to domain experts and can be discussed in the wider community for further improvement. In terms of accuracy, the procedure scores among the top ranking methods of BraTS 2017 – the state of the art in the field, currently dominated by machine-learning methods – and it is comparable in quality to manual delineation by human experts (see [4] for further details comparing our results with the 18 alternative techniques used in BraTS 2017 that were applied to at least 100 cases of the dataset). The segmentation procedure takes only a few seconds per case to complete.

In [3], VoxLogicA has been used for skin lesions segmentation, which is the first task in melanoma diagnosis. An ImgQL procedure was applied to images of skin lesions from two datasets released by ISIC (International Skin Imaging Collaboration) for the 2016 challenge – a training set (900 images) and a test set (379 images) – obtaining results, in terms of accuracy and computational efficiency, in line with the state of the art.

Graphical Processing Units (GPUs) are high-performance, massively parallel computational devices that are available in various sizes (and computing power), in diverse machines ranging from smart phones, tablets, laptops, workstations to large-scale cloud-based computing facilities. GPU computing differs from the *multi-core* paradigm of modern CPUs in many respects: the execution model is *Single Instruction Multiple Data*; the number of computation cores is high; the memory model is highly localised and synchronisation among parallel threads is very expensive. In [7] a GPU-based version of VoxLogicA was introduced. The obtained speedup on synthetic benchmarks, using an office workstation equipped with a good consumer GPU, was between one and two orders of magnitude. The main challenges that were faced in [7] concerned the minimisation of the expensive read/write operations from and to the GPU memory, and turning each algorithm into a massively parallel one. To date, VoxLogicA-GPU implements the core logical primitives of VoxLogicA on GPU, including reachability (based on connected component labelling). Such effort shares some motivation with a recent trend on implementing formal methods on GPU [5,16,17,19,20].

The work in [3,4] concerns the analysis of individual images. In our future work, we are interested in extending the technique to the analysis of medical imaging applications, such as ultrasound exams, and other video-based diagnostic techniques in real time. Such analysis would require processing of videos in real time. This paper presents a case study that aims at investigating whether spatial model checking can be used to analyse high-resolution videos in real-time. As we shall see, the GPU implementation is the key to achieve this. Since VoxLogicA cannot yet load videos directly, our experiments operate on individual video frames, saved on disk as separate png images, but these frames are loaded in a single model-checking session in batches (say, each one corresponding to 5 s of video) in order to maximise throughput. Loading single frames introduces a high overhead due to loading and saving separate files. Therefore in order to measure the "real" execution time, we defined a strategy to mitigate the impact of such overhead, which will not be present e.g., if frames are streamed from a webcam. After this, we demonstrate that the GPU implementation operates in real-time with large margins for future improvement.

As an abstract, but still feature-rich, example, we use a video of the Pac-Man video game[2]. The results show that with the spatial model checking approach we are able to precisely identify the video frames where interesting aspects of gameplay are present.

The paper is organised as follows. Section 2 provides the relevant background on spatial model checking. Section 3 presents the experimental set-up and Sect. 4 presents the results. Section 5 concludes the work and provides an outlook on further research.

2   Background: Spatial Model Checking on GPU

We briefly review the syntax of the Spatial Logic for Closure Spaces (SLCS), defined in [8,9], and its interpretation, restricted to the case of two-dimensional images which is currently handled by VoxLogicA-GPU. For the general definition on so-called *closure spaces*, and the link between (multi-dimensional) images, graphs, closure spaces and topological spatial logics we refer the reader to [1,4,9]. The syntax of the logic we use in this paper is its most up-to-date rendition, where the *surrounded* connective from [9] is a derived one, whereas reachability is primitive, as in [2,10,14]. Given set P of *atomic propositions*, with $p \in P$, the syntax of the logic is described by the following grammar:

$$\phi ::= p \mid \neg\phi \mid \phi_1 \wedge \phi_2 \mid \mathcal{N}\phi \mid \rho\,\phi_1[\phi_2] \tag{1}$$

The logic is interpreted on the pixels of an image $\mathcal{M}$ of fixed dimensions. The truth values of a formula ϕ on *all* the pixels can be rendered as a binary image of the same dimensions of $\mathcal{M}$. Therefore, in particular, **atomic propositions** correspond to binary images. However, concretely, when working on images, atomic propositions also include constraints (e.g., thresholds) on imaging features, such as intensity, or red, green, blue colour components. **Boolean operators** are defined pixel-wise: $\neg\phi$ is the complement of the binary image representing ϕ,

---

[2] PAC-MAN[TM] & ©1980 BANDAI NAMCO Entertainment Inc.

and $\phi_1 \wedge \phi_2$ is binary image intersection. The **modal** formula $\mathcal{N}\phi$ is satisfied by a pixel x that shares a vertex or an edge with any of the pixels that satisfy ϕ (adopting the so-called *Moore neighbourhood*); in imaging terminology, this is the *dilation* of the binary image corresponding to ϕ. The **reachability** formula $\rho\ \phi_1[\phi_2]$ is satisfied by a pixel x if there is a pixel y, a path π and an index ℓ such that $\pi_0 = x$, $\pi_\ell = y$, y satisfies ϕ_1, and all the intermediate pixels $\pi_1, \ldots, \pi_{\ell-1}$ (if any, hence the notation for optional [...]) satisfy ϕ_2.

Note that $\mathcal{N}\phi$ can be derived from ρ, and viceversa. In this paper we use $\mathcal{N}$ explicitly because of its specific implementation in the tool.

From the basic operators, several interesting notions can be derived, such as:

- *interior* corresponding to the imaging primitive of *erosion*;
- *surroundedness*;
- *contact* between regions (see also [10]) denoted as $\mathcal{T}$ (from 'touch').

Concerning region based analysis, the *discrete* Region Connection Calculus RCC8D of [18] has been encoded in a variant of SLCS with operators on sets of points instead of single points [10].

In `ImgQL`, the input language of `VoxLogicA`, these operators have their own syntax. In particular, in the context of the present work we will use:

- `|`, `&`, `!` for the boolean operators disjunction, conjunction and negation, respectively;
- `N` for the near operator;
- `I` for the interior operator, where `I (x) = !(N !x)`;
- `mayReach(x,y)` for the reachability operator $\rho\ x\ [y]$;
- `touch(x,y) = a & mayReach(y,x)` for the contact operator;
- `.<=` , `.>=` and so on for constraints involving constant bounds (on the side of the dot) and pixel attributes such as intensity or colour.

The tool `VoxLogicA-GPU` is a global, explicit state model checker for SLCS, aiming at high efficiency and maximum portability. `VoxLogicA-GPU` is implemented in FSharp, using the Microsoft dotnet infrastructure, and exploiting the imaging library SimpleITK and the portable GPU computing library OpenCL[3].

Efficiency is one of the major challenges, as outperforming the CPU implementation of `VoxLogicA` [4] inherently means designing in-GPU imaging primitives faster than the state-of-the-art library ITK. The focus of the first release of `VoxLogicA-GPU` has been on demonstrating its scalability. The tool takes as input an `ImgQL` specification and automatically creates a computing pipeline, consisting of a set of tasks to be run. Each task corresponds to a basic primitive (including SLCS operators, and basic imaging primitives such as thresholds). Each arrow denotes a dependency between two tasks, namely that the output of the source task should be fed as the input to the target one. Such task graph is then sent to the GPU, exploiting the so-called *events* mechanism of OpenCL

---

[3] FSharp: see https://fsharp.org. NET Core: see https://dotnet.microsoft.om. OpenCL: see https://www.khronos.org/opencl. ITK: see https://itk.org.

to describe the dependencies. The pipeline is then run on the GPU, respecting the input/output dependencies created by the events mechanism, but otherwise without a specified order.

3   Experimental Setup

The huge speedup attained with the switch to GPUs is theoretically capable of processing video streams in real time. Our work aims at verifying up to which extent this is true using `VoxLogicA-GPU`, and at establishing preliminary use cases for experimentation. Video streams are composed of several frames, each one capturing an instant of a whole scene.

Our envisaged future applications mainly concern two scenarios: that of medical imaging, as mentioned in the introduction, and the field of smart transportation (see e.g. [12]). However, first of all a preliminary study is needed, in order to assess effectiveness of the proposed method, e.g. in terms of complexity of logic formulas, interesting logical operators, and so on.

To this aim, we propose an example based on a video game, namely *Pac-Man*. We provide here a detailed description of the experimental setting, including how execution times are measured, and why we chose to use a footage of a video game as a benchmark.

Pac-Man is a famous 2D video game, released in 1980 by Bandai-Namco. The main character is Pac-Man, represented by a yellow circle, whose goal is to eat all the dots in a maze, avoiding to be captured by the coloured ghosts (Blinky, Pinky, Inky and Clyde) following him. Pac-Man can also eat *energiser pellets* (bigger, blinking dots on the same path as the smaller dots) to gain in turn the ability to catch ghosts. Once caught by Pac-Man, ghosts will re-appear in the centre of the maze. There are various reasons why this simple video game represents an interesting benchmark. The topology of the space remains the same over time, but there are several entities appearing and disappearing. These entities can be effectively specified via a declarative procedure. For this reason, the analysis does not require any kind of preprocessing: video footages have been recorded and split into multiple frames in the `png` format, and then processed directly using `VoxLogicA`.

The `ImgQL` specification of the game elements is shown in Specification 1. Pac-Man is yellow. This is specified by thresholds on the intensity of the red, green and blue components of each pixel. Similarly, for the ghosts and the dots and energiser pellets.

As can be observed in a typical video frame of the game (see Fig. 1), any auxiliary lives of Pac-Man are indicated by small Pac-Man images at the bottom of the frame. Pac-Man itself is inside the maze, so sufficiently far from the border of the frame. In `ImgQL` 'border' is an atomic proposition that holds at all pixels at the extremes of the image. So, Pac-Man itself can be characterised by satisfying the formula `pacmans`, but being sufficiently far from the border, i.e. not touching an area composed of pixels that are at a distance of less than 12 pixels from the border. The `ImgQL` specification is shown in Specification 2.

ImgQL Specification 1: Pac-Man game elements.

```
1 //find all characters and other elements
2 let pacmans = (252 .<= red(img)) & (252 .<= green(img)) &
3                 (10 .>= blue(img))
4 let blinky = (250 .<= red(img)) & (10 .>= green(img)) &
5                 (10 .>= blue(img))
6 let pinky = (250 .<= red(img)) & (175 .<= green(img)) &
7                 (190 .>= green(img)) & (245 .<= blue(img))
8 let inky = (15 .>= red(img)) & (240 .<= green(img)) &
9                 (240 .<= blue(img))
10 let clyde = (240 .<= red(img)) & (190 .>= green(img)) &
11                 (165 .<= green(img)) & (90 .>= blue(img))
12 let dotsAndPellets = (240 .<= red(img)) & (200 .>= green(img)) &
13                 (175 .<= green(img)) & (190 .>= blue(img)) &
14                 (165 .<= blue(img))
```

ImgQL Specification 2: Active Pac-Man.

```
1 let N12 (x) = N N N N N N N N N N N N x
2 let pacman = (pacmans & !touch(pacmans, N12 (border)))
```

Pellets and dots have the same colour, but pellets are larger than dots. This information can be used to distinguish them. Taking the area characterised by dotsAndPellets and shrinking this area in several steps using the interior operator results in an area comprising only the inner parts of the bigger pellets. The pellets themselves can then be retrieved by extending the thus obtained area by pixels near the remaining area (i.e. centres of the pellets) within 4 steps. This is shown in the second line of Specification 3. The dots are those pixels satisfying dotsAndPellets that are not satisfying pellets. Figure 1.3 shows the result of dots, and Fig. 1.4 shows the result of pellets. As we will see, we need to introduce the concept of "uninterrupted paths of dots", specified via the formula auxDots, consisting of all pixels that are at most 13 steps (13 times N) from a dot (including dots themselves). Figure 1.5 shows all pixels satyisfing auxDots.

ImgQL Specification 3: Dots and pellets.

```
1 let N13 (x) = N N N N N N N N N N N N N x
2 let pellets = N N N N I I I dotsAndPellets
3 let dots = N N (dotsAndPellets & !pellets)
4 let auxDots = N13 (dots)
```

The key points of the game constitute interesting spatial properties. Let's focus on the behaviour of ghosts: each of them will try to catch Pac-Man, following different routes. We can specify the situation in which Pac-Man is caught by a ghost using ImgQL as follows:

$$\text{touch(pacman, blinky) | touch(pacman, pinky)}$$
$$\text{| touch(pacman, inky) | touch(pacman, clyde)}$$

Another significant property, involving reachability, is the fact that Pac-Man can follow a path of dots and reach a pellet (recall that for a game level to be completed, Pac-Man is required to eat all dots in the maze):

$$\text{touch(pacman, mayReach(pellets, auxDots))}$$

Intuitively, the property is true if Pac-Man "touches" the beginning of a path of dots leading to a pellet. This is shown in Specification 4. In the second line of the specification the operator mayReach is used, denoting the ρ-operator of SLCS. auxReach is satisfied by all pixels of pellets and paths formed by enlarged dots as specified in the last line of Specification 3. In the last line one only needs to check whether Pac-Man touches the pixels identified by auxReach.

ImgQL Specification 4: Pac-Man reaches pellets and Pac-man caught by ghost.

```
1 let auxReach = mayReach(pellets, auxDots)
2 let result = touch(pacman, auxReach)
3 let caught = touch(pacman, blinky) | touch(pacman, pinky) |
  touch(pacman, inky) | touch(pacman, clyde)
```

This concludes the ImgQL specification of the spatial analysis for Pac-Man. The intermediate results of all definitions can be saved separately and numerical information on each frame can be printed as shown in Specification 5. This is how the images in Fig. 1 have been obtained.

ImgQL Specification 5: Saving and printing.

```
1 save "00_pacman.png" pacman
2 save "01_dots.png" dots
3 save "02_pellets.png" pellets
4 save "03_auxDots.png" auxDots
5 save "05_result.png" result

6 print "pathToPellets $NUMFRAME" volume(result) .>. 0
7 print "pacmanCaught $NUMFRAME" volume(caught) .>. 0
```

In order to check the results for each frame, a simple Python script has been written. The script accepts as input a specification fragment such as the ones we have shown so far, and generates a (possibly very large) VoxLogicA specification that repeats the given fragment for each video frame, loading each time a different one. In order to identify the result of the analysis on different frames, the placeholder ($NUMFRAME) can be used when naming the result values (see also the last line in Specification 5). This placeholder will be replaced with the number of the frame by the Python script while generating the specification. Note also that the result can be both saved as an image or printed as a boolean value. The boolean image *False* corresponds to a completely black image, so we can print the truth value of the formula volume(resultImage) . > . 0. As the volume of an image is the sum of its non-zero components, the result will clearly mirror the truth value of the formula. All tests were performed on a workstation equipped with:

- An Intel(R) Core(TM) i9-9900K CPU @ 3.60 GHz (16 cores, 32 threads);
- An NVIDIA GeForce RTX 3080 1785 MHz, 10 GB global memory.

Each test has been run 5 times, in such a way to get an approximate average running time. In our experimental setup, execution times cannot be measured directly by just running the specification. The fact that our video has been expanded to single frames on disk makes input/output times dominate over computation, thus rendering it impossible to measure in a direct way how much time exactly is spent on computation. To overcome this, VoxLogicA and VoxLogicA-GPU have been modified to accept a command line switch that will let the tool load just one image and reuse it multiple times. Note that this methodology is only used to measure performance and gives a good approximation of the processing time, whereas the loading time is negligible, as only one image is loaded. By carefully choosing, as the representative image, one that exhibits a reasonable complexity, the obtained measurements are representative enough to get a sensible indication of the total computation time. In future work, we will cater for loading video files directly, and unpacking each video frame in memory using optimized (possibly in-hardware) functionality, so that on the one hand, loading of single frames from disk will no longer affect video processing in VoxLogicA-GPU, and on the other hand the model checking result will be correct. By the above considerations, we expect the obtained performance to be in line with the measurements that we present in this paper.

4   Results

In this section, we report the results of our experiments. We recall that both the CPU and the GPU versions are tested against *contact* and *reachability* formulas, as described in the previous section. In the considered frame (Fig. 1.1), there is a way for Pac-Man to reach the bottom-right pellet by only eating dots, thus the result image will highlight Pac-Man.

We restricted the tests to a benchmark of 150 frames. This is due to the fact that the CPU version of VoxLogicA does not feature any kind of memory management mechanism, thus it suffers from memory limits (on the other hand the memory management mechanism embedded in VoxLogicA-GPU allows for larger tests to be run). Videos are RGBA videos, with a resolution of 1600×1200 and 30 fps, namely, 150 frames capture circa 5 s. In Table 1, execution times for the above mentioned formula are reported.

Table 1. Comparison between CPU and GPU execution times, reported in milliseconds

Execution time of sample formulas (150 frames)		
Formula	GPU	CPU
Pac-Man is caught by a ghost (caught)	3,800 ms	12,200 ms
Pac-Man can reach a pellet via dots (result)	3,000 ms	54,000 ms

The comparison of results shows that using GPUs enable real-time analysis. In this case, we load a pre-recorded video, but our results suggest that monitoring video streaming might be feasible using our technology. It is also interesting to note that the more involved formula actually requires less time on GPU than the simpler collision detection one. This type of results, that may be counter intuitive, depends on the operators involved in the computation:

- in the reachability formula result, connected components are computed only once per frame, namely to check if the desired path exists, and "proximity" operators, like Interior and Near, are massively used to find dots and pellets and to enlarge them, in such a way that they form a path. GPUs are more beneficial to this kind of operators, as devices' parallelism can be exploited at its best.
- in the collision detection formula caught, connected components must be computed four times for each frame; in fact, we must compute touch (which requires computing Connected Components) between Pac-Man and each ghost. Such computation affects the performance of the GPU, as multiple kernels must be called and randomised write and read on the global device memory are required.

Despite these considerations, the execution time stays far below the required real-time threshold. Note that currently it is not possible to state spatio-temporal properties in ImgQL, and no temporal analysis is performed in VoxLogicA. We leave the possibility to add temporal operators as a future work, possibly still exploiting GPUs.

One may have noted that step 5 in Fig. 1 could cause some false positives. This is due to the fact that enlarging dots using the Near operator causes the paths to touch each other in proximity of pellets. This can be actually avoided

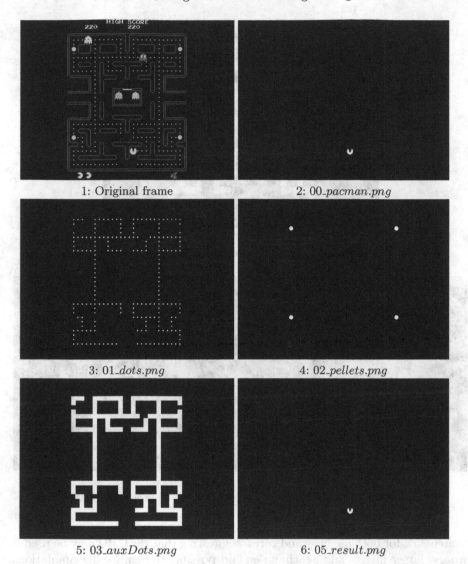

1: Original frame   2: 00_pacman.png

3: 01_dots.png   4: 02_pellets.png

5: 03_auxDots.png   6: 05_result.png

Fig. 1. Analysis of a video frame (1). Using thresholds, we isolate Pac-Man (2), dots (3) and energy pellets (4). We then enlarge dots in such a way that they touch each other, thus forming a path (5). The result for the formula *Pac-Man can reach a pellet via dots* represents Pac-Man itself (6), as it touches a path leading to a pellet.

by replacing Near with a distance operator based on Euclidean distance (see Fig. 2), whose implementation is currently in progress on VoxLogicA-GPU.

Another interesting point to note is GPU memory and cores occupation. Figure 3 shows that the GPU load is actually quite low. The *nvtop* tool, which is used to monitor processes currently running on GPU, shows that the occupation

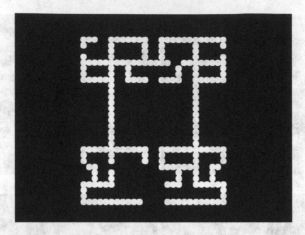

Fig. 2. Path found via the Euclidean distance operator.

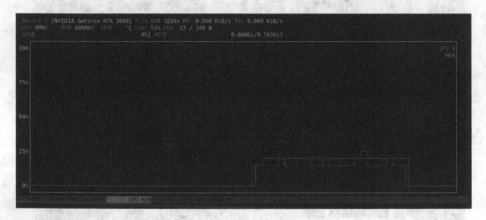

Fig. 3. Memory and cores occupation on GPU, while processing 300 frames.

is circa 25% for both memory and cores, suggesting that the GPU may be used to process larger images and benchmarks, and possibly to monitor 3D simulations.

5   Conclusions

In current work-in-progress, the results obtained in [7] have been vastly improved (ranging from a speed-up of 50× on case studies to 500× on artificial benchmarks). The aim of such optimisation was initially focused on enabling interactive calibration of analysis parameters in ImgQL specifications by end-users of VoxLogicA, and a faster analysis development cycle by domain experts, also in conjunction with a dedicated user interface. The latter is currently being developed taking also cognitive aspects of usability into account (see [6]). However, our preliminary experiments confirmed that this encouraging result can also be used for a real time analysis of video streams. Despite the fact that temporal operators are currently not available in VoxLogicA, it is possible to state and check interesting properties, and this can be done on high resolution videos, in real-time. Furthermore, we showed that the GPU is far from being stressed by the task, thus we expect the speedup to be even larger in case of higher quality videos, 3D animated simulations, or more complex properties.

Still, a large amount of execution time is devoted to I/O operations (in particular loading frames as png files). Therefore, a major goal of future work will be to provide VoxLogicA with a video loader, possibly exploiting the state-of-the-art OpenCV library[4].

As mentioned above, another goal is to implement temporal operators and a temporal model checking algorithm in VoxLogicA-GPU. This will widen the set of properties amenable to spatio-temporal model checking of video-streams, opening possibilities of new scenarios.

Our experiments will also be useful in future work for expanding the logical language with dynamic binding predicates, giving the language the ability to capture the concept of a "new entity", different from all the previously known ones which appears in a video stream at a given instant, and that may reappear later. In our physical simulation example, binding can be used e.g. to answer queries like "was Pac-Man caught twice by the same ghost x", independently from the moment in which x appears for the first time, and the identity of x.

References

1. Banci Buonamici, F., Belmonte, G., Ciancia, V., Latella, D., Massink, M.: Spatial logics and model checking for medical imaging. Int. J. Softw. Tools Technol. Transfer **22**(2), 195–217 (2019). https://doi.org/10.1007/s10009-019-00511-9
2. Bartocci, E., Bortolussi, L., Loreti, M., Nenzi, L.: Monitoring mobile and spatially distributed cyber-physical systems. In: Talpin, J., Derler, P., Schneider, K. (eds.) MEMOCODE 2017, pp. 146–155. ACM (2017)
3. Belmonte, G., Broccia, G., Ciancia, V., Latella, D., Massink, M.: Feasibility of spatial model checking for nevus segmentation. In: 2021 IEEE/ACM 9th International Conference on Formal Methods in Software Engineering (FormaliSE), pp. 1–12 (2021). https://doi.org/10.1109/FormaliSE52586.2021.00007
4. Belmonte, G., Ciancia, V., Latella, D., Massink, M.: VoxLogicA: a spatial model checker for declarative image analysis. In: Vojnar, T., Zhang, L. (eds.) TACAS 2019. LNCS, vol. 11427, pp. 281–298. Springer, Cham (2019). https://doi.org/10.1007/978-3-030-17462-0_16
5. Berkovich, S., Bonakdarpour, B., Fischmeister, S.: GPU-based runtime verification. In: IPDPS 2013, pp. 1025–1036. IEEE Computer Society (2013)
6. Broccia, G., Milazzo, P., Ölveczky, P.C.: Formal modeling and analysis of safety-critical human multitasking. Innov. Syst. Softw. Eng. **15**(2), 169–190 (2019). https://doi.org/10.1007/s11334-019-00333-7
7. Bussi, L., Ciancia, V., Gadducci, F.: Towards a spatial model checker on GPU. In: Peters, K., Willemse, T.A.C. (eds.) FORTE 2021. LNCS, vol. 12719, pp. 188–196. Springer, Cham (2021). https://doi.org/10.1007/978-3-030-78089-0_12

---

[4] See: https://opencv.org/.

8. Ciancia, V., Latella, D., Loreti, M., Massink, M.: Specifying and verifying properties of space. In: Diaz, J., Lanese, I., Sangiorgi, D. (eds.) TCS 2014. LNCS, vol. 8705, pp. 222–235. Springer, Heidelberg (2014). https://doi.org/10.1007/978-3-662-44602-7_18
9. Ciancia, V., Latella, D., Loreti, M., Massink, M.: Model checking spatial logics for closure spaces. Log. Methods Comput. Sci. **12**(4) (2016)
10. Ciancia, V., Latella, D., Massink, M.: Embedding RCC8D in the collective spatial logic CSLCS. In: Boreale, M., Corradini, F., Loreti, M., Pugliese, R. (eds.) Models, Languages, and Tools for Concurrent and Distributed Programming. LNCS, vol. 11665, pp. 260–277. Springer, Cham (2019). https://doi.org/10.1007/978-3-030-21485-2_15
11. Ciancia, V., Belmonte, G., Latella, D., Massink, M.: A hands-on introduction to spatial model checking using VoxLogicA. In: Laarman, A., Sokolova, A. (eds.) SPIN 2021. LNCS, vol. 12864, pp. 22–41. Springer, Cham (2021). https://doi.org/10.1007/978-3-030-84629-9_2
12. Ciancia, V., Gilmore, S., Grilletti, G., Latella, D., Loreti, M., Massink, M.: Spatio-temporal model checking of vehicular movement in public transport systems. Int. J. Softw. Tools Technol. Transfer **20**(3), 289–311 (2018). https://doi.org/10.1007/s10009-018-0483-8
13. Ciancia, V., Latella, D., Massink, M., Paškauskas, R., Vandin, A.: A tool-chain for statistical spatio-temporal model checking of bike sharing systems. In: Margaria, T., Steffen, B. (eds.) ISoLA 2016. LNCS, vol. 9952, pp. 657–673. Springer, Cham (2016). https://doi.org/10.1007/978-3-319-47166-2_46
14. Ciancia, V., Latella, D., Massink, M., de Vink, E.P.: Towards spatial bisimilarity for closure models: logical and coalgebraic characterisations. CoRR abs/2005.05578 (2020). https://arxiv.org/abs/2005.05578
15. Ma, M., Bartocci, E., Lifland, E., Stankovic, J.A., Feng, L.: A novel spatial-temporal specification-based monitoring system for smart cities. IEEE Internet Things J. **8**(15), 11793–11806 (2021). https://doi.org/10.1109/JIOT.2021.3069943
16. Neele, T., Wijs, A., Bošnački, D., van de Pol, J.: Partial-order reduction for GPU model checking. In: Artho, C., Legay, A., Peled, D. (eds.) ATVA 2016. LNCS, vol. 9938, pp. 357–374. Springer, Cham (2016). https://doi.org/10.1007/978-3-319-46520-3_23
17. Osama, M., Wijs, A.: Parallel SAT simplification on GPU architectures. In: Vojnar, T., Zhang, L. (eds.) TACAS 2019. LNCS, vol. 11427, pp. 21–40. Springer, Cham (2019). https://doi.org/10.1007/978-3-030-17462-0_2
18. Randell, D.A., Landini, G., Galton, A.: Discrete mereotopology for spatial reasoning in automated histological image analysis. IEEE Trans. Pattern Anal. Mach. Intell. **35**(3), 568–581 (2013). https://doi.org/10.1109/TPAMI.2012.128
19. Wijs, A., Bošnački, D.: Many-core on-the-fly model checking of safety properties using GPUs. Int. J. Softw. Tools Technol. Transfer **18**(2), 169–185 (2015). https://doi.org/10.1007/s10009-015-0379-9
20. Wijs, A., Neele, T., Bošnački, D.: GPUexplore 2.0: unleashing GPU explicit-state model checking. In: Fitzgerald, J., Heitmeyer, C., Gnesi, S., Philippou, A. (eds.) FM 2016. LNCS, vol. 9995, pp. 694–701. Springer, Cham (2016). https://doi.org/10.1007/978-3-319-48989-6_42

Data Mining and Processing Related Approaches

Privacy Risk and Data Utility Assessment on Network Data

Roberto Pellungrini(✉) (iD)

Department of Computer Science, University of Pisa, Pisa, Italy
`roberto.pellungrini@di.unipi.it`

Abstract. In the modern Internet era the usage of social networks such as Twitter, Instagram and Facebook is constantly increasing. The analysis of this type of data can help us understand interesting social phenomena, because these networks intrinsically capture the new nature of user interactions. Unfortunately, social network data may reveal personal and sensitive information about users, leading to privacy violations. In this paper, we propose a study of privacy risk for social network data. In particular, we empirically analyze a set of privacy attacks on social network data by using the privacy risk assessment framework PRUDEnce. After simulating the attacks on real data, we first analyze how the privacy risk is distributed over the whole population. Then, we study the effect of high-risk users sanitization on some common network metrics.

Keywords: Privacy · Attack models · Social networks

1 Introduction

Social networks are used by people everyday for different purposes: for interacting with friends (Facebook), for professional activities (LinkedIn), for spreading information, news and multimedia material (Twitter and Instagram). Nowadays, the analysis of social network data is fundamental to study and understand social phenomena. The social network analysis can help in understanding customer interactions and reactions [15], marketing strategies based on communities or singles users, migration flows, fake news diffusion or virus spread [16], etc. However social network data may contain sensitive and private information about the real people that actively operate in the network. Therefore, different techniques have been used to anonymize the data, the simplest way being replacing identity with pseudonymous keys. However, Backstrom et al. [3] showed that this technique is not enough for privacy protection as malicious adversaries still may succeed in re-identifying individuals using a background knowledge attack.

In order to enable a practical application of the privacy-preserving techniques proposed in the literature, Pratesi et al. in [14] proposed PRUDEnce, a framework for systematic privacy risk assessment. This framework follows the idea of the EU General Data Protection Regulation, which explicitly imposes on data controllers an assessment of the impact of data protection for the most risky

© Springer Nature Switzerland AG 2022
J. Bowles et al. (Eds.): DataMod 2021, LNCS 13268, pp. 93–106, 2022.
https://doi.org/10.1007/978-3-031-16011-0_7

processes.[1] In [14], Pratesi et al. show the applicability of their framework on mobility data. In this paper, we propose to apply PRUDEnce framework for the privacy risk assessment in social network data. This requires to first formally define a set of privacy attacks on social network data, then simulate them on real data to empirically evaluate the individual privacy risks, and then, evaluate the data utility by considering only non-risky data. In order to evaluate the data utility, we perform an analysis that highlights the degradation of the social network structure in case we only consider non-risky nodes and their connections.

The paper is organized as follows. In Sect. 2, we discuss some of the related works in the literature. In Sect. 3, we define the data structures to describe social network data according to different data aggregations. In Sect. 4, we introduce the framework used for the privacy risk assessment. In Sect. 5, we formally define the privacy attacks on social network data. In Sect. 6, we show the results of our experiments on the attack simulations. In Sect. 8, we present an analysis on the network degradation, discusses some related work. In Sect. 9, we draw our conclusions and discuss future works.

2 Related Work

The concept of privacy-by-design was initially developed by Ann Cavoukian [5] to address the ever-growing and systemic effects of Information and Communication Technologies, and of large-scale networked data systems in the 90's. This concept basically expresses the general approach of embedding privacy into the design, development and management of information. A related study on the application of the concept of privacy-by-design to social media is [7] where the authors develop a social networking privacy framework and privacy model for applying privacy-by-design principles to social networks for both desktop and mobile devices. This approach mitigates many current social network privacy issues, and leads to a more controlled form of privacy assessment.

One of the classical works in the field of privacy risk assessment is the LINDDUN methodology [6], a privacy-aware threat analysis framework based on Microsoft's STRIDE methodology [19]. PRUDEnce [14] builds on these principles, developing a privacy risk assessment framework applicable to any kind of data [12]. While the models and methodology presented in these works have been used previously on human mobility data, they are flexible enough to be adapted to social network data. For modeling the attacks, we rely on the contributions made in [1,9,17,20,21]. We apply the general structure of these attacks, tweaking some of them to our specific need, as explained in Sect. 5.

Privacy for social media networks is a high interest topic, as show in works such as [11] where the authors highlight how privacy awareness changes the perspectives and motivations of users of a social media. In the context of privacy for online social networks Liu and Terzi [10] propose a framework for computing privacy scores for each user in the network. Such scores indicate the potential risk caused by her participation in the network. Our effort in defining possible

---

[1] The EU General Data Protection Regulation can be found at http://bit.ly/1TlgbjI.

attacks and studying their applications on real network goes in the direction of offering more tools to actually provide realistic evaluation of privacy risk to individuals. In [4] Becker and Chen propose a framework called PrivAware, a tool to detect and report unintended information loss in online social networks. In [2] Ananthula et al. discuss a "Privacy Index" (PIDX) used to measure a user's privacy exposure in a social network. They have also described and calculated the "Privacy Quotient" (PQ) i.e. a metric to measure the privacy of the user's profile using a naive approach. Pensa and Blasi in [13] have proposed a supervised learning approach to calculate a privacy score of an individual in social network data based on the actual people allowed to access the profile of the individual.

3 Data Definitions

Social network have traditionally been modeled as graphs:

Definition 1 (Social Network). *We model a social network as a simple graph $G = (V, E, L, \Gamma)$, where V is the set of vertices representing individuals, $E \subseteq V \times V$ is the set of edges representing the relationships between individuals, L is a set of labels, and $\Gamma : V \rightarrow l$ is a labeling function that maps each vertex to a subset of labels l with $l \subseteq L$.*

To keep our definition simple, we assume that edges do not have any labels. In a social network, the direction of an edge indicates the relationship between vertices and can be used to distinguish the type of relationship: single-sided or mutual. For our purposes, we will assume that all relationships are mutual. From the social network graph we can derive data structures representing aggregated information. These are used to expose less information while still enabling the computation of standard network metrics. Clearly, this data transformation helps privacy preserving analyses and the respect of data minimization principle.

Definition 2 (Friendship Vector). *The friendship vector F_v of an individual $v \in V$ is a set of vertices $F_v = \langle v_1, v_2 \ldots, v_n \rangle$ representing individuals connected to v in the social network graph.*

The friendship vector of a node v essentially represents the neighborhood of the individual v at distance 1.

Definition 3 (Label vector). *The label vector of an individual v is a set of labels $LA_v = \langle la_1, la_2 \ldots, la_m \rangle$. Each $la_j = (f, l)$ (with $j \in \{1, 2, \ldots, |L|\}$) is a pair composed of a feature name f and the associated label value l. The label vector of an individual can be empty.*

Each label describes a profile feature of an individual, for example *gender*: *'female'* or *'male'*, *educational information*: *'Pisa University'* or *'Stanford University'*, etc.

Definition 4 (Degree vector). *The degree vector of an individual* v, *denoted by* $D_v = \langle d_{v_1}, d_{v_2}, \ldots, d_{v_n} \rangle$, *represents the number of friends of each friend of* v. *Thus, each element* d_{v_i} *is equal to the length of the friendship vector of the individual* v_i *in the social network graph, i.e.,* $d_{v_i} = |(F_{v_i})|$.

Definition 5 (Mutual Friendship vector). *The mutual friendship vector of an individual* v, *denoted by* $MF_v = \langle mf_1, \ldots, mf_n \rangle$, *represents the number of common friends of* v *with each one of its friends* v_i. *Thus, each element* mf_i *is equal to the cardinality of the intersection between the friendship vector of* v *and the one of* v_i, *i.e.,* $mf_i = | F_v \cap F_{v_i} |$.

Taking in consideration all of the structures defined above we can define a Social Network Dataset as follows:

Definition 6 (Social Network Dataset). *A social network dataset is a set of data structures* $\mathcal{S} = \{\mathcal{S}_1, \mathcal{S}_2, \ldots, \mathcal{S}_k\}$ *where* $\mathcal{S}_v$ $(1 \leq v \leq k)$ *is the social network data structure of an individual* v.

A Social Network Dataset represents a possible aggregation of a social network that some data provider may share or publish for some usage. A malicious adversary can attack a Social Network Dataset using some previously acquired knowledge about one or more individuals in the dataset, i.e., a background knowledge.

4   Privacy Risk Assessment Framework

Given the rapid growth in the number of services and applications based on social networks, there is increasing concern about privacy issues in published social network data. The prevention of node/individual re-identification is one of the critical issues. With some background knowledge about an individual in a social network, an adversary may perform a re-identification attack and disclose the identity of the individual. To preserve privacy, it is not sufficient to remove all identifiers, as shown in [20,21]. In this paper we want to empirically study the privacy risk in social network data using the framework proposed in [14]. PRUDEnce is a system enabling a privacy-aware ecosystem for sharing personal data. The main components of its architecture are shown in Fig. 1. The typical scenario considered is one where a Service Developer (SD) requests personal data, such as social network data, from a Data Provider (DP) to develop services or perform an analysis. The Data Provider has to guarantee the right to privacy of the individuals whose data are recorded. Thus, the data stored by DP cannot be shared directly without assessing the privacy risk of the individuals represented in the data. Once privacy risk has been assessed, DP can choose how to protect the data before sharing, selecting the privacy preserving methodology most appropriate for the data to be shared. Assuming that the Data Provider stores a database D, it aggregates, selects, and filters the dataset D to meet the requirements of the Data Analyst and produces a set of social network datasets

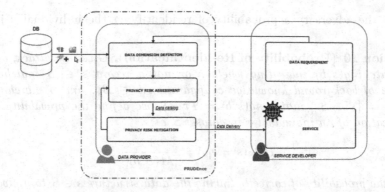

Fig. 1. PRUDence: privacy-aware data sharing ecosystem

$\{S_1, S_2, \ldots, S_k\}$ each with a different data structure and/or aggregation of the data. The Data Provider then performs the privacy risk assessment.

The privacy risk assessment component of the framework has to produce a quantitative measure of privacy risk. Such measure depends on the kind of attack simulated, the kind of data, and on the aggregation on the data itself. The simulation of a privacy attack takes place in two phases: first, we assume that a malicious adversary gathers, in some way, a *background knowledge* about an individual (e.g., a part of their friendship vector) and then the adversary uses the acquired background knowledge to re-identify the individual in the social network dataset. Every background knowledge can be configured in many ways, and for each configuration there can be many background knowledge instances. To explain how risk is computed, we give the formal definitions of these concepts:

Definition 7 (Background knowledge Category). *A background knowledge category B of an attack is the type of information known by the malicious adversary. It represents the dimensions of data considered by the adversary, i.e., the knowledge of the friendship vector, or the neighboring vector etc.*

Definition 8 (Background Knowledge Configuration). *A background knowledge configuration $B_k \in \mathcal{B} = \{B_1, B_2, ..., B_n\}$ represents the k elements of the background knowledge category $\mathcal{B}$ known to the adversary. For example, the adversary might know $k = 3$ of the friends in the friendship vector of an individual.*

Definition 9 (Background Knowledge Instance). *A background knowledge instance $b \in B_k$ is a specific information known by the adversary, i.e., the actual portion of data structure known by the adversary.*

As an example, suppose that an adversary has, as background knowledge category, the friendship vector of a user, and suppose $F_v = \langle v_1, v_2, v_3, v_4 \rangle$. If the background knowledge configuration that we assume for the adversary is B_2, a possible instance could be $b = v_1, v_4$ or $b = v_3, v_4$ for example. Each instance gives to the adversary a probability of re-identifying the individual v in the dataset.

Definition 10 (Probability of Re-identification). *Given an attack, a function $matching(s, b)$ indicating whether or not a record $s \in S$ matches the instance of background knowledge configuration $b \in B_k$, and a matching set $M(S, b) = \{s \in S \mid matching(s, b) = True\}$, we define the probability of re-identification of an individual v in dataset S as:*

$$PR_S(s = v|b) = \frac{1}{|M(S, b)|}$$

that is the probability of correctly linking the data structure $s \in S$ to v given the background knowledge instance b.

Note that $PR_S(s = v|b) = 0$, in case an individual v does not belong to S.

PRUDEnce is a worst-case scenario framework, so when simulating an attack we have to assume that the adversary has access to the worst possible background knowledge instance. We take the maximum probability of re-identification among all $b \in B_k$ as risk of the re-identification risk for that individual:

Definition 11 (Risk of re-identification). *The risk of re-identification of an individual v is $Risk(v, S) = \max PR_S(s = v \mid b), \forall b \in B_k$, i.e., the maximum probability of re-identification.*

Our definition of probability of re-identification and privacy risk derives from the work of Sweeney in [18].

To better understand these concepts, we provide an example of risk computation definitions of probability and risk of re-identification.

Let us consider a set of individuals (nodes) $V = \{1, 2, 3, 4, 5, 6, 7\}$ and the corresponding dataset S composed of the friendship vectors of individuals:

$F_1 = \langle$ '3', '4', '6' $\rangle$ $F_2 = \langle$ '4', '6' $\rangle$
$F_3 = \langle$ '1', '5', '7' $\rangle$ $F_4 = \langle$ '1', '2', '6' $\rangle$
$F_5 = \langle$ '3', '7' $\rangle$ $F_6 = \langle$ '1', '2', '4', '7' $\rangle$
$F_7 = \langle$ '3', '5', '6' $\rangle$

Let us assume an adversary wants to perform an attack on individual 6 and knows two friends of that individual. The background knowledge configuration in this case is B_2. We compute the privacy risk of the individual 6, given the dataset S of friendship vectors and the knowledge of the adversary as follows:

1. We compute every possible instance $b \in B_2$ which are: $\{(1, 2), (1, 4), (1, 7), (2, 4), (2, 7), (4, 7)\}$
2. We compute the probability of re-identification for each background knowledge instance, matching it with the dataset S and counting the matching individuals. For example, the first instance $b = (1, 2)$ has the probability of re-identification $PR_S(s = 6|(1, 2)) = \frac{1}{2}$ because both 4 and 6 include $b = (1, 2)$ in their friendship vectors. We do this for every instance, obtaining the following values: $\frac{1}{2}, 1, \frac{1}{2}, 1, 1, 1$.
3. We take the maximum probability of re-identification as risk for individual 6: $Risk(6, S) = max(\frac{1}{2}, 1, \frac{1}{2}, 1, 1, 1) = 1$

5   Privacy Attack on Social Networks

Given the privacy framework we presented, the definition of an attack depends entirely on the matching function used to understand if a particular background knowledge instance can be found in the data structure of an individual. In this section, we describe the different type of attacks detailing their matching function.

5.1   Neighborhood Attack

The *neighborhood attack* considers an adversary who only knows a certain number of friends/neighbors of an individual. More technically, the adversary has an information about the nodes which are connected to the victim node in the social network graph. This type of attack was introduced in [20]. Background knowledge instances for this kind of attack are portions of the friendship vector F_v of an individual.

Definition 12 (Neighborhood Attack Matching). *Given the instance b, we define the matching function of the neighborhood attack as follows:*

$$Matching(b, F_v) = \begin{cases} true & b \subseteq F_v \\ false & otherwise \end{cases} \tag{1}$$

5.2   Label Pair Attack

The *label pair attack* considers an adversary who knows a certain number of pairs of features with their values of an individual. Each label pair in key-value format $la_i = (f, l)$ is distinct in a label vector of an individual. Similar type attack has been defined in [9] by using the label pair knowledge on two connected nodes. In our work, we consider that an adversary uses label pair knowledge of just one individual and it may be sufficient for his re-identification within S. Therefore, background knowledge instances for this kind of attack are portions of the label pair vector LA_v of an individual.

Definition 13 (Label Pair Attack Matching). *Given the instance b, we define the matching function of the label pair attack as:*

$$Matching(b, LA_v) = \begin{cases} true & b \subseteq LA_v \\ false & otherwise \end{cases} \tag{2}$$

5.3   Neighborhood and Label Pair Attack

Starting from the previous two attacks, we define a new and stronger attack that we call *neighborhood and label pair attack*. In this case, we consider an adversary knowing a certain number of friends/neighbors and a certain number of feature labels of an individual at the same time. In other words, it combines the background knowledge of the two previous attacks.

Definition 14 (Neighborhood and Label Pair Attack Matching). *Given the instance $b = (b', b'')$, we define the matching function of the neighborhood and label pair attack as:*

$$Matching(b, F_v, LA_v) = \begin{cases} true & b' \subseteq F_v \ \wedge \ b'' \subseteq LA_v \\ false & otherwise \end{cases} \qquad (3)$$

5.4 Friendship Degree Attack

In a *friendship degree attack*, the adversary knows the degree of a number of friends of the victim as well as the degree of the victim. This type of attack has been defined in [20]. A background knowledge instance for this kind of attack will be a portion of the degree vector D_v of an individual.

Definition 15 (Friendship Degree Attack Matching). *Given the instance b, we define the matching function of the friendship degree attack as:*

$$Matching(b, D_v) = \begin{cases} true & len(D_v) \wedge d \in D_v \forall d \in b \\ false & otherwise \end{cases} \qquad (4)$$

5.5 Mutual Friend Attack

In a *mutual friend attack*, the adversary knows the number of mutual friends of the victim and some of its neighbors. This type of attack has been already defined in [17]. A background knowledge instance for this kind of attack will be a portion of the mutual friendship vector MF_v of an individual.

Definition 16 (Mutual Friend Attack Matching). *Given the instance b, we define the matching function of the mutual friend attack as:*

$$Matching(b, MF_v) = \begin{cases} true & b \subseteq MF_v \\ false & otherwise \end{cases} \qquad (5)$$

5.6 Neighborhood Pair Attack

In a *neighborhood pair attack*, the adversary knows subset of the friends of the victim who are friends with each other, that is a subset of F_v in which v_i and v_j are connected to each other $v_i \in F_{v_j}$, $v_j \in F_{v_i}$ and $v_i, v_j \in F_v$. Similar type of attack has been already defined in [1]. With respect to the original definition, in our work, we reduce the knowledge of adversary by eliminating the degree knowledge of the victim about the individual, because we would like to simulate a less powerful kind of attack.

Definition 17 (Neighborhood Pair Attack Matching). *Given the instance b, we define the matching function of the neighborhood pair attack as:*

$$Matching(b, F_v) = \begin{cases} true & v_i \in F_{v_j} \wedge v_j \in F_{v_i} \wedge v_i, v_j \in F_v \forall (v_i, v_j) \in b \\ false & otherwise \end{cases} \qquad (6)$$

6   Experimental Dataset

In our work, we use the Facebook Dataset provided by Stanford University's "Stanford Large Network Dataset Collection" [8]. This dataset includes node features (profiles), circles and ego networks. Nodes have been anonymized by replacing the Facebook-internal id's for each user with a new value. Feature vectors from this dataset have also been provided while the interpretation of those features has been anonymized. After aggregating all data, we obtain a social network graph of 4039 nodes and 88,234 edges. Roughly half of the all individuals have 30 friends/neighbors or less. In Fig. 2 we can see some visual information about the dataset.

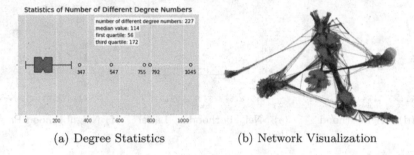

(a) Degree Statistics   (b) Network Visualization

Fig. 2. Visual information about Stamford Facebook dataset

7   Privacy Risk Assessment Results

In this section, we present the results of the simulation of attacks defined in Sect. 5. We simulated all the defined attacks setting the background knowledge configuration value to $k = 1, 2, 3, 4$, that is with four different lengths of the adversary background knowledge. We discretized the privacy risk in six intervals: $[0.0], (0.0, 0.1], (0.1, 0.2], (0.2, 0.3], (0.3, 0.5]$ and $(0.5, 1.0]$ from the lowest privacy risk to the highest.

Figure 3 shows as privacy risk for the attacks on network data varies significantly. In general and as expected, the number of individuals in the highest risk level and lowest risk level increases while the background knowledge configuration value k increases. We can observe that, for most of the attacks, we reach a sort of plateau increasing k to values 3 and 4. This is a phenomenon observed also in other types of data [12]. The most interesting results can be seen for the neighborhood label pair attack: with respect to the simple label attack or neighborhood attack, the mixed attack leads to an increase of the number of high risk individuals by a great margin. The mutual friend attack is weaker with respect to all the others. Indeed, in each setup of the background knowledge configuration value k, many individuals belong to the privacy risk level $(0.0, 0.1]$. This is not surprising since the Mutual Friend attacks uses the number of mutual

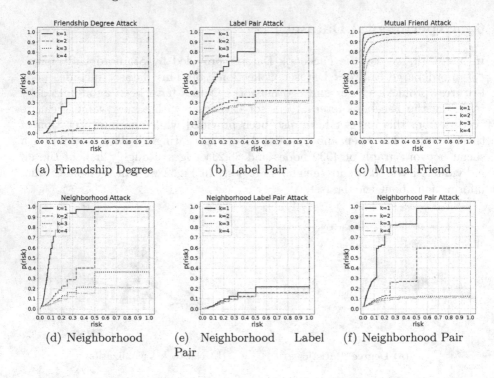

Fig. 3. Cumulative distributions of privacy risk for social network data.

friends of one node, which has a pretty even distribution over the entire network. Overall, the results suggest that basic topological information such as immediate neighborhood yield sufficient information for powerful privacy attacks, and that even a small amount of information can result in significant risk for the entire network.

8   Analysis on Network Degradation

Given the risk found in our assessment, we now remove from the data those individuals that are at or above a certain threshold of privacy risk and try to understand what impact will this have on the network: removing certain nodes from the network may lead to a disconnected networks. In these cases we compute the metrics and statistics on the biggest component of the unconnected network, thus we exclusively study the network's giant component. In order to verify the network degradation varying the minimum privacy risk guaranteed we compute: the total number of nodes preserved in the network, number of nodes preserved in the giant component, the total number of edges between individuals in the giant component and number of disconnected components generated.

We chose four thresholds of the privacy risk for all possible attacks. Thus, for each attack and background knowledge configuration value we created four distinct datasets which are:

- D_1: The dataset with all individuals
- $D_{0.5}$ The dataset with individuals whose privacy risk is between 0.0 and 0.5 included.
- $D_{0.33}$ The dataset with individuals whose privacy risk is between 0.0 and 0.333 included.
- $D_{0.25}$ The dataset with individuals whose privacy risk is between 0.0 and 0.25 included.

Tables 1 and 2 show the results of degradation analysis for the above statistics. For each attack the tables report the statistics for both $k = 1$ and $k = 4$ (the lowest and the greatest adversary knowledge). In these tables we indicate with **NA** the neighborhood attack, **LA** the label pair attack, **NLA** the neighborhood and label pair attack, **FDA** the friendship degree attack, **MFA** the mutual friend attack and **NPA** the neighborhood pair attack.

The results indicates that also considering an attack with a weak background knowledge the effect of taking into consideration only non-risky nodes has an important negative impact on the network quality. First of all, we can observe that for any attack there is an increment of the disconnected components in the networks (Table 1), that leads to a decrease in connectivity for the network. This effect is present even with weak attacks such as the *mutual friend attack*.

Tables 2 and 3 show that both the number of nodes in the whole network and in the giant component are mainly affected by the consequences of attacks based on the neighborhood information such as *neighborhood attack, friendship degree attack* and *neighborhood pair attack*.

Instead, Table 4 show that the number of edges is sensitive to the attacks that take into consideration the relationship between nodes such as the *friendship degree attack*.

Figure 4 shows what happens to the social network structure under the *mutual friend attack*, varying k. We can see how the network changes when we remove individuals with risk equal to 1 varying the background knowledge configuration. Even more evident effects can be seen for more powerful attacks.

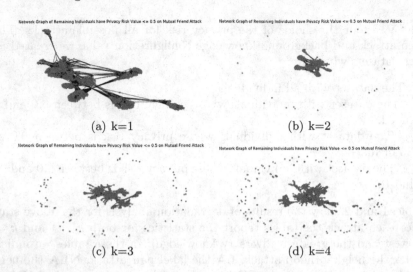

(a) k=1   (b) k=2

(c) k=3   (d) k=4

Fig. 4. Cumulative distributions of privacy risk for social network data.

Table 1. Number of disconnected components varying privacy risk.

	NA		LA		NLA		FDA		MFA		NPA	
	$k=1$	$k=4$	$k=1$	$k=4$	$k=1$	$k=4$	$k=1$	$k=4$	$k=1$	$k=4$	$k=1$	$k=4$
D_1	1	1	1	1	1	1	1	1	1	1	1	1
$D_{0.5}$	91	453	1	160	246	150	131	247	1	120	1	431
$D_{0.33}$	171	460	78	159	227	143	143	239	19	120	112	413
$D_{0.25}$	226	412	84	157	203	140	162	239	19	120	112	405

Table 2. Number of Nodes in the network varying privacy risk.

	NA		LA		NLA		FDA		MFA		NPA	
	$k=1$	$k=4$	$k=1$	$k=4$	$k=1$	$k=4$	$k=1$	$k=4$	$k=1$	$k=4$	$k=1$	$k=4$
D_1	4039	4039	4039	4039	4039	4039	4039	4039	4039	4039	4039	4039
$D_{0.5}$	4029	907	4026	1282	883	976	2573	295	4039	2982	3971	511
$D_{0.33}$	3940	700	3251	1178	648	937	1836	276	4021	2982	3351	488
$D_{0.25}$	3792	579	2885	1131	498	925	1378	276	4021	2982	3313	472

Table 3. Number of nodes in the giant component varying privacy risk.

	NA		LA		NLA		FDA		MFA		NPA	
	$k=1$	$k=4$	$k=1$	$k=4$	$k=1$	$k=4$	$k=1$	$k=4$	$k=1$	$k=4$	$k=1$	$k=4$
D_1	4039	4039	4039	4039	4039	4039	4039	4039	4039	4039	4039	4039
$D_{0.5}$	3732	25	4026	506	192	348	1426	7	4039	2226	3971	13
$D_{0.33}$	3507	23	2995	451	118	337	800	6	4003	2226	2566	13
$D_{0.25}$	3293	20	2618	429	83	335	326	6	4003	2226	2532	13

Table 4. Number of edges in the giant component varying privacy risk.

	NA		LA		NLA		FDA		MFA		NPA	
	k = 1	k = 4	k = 1	k = 4	k = 1	k = 4	k = 1	k = 4	k = 1	k = 4	k = 1	k = 4
D_1	88234	88234	88234	88234	88234	88234	88234	88234	88234	88234	88234	88234
$D_{0.5}$	82305	88	87688	2940	545	1587	12310	21	88234	15160	87744	71
$D_{0.33}$	80335	223	46610	2506	851	1528	4527	15	82800	15160	30900	71
$D_{0.25}$	77368	163	34520	2276	211	1503	1753	15	82800	15160	30758	71

9 Conclusions and Future Works

Social network data are a precious proxy to improve our understanding of social dynamics. Nevertheless, it contains sensitive information which, if analyzed with malicious intent, can lead to privacy violations for the individuals involved. In this paper, we proposed to apply PRUDEnce framework for assessing privacy risk in social networks and for evaluating the network degradation in case we consider only non-risky individuals and their connections. Our study indicates that for social network, privacy attacks can yield high privacy risk, even when the background knowledge is based on aggregated structures. We also showed how basic sanitization of the network is difficult, due to several properties of the network being disrupted by the cancellation of high risk nodes. PRUDEnce demands high computational costs for attack simulations. In order to address this problem it would be interesting to investigate the possibility to apply machine learning methods able to learn the relationship between some graph properties and the privacy risk, in order to predict the node privacy exposure.

Acknowledgments. This work has been funded by the European projects SoBigData-PlusPlus (Grant Id 871042).

References

1. Abawajy, J.H., Ninggal, M.I.H., Herawan, T.: Vertex re-identification attack using neighbourhood-pair properties. Concurr. Comput. Pract. Exp. **28**(10), 2906–2919 (2016). https://doi.org/10.1002/cpe.3687
2. Ananthula, S., Abuzaghleh, O., Alla, N.B., Chaganti, S.P., Kaja, P.C., Mogilineedi, D.: Measuring privacy in online social networks. Int. J. Secur. Priv. Trust Manag. **4**(2), 01–09 (2015). https://doi.org/10.5121/ijsptm.2015.4201. www.airccse.org/journal/ijsptm/papers/4215ijsptm01.pdf
3. Backstrom, L., Dwork, C., Kleinberg, J.: Wherefore art thou R3579X? Anonymized social networks, hidden patterns, and structural steganography. In: Proceedings of the 16th International Conference on World Wide Web, WWW 2007, pp. 181–190. ACM, New York (2007). https://doi.org/10.1145/1242572.1242598
4. Becker, J., Chen, H.: Measuring Privacy Risk in Online Social Networks
5. Cavoukian, A.: Privacy by design the 7 foundational principles, August 2009. www.iab.org/wp-content/IAB-uploads/2011/03/fred_carter.pdf
6. Deng, M., Wuyts, K., Scandariato, R., Preneel, B., Joosen, W.: A privacy threat analysis framework: supporting the elicitation and fulfillment of privacy requirements. Requir. Eng. **16**(1), 3–32 (2011). https://doi.org/10.1007/s00766-010-0115-7

7. Islam, M.B., Iannella, R.: Privacy by design: does it matter for social networks? In: Privacy and Identity Management for Life - 7th IFIP WG 9.2, 9.6/11.7, 11.4, 11.6/PrimeLife International Summer School, Trento, Italy, 5–9 September 2011, Revised Selected Papers, pp. 207–220 (2011)
8. Leskovec, J., Krevl, A.: SNAP Datasets: Stanford large network dataset collection, June 2014. http://snap.stanford.edu/data
9. Liu, C., Yin, D., Li, H., Wang, W., Yang, W.: Preserving privacy in social networks against label pair attacks. In: Ma, L., Khreishah, A., Zhang, Y., Yan, M. (eds.) WASA 2017. LNCS, vol. 10251, pp. 381–392. Springer, Cham (2017). https://doi.org/10.1007/978-3-319-60033-8_34
10. Liu, K., Terzi, E.: A framework for computing the privacy scores of users in online social networks. TKDD 5(1), 6:1–6:30 (2010). https://doi.org/10.1145/1870096.1870102
11. Mvungi, B., Iwaihara, M.: Associations between privacy, risk awareness, and interactive motivations of social networking service users, and motivation prediction from observable features. Comput. Hum. Behav. 44, 20–34 (2015). https://doi.org/10.1016/j.chb.2014.11.023
12. Pellungrini, R., Pappalardo, L., Pratesi, F., Monreale, A.: Analyzing privacy risk in human mobility data. In: Mazzara, M., Ober, I., Salaün, G. (eds.) STAF 2018. LNCS, vol. 11176, pp. 114–129. Springer, Cham (2018). https://doi.org/10.1007/978-3-030-04771-9_10
13. Pensa, R.G., Di Blasi, G.: A semi-supervised approach to measuring user privacy in online social networks. In: Calders, T., Ceci, M., Malerba, D. (eds.) DS 2016. LNCS (LNAI), vol. 9956, pp. 392–407. Springer, Cham (2016). https://doi.org/10.1007/978-3-319-46307-0_25
14. Pratesi, F., Monreale, A., Trasarti, R., Giannotti, F., Pedreschi, D., Yanagihara, T.: PRUDEnce: a system for assessing privacy risk vs utility in data sharing ecosystems. Trans. Data Priv. 11, 139–167 (2018)
15. Rossetti, G., Milli, L., Giannotti, F., Pedreschi, D.: Forecasting success via early adoptions analysis: a data-driven study. PLoS ONE 12(12), e0189096 (2017)
16. Rossetti, G., Milli, L., Rinzivillo, S., Sîrbu, A., Pedreschi, D., Giannotti, F.: NDLIB: a python library to model and analyze diffusion processes over complex networks. Int. J. Data Sci. Anal. 5(1), 61–79 (2017). https://doi.org/10.1007/s41060-017-0086-6
17. Sun, C., Yu, P.S., Kong, X., Fu, Y.: Privacy preserving social network publication against mutual friend attacks. Trans. Data Priv. 7(2), 71–97 (2014). www.tdp.cat/issues11/abs.a195a14.php
18. Sweeney, L.: k-anonymity: a model for protecting privacy. Int. J. Uncertainty Fuzziness Knowl.-Based Syst. 10(05), 557–570 (2002). https://doi.org/10.1142/S0218488502001648
19. Swiderski, F., Snyder, W.: Threat Modeling. O'Reilly Media Inc., New York (2009). oCLC: 609857070
20. Tai, C., Yu, P.S., Yang, D., Chen, M.: Privacy-preserving social network publication against friendship attacks. In: Proceedings of the 17th ACM SIGKDD International Conference on Knowledge Discovery and Data Mining, San Diego, CA, USA, 21–24 August 2011, pp. 1262–1270 (2011)
21. Zhou, B., Pei, J.: Preserving privacy in social networks against neighborhood attacks. In: Proceedings of the 24th International Conference on Data Engineering, ICDE 2008, Cancún, Mexico, 7–12 April 2008, pp. 506–515 (2008)

Detecting Anxiety Trends Using Wearable Sensor Data in Real-World Situations

Marissa Gray[1], Shweta Majumder[1], Kate Nelson[1],
and Reshma Munbodh[2,3]

[1] School of Engineering, Brown University, Providence, RI, USA
[2] Department of Radiation Oncology, Alpert Medical School of Brown University,
Providence, RI, USA
[3] Department of Radiation Oncology, Columbia University Irving Medical Center,
New York, NY, USA
reshma.munbodh@columbia.edu

Abstract. Anxiety can manifest through a range of physiological changes. We develop methods to detect anxiety among medical residents making case presentations in a clinical setting using wearable sensors and machine learning. A number of classifiers are tested on different features extracted from real-time physiological measurements. Our results indicate that anxiety can be detected among healthy volunteers in clinical setting and serve as an introduction to future wearable sensing studies for applications in radiation oncology.

Keywords: Wearable sensors · Machine learning · Anxiety detection · Radiation oncology · Heart Rate Variability (HRV)

1 Introduction

It is well known that different mental states can manifest themselves through physiological signals. Particularly, anxiety and stress, which are the body's adaptive neural responses to threats, have been attributed to physiological changes in the body [1]. Our brain detects certain situations to be stressful including loss of control, unpredictability and level of threat to self [2]. After the brain processes a situation as "stressful," it triggers a pathway that ultimately activates the sympathetic nervous system (SNS), which leads to various physiological and behavioral changes that are detectable and distinguishable from baseline (rested) physiology [1–3]. Thus, physiological signals can be objective biomarkers to detect anxiety and stress. Heart rate (HR), heart rate variability (HRV), skin conductance or electrodermal activity (EDA)[1], and body movement or accelerometry (ACC), have been correlated successfully with stress and anxiety in a number of

---

[1] The variation in electrical conductance of the skin due to sweat secretion.

M. Gray and S. Majumder—These authors contributed equally to this work.

© Springer Nature Switzerland AG 2022
J. Bowles et al. (Eds.): DataMod 2021, LNCS 13268, pp. 107–117, 2022.
https://doi.org/10.1007/978-3-031-16011-0_8

situations including public speaking, mental health monitoring, and on-the-job anxiety [4–7].

Although the SNS is responsible for the body's physical responses to stressors, it works in tandem with the parasympathetic nervous system (PNS), which responds to rest and relaxation. These complimentary systems are highly involved in activities of the heart. Increases in sympathetic activity relate to an increased heart rate whereas heart rate decreases can be attributed to relative increases in parasympathetic activity. This dynamic balance can be altered due to different neurological or psychological activities [12]. Thus, it is not surprising that anxiety can have measurable impacts on the heart rate activity [7].

Public speaking, an essential skill for learning and career development, is also a task that contributes to social stress and anxiety among many individuals. The National Institute of Mental Health states that around 73% of the U.S. population has a fear of public speaking even though it is a common occurrence in everyday life [26]. For many, it is a regular part of their professional careers. Because there is a high prevalence of public speaking anxiety, many researchers have used wearable sensors to detect physiological features of anxiety during public speaking tasks. However, most of these experiments have been held in laboratory settings with controlled tests on subjects [9]. Although there have been studies focused on targeted groups of people in real-world settings, they have often been limited in scope and to controlled activities. Few studies have focused on real-time anxiety detection in real-world activities [4,5]. Here, we present a feasibility study to detect anxiety throughout real-world public speaking situations that are an essential job function. Specifically, we address the detection of anxiety among medical residents making case presentations in a hospital-based radiation oncology department.

2   Related Work

Previously, wearable sensors have been used to detect physiological signals of stress and anxiety which are then used to train classifier algorithms that aim to quantify stressful or anxious states [8,9]. Studies analyzing HRV, EDA [9,10], and ACC [11] have been conducted in a wide range of settings. However, most of these studies are carefully controlled with participants undergoing specific public speaking tests such as the Trier Social Stress Test [24] and the Maastricht Acute Stress Test [25]. In these studies, physiological signals are analyzed using a variety of supervised learning techniques such as support vector machines (SVM), decision trees, k-Nearest Neighbors (KNN), random forests, logistic regression, and multilayer perceptron [22,23,26]. The acquired physiological signals vary between studies. Several studies acquire multimodal sensor information such as electrocardiography (ECG), electroencephalography (EEG), photoplethymography (PPG), and electrodermal activity (EDA) [25,26], while others focus on a single physiological signal. Lee et al. conducted a study that analyzed only EDA data from student volunteers in a real-world classroom setting [4]. The EDA data was collected from students while they were delivering regular presentations in class. After processing, the EDA data was analyzed using k-means clustering to classify data into two groups based on anxiety levels. Although this study collected physiological data in a real-world setting, researchers focused on one type of signal and a single classification method.

Heart activity is measured by looking at changes in the volume of blood at a localized area of the body, such as the wrist and is commonly detected by a PPG sensor [13,14]. PPG uses light to measure variations of blood volume. Several features from time series and frequency domain data of PPG data can be extracted and derived. These features, such as HRV, have been shown to be indicators of heart activity and can be used to gain insight into the person's psychological state [1].

In this study, we use wearable sensors to collect real-time HRV data from healthy subjects who are performing an essential job function that involves public speaking to a group of supervisors. Supervised machine learning techniques are applied to the HRV data with the aim of identifying how to best classify and predict anxiety in the subjects. Here we are testing multiple classification methods of one type of physiological signal (HRV). Our overall goal is to use this knowledge to develop real-time methods of detecting and analyzing anxiety experienced in real-world situations.

3 Methods

Healthy subjects (N = 3) were recruited from a group of radiation oncology medical residents. The subjects were studied during a known anxiety-inducing activity in medical residents: presentations during chart rounds [15–17]. During these regular presentations, residents sit and review patients' records with peers and supervising physicians. To acquire data, the subjects were fitted with an Empatica E4[2] wearable sensor on the wrist. The Empatica E4 acquires blood volume pulse (BVP), EDA, accelerometry data (ACC), and body temperature (BT). These signals were recorded for approximately 20 min before, during chart rounds (up to one hour) and after chart rounds (at least 5 min). The residents were seated during the chart rounds and their presentations. They were instructed to remain as still as possible so that the physiological measures would not be affected by motion. Deidentified physiological data was recorded in real-time and transferred to the cloud-based storage system. Residents were asked to mark the start and end of chart rounds in addition to the time they presented their cases during chart rounds using the event marking capability on the Empatica E4. Thus, the 3 main sections of the data are the baseline period (starting 20 min before chart rounds), the chart round period (lasting up to 1 h), and the recovery period (at least 5 min after chart rounds end). Each subject was involved in 2–3 chart rounds sessions. Hence, we collected a total of seven sets of data during seven different chart round sessions from the three subjects.

---

[2] https://www.empatica.com/en-gb/research/e4/.

3.1   Extraction of HRV Features

In this study, we use time-domain and frequency-domain HRV features to detect anxiety. Extraction of the HRV features is described below.

In the Empatica E4, heart activity is measured through BVP at a sampling rate 64 Hz. The sensor has a built-in algorithm that calculates and displays a time series of inter-beat intervals (IBIs), which is the time between two consecutive heart beats, in real-time. The IBI conversion algorithm also removes spurious peaks that can occur due to rigorous movement, and thus can lead to data loss during high intensity movements [18]. From the time series of IBIs, the instantaneous heart rate (HR) in beats per minute (bpm) is given by Eq. 1.

$$HR = \frac{60}{IBI} \, bpm \qquad (1)$$

In order to account for variations in inherent heart rate among study subjects, the heart rate time series for each experimental session was normalized using the mean of the baseline heart rate data from the experiment. For the normalization, the mean of the truncated baseline data is taken by excluding 90 s of data from both the start and the end of the baseline section (see the red section of Fig. 1). The first 90 s of the data was excluded because the raw BVP signal required some time to stabilize after the device is turned on due to signal noise observed within the first few minutes of data collection.

A 90-s window with 75% overlap was used to extract HRV features from the IBI, interpolated IBI (IIBI) and HR time series. The 75% overlap was chosen to have sufficient meaningful data points for HRV feature extraction even with the short time window [9]. The time-domain HRV features extracted for each window were:

- SDNN: Standard deviation of the inter-beat intervals
- nAVHR: Normalized average heart rate
- nMAXHR: Normalized maximum heart rate
- nMINHR: Normalized minimum heart rate
- nPNN90: Normalized 90-th percentile heart rate
- NN50: The number of IBIs in a time window which differ by more than 50ms from their preceding IBI
- PNN50: The proportion of the IBIs which differ by more than 50ms from their preceding IBI in the time window.

From the IIBI time-series, a Welch's periodogram is computed [2]. Welch's method for periodogram estimation [19] uses fast Fourier transforms (FFT) on overlapping segments of the time series and averages the FFT power to estimate the power spectrum for the signal. Frequency domain HRV features extracted for each time window were:

- VLF: Band-power of the very low frequency (<0.04 Hz).
- LF: Band-power of the low frequency (0.04 Hz–0.15 Hz).
- HF: Band-power of the high frequency (0.15 Hz–0.4 Hz)
- HF/LF: The ratio of high frequency to low frequency.

3.2   Data Labeling

For data labeling, features from only the truncated baseline are were labeled as '0'. From the chart rounds data, features from 90 s before the start of the presentation to 3–5 min after the start of the presentation were labeled as '1' (the time duration depended on each session). In general, the presentation sessions lasted from 3 to 15 min. An example of the segments used to label the training data is shown in Fig. 1.

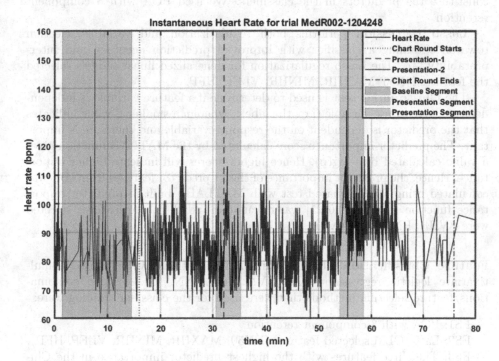

Fig. 1. How the dataset is segmented shown on the IBI time series (blue plot). Black vertical lines from left to right: i) Chart round starts, ii) Presentation 1, iii) Presentation 2, iii) Chart Round ends. Segments: i) Red: Baseline segment, ii) Green: Presentation segment (Color figure online)

3.3   Classifier Training and Validation

The labeled features (0 = not anxious and 1 = anxious) from all the first chart round sessions of each subject (N = 3) were combined into a training set. The training set was fed into the different classification algorithms with 10-fold cross validation in the MATLAB Classification Learner App and the prediction accuracy on the training sets was recorded.

Feature Selection: Three different feature selection methods were used: (1) Principal component analysis (PCA), (2) Least absolute shrinkage and selection operator (Lasso) regression and (3) the Chi-squared test.

PCA is an unsupervised dimension reduction method used to derive a low-dimensional feature set from a large number of variables [27]. The lower dimensional feature set is obtained by projecting the multivariate data points onto the first few principal components, which are selected to maximize the variance of the projected data. These projections or linear combinations of the variables constitute the predictors in the classifiers. We used PCA with 3 component retention.

Lasso regression performs both regularization and variable selection towards obtaining a classifier with improved prediction accuracy and interpretability [27]. The Lasso regularization for generalized linear models selected the features NN50, MAXHR, MINHR, VLFP, HFP.

The **Chi-squared test** is used to determine if a feature variable is independent of the response variable (i.e., the label), wherein a smaller p-value indicates that the predictor is dependent on the response variable and therefore is important. The predictor importance score calculated by the MATLAB function gives a value calculated by $-\log(p)$. Hence higher scores will indicate higher importance. Hence, the predictor importance of the 11 predictor features from IBIs was calculated using a Chi-squared test with MATLAB's built-in predictor importance function (fscchi2) [20,21] was calculated and the three features selected were AVHR, PNN90, MAXHR.

Feature Classification: The classification algorithms evaluated were: multivariate logistic regression (LR), SVM and KNN. The feature combinations/feature selection methods that were used for the classifier training were:

- FS1: PCA with 3 component retention
- FS2: Lasso GLM selected features (NN50, MAXHR, MINHR, VLFP, HFP).
- FS3: The three features with the highest predictor importance in the Chi-squred test (AVHR, PNN90, MAXHR).

3.4   Classifier Testing

The three trained classifier models (LR, SVM and KNN) were then used to predict anxiety on labeled features from the new and repeated chart round sessions for the participants (4 sessions). These test data were labeled similarly as the training data (see Sect. 3.2). Using the predicted labels from each trained classifier models on test data, classifier performances metrics such as the testing accuracy, recall and precision were calculated to compare the model performances.

4   Results

In general, presenters are aware that it is their turn to speak about 20–30 s before the start of their presentation. Verbal accounts from the residents indicated that they were aware that it was their turn to speak about 20–30 s before the start of their presentation.

As mentioned in Sect. 3.3, the labeled features from the first chart round session for each participant were used for training, and validation of different classification algorithms with the different feature selection methods. Testing was done on the remaining chart round sessions to verify testing accuracy, recall, precision and F-measure on new sets of experiments. Two-dimensional grouped scatter plots were generated of the different features extracted from IBI and HR in all the experiments. Figure 2 shows a graph of the standard deviation of the IBIs plotted against the average normalized heart rate for the baseline period and the period surrounding the presentations.

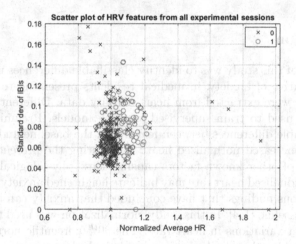

Fig. 2. Comparison of standard deviation of the IBIs with the average normalized heart rate in all 7 experimental sessions. 0 = Baseline/"Not Anxious" in Red, 1 = Presenting/"Anxious" in Blue (Color figure online)

The accuracy (on both test and training data), and precision, recall and F-measure (on test data only) of each of the classifiers with different feature combinations are shown in Table 1.

Table 1. Performance of different classifiers on different feature combinations. The accuracy (acc.), recall, precision (prec.) and F-measure (F-meas.) for SVM, KNN and LR are shown for Feature set 1 (FS1), Feature set 2 (FS2), and Feature set 3 (FS3)

Features	Classifier	Training	Testing			
		Acc.	Acc.	Recall	Prec.	F-Meas.
FS1	SVM	86.4	58.2	0.02	0.14	0.03
	KNN	89.1	71.2	0.41	0.73	0.52
	LR	86.4	62.1	0.03	0.67	0.06
FS2	SVM	90.9	61.4	0.32	0.5	0.39
	KNN	94.1	63.4	0.22	0.56	0.31
	LR	87.7	54.9	0.08	0.25	0.13
FS3	SVM	92.7	73.2	0.51	0.71	0.59
	KNN	93.6	69.9	0.44	0.67	0.53
	LR	86.8	67.3	0.15	1	0.26

5 Discussion

The main goal of this study was to identify classifiable differences in heart activity data, indicative of anxiety, in medical residents presenting to an audience. Eleven features were extracted from heart activity data. Different feature combinations were used to train supervised learning models. Preliminary analysis showed classifiable differences between features of the baseline and presentation data, with an increased normalized heart rate during the presentation period. In the absence of other known factors causing these physiological changes, the increased individualised heart rate may indicate heightened anxiety and is consistent with previous findings that have concluded that anxiety can increase heart rate from the baseline [1,4]. In this study, normalization was used to account for the inter-subject variations in heart rate. The 90th percentile normalized heart rate was not used in other similar papers, but it ranked as second most important feature in our predictor importance analysis using Chi-squared test.

A specific challenge for this study is the lack of set thresholds for heart rate and other heart activity metrics that indicate anxiety. Therefore, we need to compare the heart rate data at baseline (rest) to heart rate during the anxiety-inducing situation. Modeling situational anxiety in a real-life scenario can bring about its own challenges: the lack of a controlled environment can corrupt data through movements and environmental changes. In this study, the labeling of the data was particularly challenging and it was necessary to make certain assumptions as to when the subjects were anxious.

A unique aspect of the data labeling employed in the project was to label only a fixed-time segment around the presentation as "anxious" rather than the whole presentation segment since the subjects might not stay anxious throughout chart rounds. Model accuracy on training data was highest when all HRV features were used to train an optimizable KNN. However, the high number of features in this model may indicate overfitting of the data. In this study, KNN on FS3 had the highest accuracy, recall, precision and F-score on the test data. Interestingly, SVM was the classifier of choice in similar studies in the literature. A limitation of this study is the low sample size (n = 7). To increase the number of data points from each experiment, a 75% overlap was used with the 90-s window for feature extraction, which is slightly higher than the recommended overlap.

From the initial results, we can see that there is distinguishable differences between HRV features between the baseline state and early presentation state. Also, KNN worked the best for all feature selection methods with the best testing accuracy with PCA.

This early study served as a feasibility study and an introduction to future wearable sensing studies for applications in real-world settings. In the future, as we increase the number of subjects in the study, we plan to investigate different machine learning methods to construct the classifiers including alternate schemes for splitting the data into training and test sets. We are also exploring other machine learning methods such as unsupervised learning methods which automatically group the data into distinct clusters. We plan to extend this study to include EDA and accelerometry data in the future.

Acknowledgment. We would like to thank Dr. David Wazer, Dr. Elana Nack, Dr. Imran Chowdhury and Dr. Jeff Huang for their support.

References

1. Thayer, J.F., Åhs, F., Fredrikson, M., Sollers, J.J., Wager, T.D.: A meta-analysis of heart rate variability and neuroimaging studies: implications for heart rate variability as a marker of stress and health. Neurosci. Biobehav. Rev. **36**(2), 747–756 (2012). https://doi.org/10.1016/j.neubiorev.2011.11.009
2. Ollander, S., Godin, C., Campagne, A., Charbonnier, S.: A comparison of wearable and stationary sensors for stress detection. In: 2016 IEEE International Conference on Systems, Man, and Cybernetics (SMC), Budapest, Hungary, pp. 004362–004366, October 2016. https://doi.org/10.1109/SMC.2016.7844917
3. Understanding the stress response - Chronic activation of this survival mechanism impairs health. Harvard Health Online, March 2011
4. Lee, H., Kleinsmith, A.: Public speaking anxiety in a real classroom: towards developing a reflection system. In: Extended Abstracts of the 2019 CHI Conference on Human Factors in Computing Systems, Glasgow, Scotland, UK, pp. 1–6, May 2019. https://doi.org/10.1145/3290607.3312875
5. Choi, B., Jebelli, H., Lee, S.: Feasibility analysis of electrodermal activity (EDA) acquired from wearable sensors to assess construction workers' perceived risk. Saf. Sci. **115**, 110–120 (2019). https://doi.org/10.1016/j.ssci.2019.01.022
6. Oskooei, A., Chau, S.M., Weiss, J., Sridhar, A., Martínez, M.R., Michel, B.: DeStress: deep learning for unsupervised identification of mental stress in firefighters from heart-rate variability (HRV) data. arXiv:1911.13213 [cs, eess, stat], November 2019. Accessed 10 Nov 2020
7. Fuentes-García, J.P., Clemente-Suárez, V.J., Marazuela-Martínez, M.Á., Tornero-Aguilera, J.F., Villafaina, S.: Impact of real and simulated flights on psychophysiological response of military pilots. IJERPH **18**(2), 787 (2021). https://doi.org/10.3390/ijerph18020787

8. Carreiro, S., Chintha, K.K., Shrestha, S., Chapman, B., Smelson, D., Indic, P.: Wearable sensor-based detection of stress and craving in patients during treatment for substance use disorder: a mixed methods pilot study. Drug Alcohol Depend. **209**, 107929 (2020). https://doi.org/10.1016/j.drugalcdep.2020.107929

9. Delmastro, F., Martino, F.D., Dolciotti, C.: Cognitive training and stress detection in MCI frail older people through wearable sensors and machine learning. IEEE Access **8**, 65573–65590 (2020). https://doi.org/10.1109/ACCESS.2020.2985301

10. Can, Y.S., Arnrich, B., Ersoy, C.: Stress detection in daily life scenarios using smart phones and wearable sensors: a survey. J. Biomed. Inform. **92**, 103139 (2019). https://doi.org/10.1016/j.jbi.2019.103139

11. McGinnis, R.S., et al.: Rapid anxiety and depression diagnosis in young children enabled by wearable sensors and machine learning. In: 2018 40th Annual International Conference of the IEEE Engineering in Medicine and Biology Society (EMBC), Honolulu, HI, pp. 3983–3986, July 2018. https://doi.org/10.1109/EMBC.2018.8513327

12. Shaffer, F., Ginsberg, J.P.: An overview of heart rate variability metrics and norms. Front. Public Health **5**, 258 (2017). https://doi.org/10.3389/fpubh.2017.00258

13. "Empatica Support," E4 Wristband Data, 23 January 2020. https://support.empatica.com/hc/en-us/sections/200582445-E4-wristband-data

14. Jones, D.: The Blood Volume Pulse - Biofeedback Basics, 10 May 2018. https://www.biofeedback-tech.com/articles/2016/3/24/the-blood-volume-pulse-biofeedback-basics

15. Johnson, D.: We Are Expected To Be Public Speakers, But Never Taught, 02 April 2019. https://opmed.doximity.com/articles/we-are-expected-to-be-public-speakers-but-never-taught?csrfattempted=yes

16. Kavanagh, J.: Giving presentations without palpitations. BMJ **332**(7555), s242–s243 (2006). https://doi.org/10.1136/bmj.332.7555.s242

17. Tejwani, V., Ha, D., Isada, C.: Observations: public speaking anxiety in graduate medical education-a matter of interpersonal and communication skills? J. Grad. Med. Educ. **8**(1), 111 (2016). https://doi.org/10.4300/JGME-D-15-00500.1

18. "Empatica Support," Utilizing the PPG/BVP signal, 23 January 2020. https://support.empatica.com/hc/en-us/sections/200582445-E4-wristband-data

19. Welch, P.: The use of fast Fourier transform for the estimation of power spectra: a method based on time averaging over short, modified periodograms. IEEE Trans. Audio Electroacoust. **15**(2), 70–73 (1967). https://doi.org/10.1109/TAU.1967.1161901

20. Univariate feature ranking for classification using chi-square tests. MATLAB (2021)

21. Gajawada, S.: "Towards Data Science," Chi-Square Test for Feature Selection in Machine learning. https://towardsdatascience.com/chi-square-test-for-feature-selection-in-machine-learning-206b1f0b8223

22. Gjoreski, M., Luštrek, M., Gams, M., Gjoreski, H.: Monitoring stress with a wrist device using context. J. Biomed. Inform. **73**, 159–170 (2017). https://doi.org/10.1016/j.jbi.2017.08.006

23. Shaukat-Jali, R., van Zalk, N., Boyle, D.E.: Detecting subclinical social anxiety using physiological data from a wrist-worn wearable: small scale feasibility study. JMIR Formative Res. **5**(10) (2021). https://doi.org/10.2196/32656

24. Mozos, O.M., Sandulescu, V., Andrews, S., et al.: Stress detection using wearable physiological and sociometric sensors. Int. J. Neural Syst. 1–17 (2005). https://core.ac.uk/reader/76958656?utmsource=linkout

25. Betti, S., Lova, R.M., Rovine, E., et al.: Evaluation of an integrated system of wearable physiological sensors for stress monitoring in working environments. IEEE Trans. Biomed. Eng. **65**(8), 1748–1758 (2018). https://doi.org/10.1109/TBME.2017.2764507
26. Arsalan, A., Majid, M.: Human stress classification during public speaking using physiological signals. Comput. Biol. Med. **133**, 10437 (2021). https://doi.org/10.1016/j.compbiomed.2021.104377
27. James, G., Witten, D., Hastie, T., Tibshirani, R.: An Introduction to Statistical Learning: with Applications in R, 2nd edn., pp. 227–250. Springer, New York (2022). https://doi.org/10.1007/978-1-4614-7138-7

Other Approaches

Combining Quantitative Data
with Logic-Based Specifications
for Parameter Inference

Paul Piho$^{(\boxtimes)}$ and Jane Hillston

University of Edinburgh, Edinburgh, UK
`ppiho@ic.ac.uk`

Abstract. Continuous time Markov chains are a common mathematical model for a range of natural and computer systems. An important part of constructing such models is fitting the model parameters based on some observed data or prior domain knowledge. In this paper we consider the problem of fitting model parameters with respect to a mix of quantitative data and data formulated as temporal logic formulae. Our approach works by defining a set of conditions that capture the dynamics inferred by the quantitative data. This allows for a straightforward way to combine the information from the quantitative and logically specified knowledge into one parameter inference problem via rejection sampling.

1 Introduction

Quantitative models like continuous time Markov chains facilitate the understanding of processes and phenomena from a variety of areas like performance modelling, epidemiology and biology. A large part of constructing these models deals with fitting the model parameters using existing data or prior domain knowledge. In the context of formal methods such parameter inference problems have been considered in [4,5] where logic specifications are used to specify the constraints on the behaviour of the model. The emphasis is on identifying parameters for which a given logical formula holds or parameters where the probability of satisfying the formula is maximised. These ideas can be used effectively in the area of control where the logic specifications are used to define the requirements for a successful controller [17]. Outside of formal methods, the inference problems are generally based on fitting the model parameters using existing observed data. The observed data can come in the form of quantitative data, like measured time trajectories, or qualitative data [14].

In this work we concentrate on parameter inference for models where the knowledge about the behaviour of the system comes in different forms. Firstly, we have observed time trajectories corresponding to a part of the modelled system's behaviour. Secondly, we have aspects of the system behaviour that are not directly measured but where the prior knowledge about the system's behaviour can be given through a logic-based specification. We combine those two sources of

© Springer Nature Switzerland AG 2022
J. Bowles et al. (Eds.): DataMod 2021, LNCS 13268, pp. 121–137, 2022.
https://doi.org/10.1007/978-3-031-16011-0_9

information into a single parameter inference problem. The benefit such integration brings is that lack of time-series data about parts of the system's behaviour can be compensated via a logic-based high level specification.

To that end, we implement a rejection sampling-based algorithm where samples of parameters from a defined prior distribution are accepted as posterior samples if the corresponding model trajectories are close enough to the quantitative data and also satisfy the logic specification. The decision on whether or not model trajectories are close to the available quantitative data is made in two ways. One follows standard approximate Bayesian computation [15] by defining a discrepancy measure between statistics of the quantitative data and simulated model trajectories. Secondly, we propose an approach where the observed data is translated into a logical specification capturing the temporal dynamics of the data. This specification is then combined with the logical specification corresponding to the knowledge about the system's properties. We then study the resulting posterior distributions empirically by considering the quantities corresponding to expected satisfaction probability of a logical specification over the recovered approximate posterior distributions.

We start by giving an overview of the related work in Sect. 2 and the required background in Sect. 3. In Sect. 4 we introduce the main contribution of the paper—a method for performing inference based on both quantitative data and logical specifications. In Sect. 5 we present computational experiment results for two illustrative examples—a rumour spread and a client server model. Finally, we end in Sect. 6 with conclusions and further work.

2   Related Work

Often the most useful types of data for inferring parameters of stochastic models are experimental time courses. However, these can be supplemented or replaced by observations or prior knowledge about the behaviour of a system in the form of categorical or qualitative characterisations. Several recent papers present work on parameter fitting for non-stochastic models of dynamics based on such data [12–14]. All of these consider deterministic ordinary differential equation models. In [12] the qualitative observations are formalised as inequality constraints on the model output. The parameter identification is then treated as a constrained optimisation problem through a heuristically constructed objective function. In [13] this work is extended to give a Bayesian formulation of parameter inference from qualitative data. The authors of [14] take an alternative approach where the best quantitative representation of the qualitative observations in the form of categorical data is found via optimal scaling methods. The found quantitative representation is referred to as surrogate data. This approach is based on an assumption that the qualitative data comes in the form of ordered categorical data, like "low", "high" and "very high", directly corresponding to quantitative trajectories. In the context of formal methods, the authors of [4] propose a method of fitting model parameters based on a logic specification by framing the problem in a Bayesian optimisation framework. However, integration of quantitative and logically specified knowledge remains an open issue.

3   Background

In this section we present an overview of the necessary background topics. Specifically, we introduce the main models of study, called *parametric continuous time Markov chains* and the related statistical model checking and inference problems.

3.1   Parametric Continuous Time Markov Chains

In this paper we consider discrete-state stochastic models, namely continuous time Markov chains. We give the following definition, common in the verification literature [2].

Definition 1. *A continous time Markov chain is a model of the form* $\mathcal{M} = \{S, \mathbb{Q}, A, L\}$ *where*

- $S = \{s_0, s_1, \cdots, s_n\}$ *is a finite set of states.*
- $\mathbb{Q}$ *is the transition rate matrix. In particular,* $\mathbb{Q}$ *is a* $|S| \times |S|$ *matrix such that the off-diagonals are non-negative and the diagonal elements*

$$a_{ii} = -\sum_{i \neq j} a_{ji} \tag{1}$$

- $L : S \rightarrow 2^A$ *is a labelling function mapping a state* $s \in S$ *to a subset of atomic propositions* A *that hold for* s.

An infinite path of a CTMC $\mathcal{M}$ is a sequence $s_0 t_0 s_1 t_1 \ldots$ where the transition rate $a_{i,i+1} > 0$ and $t_i > 0$ for all $i \geq 0$. The state s_0 denotes the initial state of the CTMC and is assumed to be fixed. The time t_i represents the time CTMC spends in a given state. The times t_i, called holding times, are drawn from the exponential distribution with rate parameter $-a_{ii}$. A trace of $\mathcal{M}$ is the mapping of path $s_0 t_0 s_1 t_1 \ldots$ through the labelling function L.

The state of the CTMC remains constant between jumps. Thus, in addition to the trace we can give the trajectory of a CTMC as a left-continuous function $\omega : \mathbb{R}_{\geq 0} \rightarrow S$ that is constant for the duration of the holding time and then jumps to the next state. We can simulate the CTMC via, for example, Gillespie's stochastic simulation algorithm [8]. Finally, we give a definition of the parametric extension of continuous time Markov chains.

Definition 2. *A parametric continuous time Markov chain over parameter vector* θ *is a model of the form* $\mathcal{M}_\theta = \{S, \mathbb{Q}_\theta, A, L\}$ *where* S, A *and* L *are defined as before. Additionally,*

- $\theta = (\theta_1, \cdots, \theta_k)$ *is the vector of parameters taking values in some domain* $D \subset \mathbb{R}_{\geq 0}^k$.
- $\mathbb{Q}_\theta$ *is the parametric transition rate matrix such that each entry in* $\mathbb{Q}_\theta$ *depends polynomially on* $\theta_1, \cdots, \theta_k$.

In particular, $\mathcal{M}_\theta$ *defines a family of continuous time Markov chains with parameters* θ *varying in a domain* D.

CTMC-based models are often expressed in a high-level modelling language such as stochastic process algebras [7,9], generalised stochastic Petri nets [3] or Chemical Reaction Network (CRN) models [1]. For simplicity we consider the latter option defined as follows:

Definition 3. *A chemical reaction network model is defined by a*

- *a vector of population variables* $\mathbf{X} = (X_1, X_2, \cdots, X_n) \in \mathbb{N}^n$ *counting the number of different agents in the system.*
- *a set of reaction rules in the form*

$$r_1 X_1 + \cdots + r_n X_n \xrightarrow{\tau(\mathbf{X}, \theta)} s_1 X_1 + \cdots + s_n X_n$$

where r_i and s_i are the counts of agents consumed (respectively produced) in a reaction. τ is the rate function depending on the state of the model $\mathbf{X}$ and a vector of model parameters θ.

The dynamics of the reaction network are interpreted as a parametric CTMC, or a CTMC if the model parameters θ are fixed, where each state in the CTMC corresponds to a vector of counts.

Example 1. In order to illustrate the ideas let us consider the following susceptible-infected-recovered (SIR) model defined as a CRN

$$S + I \xrightarrow{k_I} I + I \qquad\qquad I \xrightarrow{k_R} R$$

where S gives the number of susceptible, I the number of infected and R the number of recovered individuals in the system. The first type of transition corresponds to infected and susceptible individuals interacting, resulting in the number of infected individuals increasing and the number of susceptible decreasing. In particular, the susceptible agent turns into an infected one. The second type of transition corresponds to recovery of an infected individual and results in the number of infected decreasing and the number of recovered increasing. The states of the underlying CTMC keep track of the counts of different individuals in the system. The model parameters are given by the vector (k_I, k_R) resulting in transition rates $k_I \times S \times I$ and $k_R \times I$ for infection spread and recovery respectively.

3.2 Statistical Model Checking

An important problem in statistical model checking is estimating the probability that a model satisfies a given logical specification [10]. In this paper we assume that the logical properties are defined in the time-bounded fragment of metric interval temporal logic (MiTL) [11]. MiTL is a linear temporal logic for continuous time trajectories with the syntax given by

$$\varphi ::= true \mid \mu \mid \neg\varphi \mid \varphi_1 \wedge \varphi_2 \mid \varphi_1 U_{[T_1, T_2]} \varphi_2 \qquad (2)$$

where $U_{[T_1,T_2]}$ denotes the time-bounded until operator. The atomic propositions are inequalities on population variables of a CRN model. A MiTL formula is interpreted over a real-value function of time $\mathbf{x}(t)$ that corresponds to
a trajectory of a CTMC. The time-bounded *until* is then defined as follows:
$\mathbf{x}, t \models \varphi_1 U_{[T_1,T_2]}\varphi_2$ if and only if there exists a time t_1 in the interval $[t+T_1, t+T_2]$
such that $\mathbf{x}, t_1 \models \varphi_2$ and for all t_0 in the interval $[t, t_1]$ we have $\mathbf{x}, t_0 \models \varphi_1$. Other
temporal modalities can then be defined using the *until* operator. For example,
time-bounded *eventually* and *always* are given by $F_{[T_1,T_2]}\varphi \equiv true\ U_{[T_1,T_2]}\varphi$ and
$G_{[T_1,T_2]}\varphi \equiv \neg F_{[T_1,T_2]}\neg\varphi$ respectively.

One of the quantities of interest is the satisfaction probability with respect
to a MiTL formula. This is defined as follows.

Definition 4. *Let* $\mathcal{M}_\theta$ *be pCTMC over parameter vector* $\theta \in D \subset \mathbb{R}_{\geq 0}^k$ *and* φ
be a temporal logic formula. The satisfaction probability associated with φ *is the*
probability

$$f_\varphi(\theta) = P(\varphi = true \mid \mathcal{M}_\theta). \tag{3}$$

Statistical model checking provides a way to estimate the defined satisfaction
probability and relies on analysing a set of simulated trajectories of the model
$\mathcal{M}_\theta$ for different parameter values θ. Supposing $\mathcal{D}_\theta$ is a set of N trajectories for
θ we can give a Monte Carlo estimate of the satisfaction probability

$$f_\varphi(\theta) \approx \bar{f}_\varphi(\theta) = \frac{1}{|N|} \sum_{t \in \mathcal{D}_\theta} \mathbb{1}[t \models \varphi]. \tag{4}$$

In particular, we take a mean over the trajectories in $\mathcal{D}_\theta$ with respect to the
indicator function that returns 1 if the trajectory satisfies the temporal logic
formula φ and 0 otherwise. Note that this corresponds to the maximum likelihood
estimate of the parameter of a Bernoulli distribution. Thus the variance of the
estimate is given by

$$Var(\bar{f}_\varphi(\theta)) = \frac{\bar{f}_\varphi(\theta)(1 - \bar{f}_\varphi(\theta))}{N}. \tag{5}$$

The size of the simulated data set $\mathcal{D}_\theta$ can then be chosen such that the variance of the estimate gives acceptable confidence for the intended application. An
alternative to statistical methods for estimating the defined satisfaction probability are numerical approximation methods [6] which suffer greatly from state
space explosion.

3.3   Approximate Parameter Inference

Parameter inference for stochastic systems in general, and continuous time
Markov chains in particular, is a difficult problem. Supposing we have a pCTMC
model $\mathcal{M}_\theta$ and a set of observed data $\mathcal{D}$. The aim of parameter inference is to
describe the distribution over parameters θ such that the pCTMC $\mathcal{M}_\theta$ offers

a good model for the data. In the Bayesian setting we are looking to find the posterior distribution over model parameters θ

$$p(\theta|\mathcal{D}) \propto p(\mathcal{D}|\theta)p(\theta)$$

given the observed data $\mathcal{D}$. The posterior is proportional to the product of the likelihood $p(\mathcal{D}|\theta)$ and the prior $p(\theta)$. In the context of parameter inference of stochastic systems like CTMCs the likelihood term is usually computationally intractable. Because of this, the methods that rely on computing the likelihood are infeasible. Thus, likelihood-free methods such as approximate Bayesian computation [15] and synthetic likelihood methods [16] are commonly used to identify model parameter values such that the data simulated by the stochastic model resembles the observed data.

In this section we concentrate on approximate Bayesian computation (ABC). The idea is to simulate the model for different parameters and compare the outcomes with the observed data. Let us consider the observed data $\mathcal{D}$ and the data $\mathcal{D}_\theta$ simulated from a model $\mathcal{M}_\theta$ with a parameter value θ. In this paper we think of both $\mathcal{D}$ and $\mathcal{D}_\theta$ as sets of time-trajectories. The first step in such methods is to reduce the observed data set $\mathcal{D}$ to appropriate summary statistics. Let $\mathcal{D} = \{z_1, \cdots, z_n\}$ denote the observed data set and let the function $S_n : \mathbb{R}^n \to \mathbb{R}^d$ represent the chosen vector of summary statistics. The likelihood $\mathcal{L}(\theta)$ is approximated by

$$L(\theta) = p(S_n(\mathcal{D})|\theta)$$

which is the likelihood of data $\mathcal{D}$ under the summary statistic S_n. This likelihood however is also not known and in practice $L(\theta)$ is approximated further.

The method we consider is based on the summary statistics $S_n(\mathcal{D}_\theta)$ computed from the simulated data $\mathcal{D}_\theta$. In particular, consider the standard ABC rejection sampler. This method relies on defining a discrepancy measure

$$\Delta_\theta = \|S_n(\mathcal{D}) - S_n(\mathcal{D}_\theta)\|$$

for some norm $\|\cdot\|$. ABC methods proceed to draw samples θ from the prior distribution and simulate the corresponding summary statistics $S_n(\mathcal{D}_\theta)$. The parameters θ sampled from the prior $p(\theta)$ are retained as samples from the posterior $p(\theta|\mathcal{D})$ if the corresponding summary statistics $S_n(\mathcal{D})$ and $S_n(\mathcal{D}_\theta)$ are within a chosen distance ϵ of each other. In other words, θ is retained as a posterior sample if the acceptance criterion $\Delta_\theta < \epsilon$ is satisfied.

The notable problem with this approach is the sensitivity of the results to the choice of the discrepancy measure Δ_θ and the threshold. In this paper we work with the discrepancy measure defined in terms of the Euclidean distance between the summary statistics. The choice of the threshold value is generally less obvious and several values need to be tried to find a performing one. Setting the value too high will result in a rejection sampler that discriminates poorly between different parameter values of the model. Setting the value too low results in computation time blowing up as too many samples are rejected.

Another common class of likelihood-free inference methods is synthetic likelihood methods where the intractable likelihood $p(S_n(\mathcal{D}|\theta)$ is approximated by a normal likelihood. The likelihood is then used in a Markov chain Monte Carlo scheme like the Metropolis-Hastings algorithm. Such methods are out of the scope of this paper and are left for future work.

4   Inference

In this section we discuss the main contribution of this paper—a method for performing inference with quantitative and logically specified information about a system's behaviour. The Bayesian inference problem we are looking to solve is constructing the posterior for model parameters θ under the evidence from observed data $\mathcal{D}$ and logical specification φ. From the Bayes' theorem we know that the posterior of interest is proportional to likelihood multiplied by the prior:

$$p(\theta|\mathcal{D}, \varphi) \propto p(\mathcal{D}, \varphi|\theta)p(\theta)$$

The likelihood $p(\mathcal{D}, \varphi|\theta)$ in the case of continuous time Markov chain models is generally intractable. Further, the likelihood $p(\mathcal{D}, \varphi|\theta)$ which considers both quantitative and logic-based specifications is more complex than considering the quantitative and logic-based specifications independently. In particular, it is clear that conditional on the parameter θ the likelihood of $\mathcal{D}$ and φ are not independent. From the law of conditional probability we know that either

$$p(\mathcal{D}, \varphi|\theta) = p(\mathcal{D}|\theta, \varphi)p(\varphi|\theta)$$

or

$$p(\mathcal{D}, \varphi|\theta) = p(\varphi|\theta, \mathcal{D})p(\mathcal{D}|\theta)$$

It is not clear how to treat the conditional likelihoods $p(\mathcal{D}|\theta, \varphi)$ and $p(\varphi|\theta, \mathcal{D})$ corresponding to the likelihoods of observed data given parameter θ and specification φ holding and the likelihood of φ holding given observed data $\mathcal{D}$. Neither the ABC methods or synthetic likelihood methods mentioned in Sect. 3.3 can be applied directly to the problem at hand. In the case of ABC the challenge is defining a set of summary statistics from the available (quantitative and logical) data and a corresponding discrepancy measure. In the case of synthetic likelihood methods we also have a problem with defining a set of summary statistics that are approximately Gaussian.

In order to overcome these challenges we propose the following approach. The quantitative data in the form of observed trajectories is translated into a logical specification $\varphi_{\mathcal{D}}$. The joint likelihood $p(\varphi_{\mathcal{D}}, \varphi|\theta)$ can then be estimated via statistical model checking methods. The main difficulty is in constructing the specification $\varphi_{\mathcal{D}}$ from the quantitative data $\mathcal{D}$ such that the posterior $p(\varphi_{\mathcal{D}}, \varphi|\theta)$ approximates well the posterior $p(\mathcal{D}, \varphi|\theta)$. Note that this problem of choosing a suitable way to transform the quantitative observations into logical specification is in spirit similar to choosing a set of summary statistics and a discrepancy measure in ABC. Once we have an appropriately constructed logical specification we can use rejection sampling to sample from the approximate posterior $p(\theta|\varphi, \varphi_D)$.

4.1   Quantitative Data

The most trivial method for transforming the observed trajectories to a logical specification is to define a discrepancy measure $\Delta_\theta = \|S_n(\mathcal{D}) - S_n(\mathcal{D}_\theta)\|$ and a threshold ϵ as done for ABC. We then consider a property that is satisfied when the discrepancy is less than ϵ. Suppose then that φ denotes the logical specification corresponding to the knowledge about the system's properties. When implementing the rejection sampling we only keep the samples θ for which both the discrepancy measure is below a threshold and the logical specification for the system's properties is satisfied.

Alternatively we can convert the quantitative data into the same logic, MiTL, as the specification of the system's properties. Suppose $\mathcal{D} = \{z_1, \cdots, z_n\}$ are time trajectories observed at a finite number of points. Each trajectory z_i consists of a set

$$\{(y_0^i, t_0), (y_1^i, t_1), \ldots (y_m^i, t_m)\}$$

where y_j^i is a measured vector of data points at time t_j. As with the approximate Bayesian computation we consider the summary statistics $S_n(\mathcal{D}) = \{s_1, \cdots, s_m\}$ at times $t_0, \cdots, t_m$. Recall that $\omega(t)$ is the function that maps a CTMC to its summary statistic at time t. We say that the trajectory is close to a point (s_j, t_j) if for a small time ϵ_t and a time interval $[t_j - \epsilon_t, t_j + \epsilon_t]$ there exists a time $t \in [t_j - \epsilon_t, t_j + \epsilon_t]$ such that $d(\omega(t), s_j) < \delta$ where d is a distance measure defined between the state space of the CTMC model and summary statistic of the observed trajectories. For chosen tolerances ϵ_t and δ this can be encoded as a MiTL specification in the following way

$$F_{[t_j - \epsilon_t, t_j + \epsilon_t]}\{d(\omega(t), s_j) < \delta\}. \tag{6}$$

That is, eventually in the given time interval the discrepancy between the trajectory and the summary statistic from observations is less than δ. A useful special case is when $\epsilon_t = 0.0$ which gives

$$F_{[t_j, t_j]}\{d(\omega(t), s_j) < \delta\}. \tag{7}$$

meaning at time t_j the inequality $d(\omega(t), s_j) < \delta$ holds. In the rest of the paper we are going to work with this special case.

Let us denote this formula by φ_i. The full specification corresponding to the observed time trajectories is then given by the conjunction $\varphi_D = \bigwedge_{i \in \{1, \cdots, m\}} \varphi_i$ corresponding to the model trajectories close to the observed quantitative data. This can be taken together with the logical specification φ for the system's properties. In particular, the assumption is that $p(\mathcal{D}, \varphi|\theta)$ is approximately proportional to $p(\varphi_D, \varphi|\theta)$.

Similarly to ABC we can then implement rejection sampling from the posterior

$$p(\theta|\varphi_D, \varphi) \propto p(\varphi_D, \varphi|\theta)p(\theta) \tag{8}$$

by randomly sampling from the prior $p(\theta)$ and accepting those samples for which the model $\mathcal{M}_\theta$ satisfies the constructed logical specification. Note that the rejection sampling will only accept samples if there is part of the parameter space covered by the prior where both the satisfaction probability to both φ_D and φ are non-zero.

4.2   Expected Satisfaction Probability

The assumption in the previous section that $p(\mathcal{D}, \varphi | \theta)$ is approximately proportional to $p(\varphi_D, \varphi | \theta)$ is difficult to verify in practice. Moreover, as discussed we do not have access to the true posterior $p(\theta | \mathcal{D}, \varphi)$. Thus, in order to study the resulting posteriors we compare the expected satisfaction probabilities calculated over the approximate posterior distributions $p(\theta | \varphi_D)$, $p(\theta | \varphi)$ and $p(\theta | \varphi_D, \varphi)$.

Suppose φ is a logical property and $p(\theta | \mathcal{D})$ is a posterior distribution. We can compute the expected satisfaction probabilities over the distribution as

$$\int_\theta f_\varphi(\theta) p(\theta | \mathcal{D}) d\theta. \tag{9}$$

For example, with respect to the posterior arising from the logical specification for quantitative data we have

$$\mathbb{E}_{\varphi_D}[f_\varphi(\theta)] = \int_\theta f_\varphi(\theta) p(\theta | \varphi_D) d\theta. \tag{10}$$

Clearly, analytical solution of this will be infeasible as neither the satisfaction probability function $f_\varphi(\theta)$ nor the posterior density $p(\theta | \varphi_D)$ have analytical forms. However the expectation can be estimated from the posterior samples $\mathcal{S}$ by giving the following Monte Carlo estimate

$$\mathbb{E}_{\varphi_D}[f_\varphi(\theta)] \approx \frac{1}{|\mathcal{S}|} \sum_{s \in \mathcal{S}} f_\varphi(s). \tag{11}$$

The satisfaction probability $f_\varphi(s)$ requires another Monte Carlo estimate as described in Sect. 3.2. Thus, for example, we can study the change in expected satisfaction probability of properties φ and φ_D when going from posterior $p(\theta | \varphi)$ to $p(\theta | \varphi, \varphi_D)$. This serves as a proxy for the trade-off being made when attempting to fit a posterior distribution with respect to both quantitative and logic-based specification of the system's properties.

5   Results

In this section we present parameter inference results for two examples. Namely, a rumour spread model [4] and a client-server model, both defined as CRNs. In both cases the quantitative data considered are samples of trajectories at a given set of times. Both approaches of describing the time trajectory as a logical property presented in the previous section require us to specify a threshold parameter and are analogous to each other in the context of rejection sampling.

5.1   Rumour Spread Model

To illustrate the proposed method we are going to first consider a simple rumour spread model. This model is a variant of the commonly studied susceptible-infected-recovered model from epidemiology. The agents in the model can be in one of three states—ignorant I, spreading S or repressing R. As a chemical reaction network the model is given as follows.

$$S + I \xrightarrow{k_I} S + S$$

$$S + S \xrightarrow{k_R} S + R$$

$$R + S \xrightarrow{k_R} R + R$$

In particular, the rumour spreads from spreading individuals to ignorant. Only novel rumours are deemed worthy of sharing and thus if two spreaders meet, one of them will stop spreading the rumour. Finally, a repressing individual will quash the rumour if they meet a spreading individual, and turn them into a repressor. We assume two parameters k_I and k_R governing the rates at which ignorants become spreaders and spreading individuals are converted to repressing ones. The initial state of the model is given by 10 ignorants and 5 spreaders.

The experimental set up is as follows. For the quantitative data we assume that only one of the species in the chemical reaction network is directly observed. In particular, suppose only the number of repressors is quantitatively measured. The quantitative observations are taken to be the mean values of 1000 trajectories simulated from the model with fixed parameters at 6 equally spaced time-points in the time-interval $[0.0, 5.0]$. We repeat the experiment for 3 different parameter combinations from the half-open intervals $k_I \in (0.0, 1.0]$ and $k_R \in (0.0, 1.0]$. Namely, we consider $\{k_I = 0.2, k_R = 0.5\}$, $\{k_I = 0.4, k_R = 0.8\}$ and $\{k_I = 0.1, k_R = 0.1\}$. We then construct the discrepancy measure and MiTL-based logic specifications for the quantitative data as described in Sect. 4.

For the logical property let us suppose the following condition:

$$G_{[0,1.0]}\{I > S\}. \tag{12}$$

That is, in the time-interval $[0.0, 1.0]$ the number of ignorants is greater than the number of spreaders. Clearly, this indirectly constrains the rate at which the rumour spreads. Note that we have now said something about all three populations in the model.

The parameter for the MiTL formula construction and rejection criterion for the approximate Bayesian inference construction is chosen such that the rejection rates are similar between the two conditions. In particular, we fix the acceptance criterion parameter for the ABC as $\epsilon = 1.0$. With that in mind, choosing the parameters for the MiTL formula construction to be $\delta = \sqrt{\frac{1}{6}}$ and $\epsilon_t = 0.0$ ensures that a parameter accepted based on the MiTL formula is also accepted by the Euclidean metric-based condition. In this case this selection of parameters also happens to give a similar acceptance rate between the two methods.

(a) Quantitative.   (b) Logical property.   (c) Quantitative and logical property.

Fig. 1. Plot of the kernel density estimator based on accepted parameters for the rumour spread model. The quantitative data was sampled from the model with parameters $k_I = 0.2$ and $k_R = 0.5$. (a) shows the approximate posterior based on quantitative information only. (b) shows the posterior based on logical properties only. (c) shows the posterior for the combined information as found by method in Sect. 4.

(a) Quantitative.   (b) Logical property.   (c) Quantitative and logical property.

Fig. 2. Same as Fig. 1 but with the quantitative data sampled from the model with parameters $k_I = 0.4$ and $k_R = 0.8$.

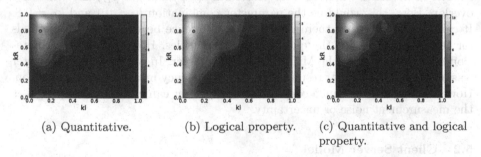

(a) Quantitative.   (b) Logical property.   (c) Quantitative and logical property.

Fig. 3. Same as Fig. 1 but with the quantitative data sampled from the model with parameters $k_I = 0.1$ and $k_R = 0.8$.

Figures 1, 2 and 3 show the distributions resulting from the rejection sampling based on combined quantitative data and the logical property as well as each separately. For each posterior we gathered 1000 samples. As discussed in Sect. 4.2 we assess the method by comparing the recovered posterior distribution when only quantitative data, only the logical property and both sets of informa-

Table 1. Expected satisfaction probabilities under different combinations of logical specifications.

Parameters	Formula	Expect. sat. w.r.t		
		$p(\theta|\varphi_D)$	$p(\theta|\varphi)$	$p(\theta|\varphi, \varphi_D)$
$(0.2, 0.5)$				
MiTL	φ	0.37	0.63	0.39
	φ_D	0.021	0.009	0.017
Discrepancy measure	φ	0.39	0.63	0.41
	φ_D	0.033	0.015	0.028
$(0.4, 0.8)$				
MiTL	φ	0.20	0.64	0.21
	φ_D	0.11	0.048	0.12
Discrepancy measure	φ	0.21	0.64	0.23
	φ_D	0.12	0.056	0.13
$(0.1, 0.8)$				
MiTL	φ	0.62	0.63	0.61
	φ_D	0.11	0.077	0.11
Discrepancy measure	φ	0.64	0.63	0.64
	φ_D	0.13	0.095	0.13

tion are used. In particular, Table 1 shows the trade-offs that are made to make the posterior agree with both types of data as closely as possible. The trade-off is smaller in the cases where the two posteriors $p(\theta|\varphi)$ and $p(\theta|\varphi_D)$ have the most overlap. Here, this would be the parameter combination $k_I = 0.1$ and $k_R = 0.8$. It can also be seen that there is very little difference between the two methods for taking into account the quantitative trajectories. However, the interpretation or construction of the MiTL method is simpler. In our case the parameter was chosen to give similar results with the discrepancy measure-based condition. However, the MiTL formula construction parameter can easily be interpreted as the measurement noise or uncertainty.

5.2   Client Server Model

As the second example we consider the client-server model implemented as the following chemical reaction network

$$Client + Server \xrightarrow{k_{req}} ClientThink + Server$$

$$ClientThink \xrightarrow{k_{thk}} Client$$

$$Server \xrightarrow{k_{brk}} ServerBroken$$

$$ServerBroken \xrightarrow{k_{fix}} Server$$

The model consists of two types of agents, clients and servers. The clients request data from the server, receive the requested data and perform some independent action with the data. The servers in addition to serving the clients are susceptible to failure. The initial state of the model is given by 20 clients and 3 servers.

The model parameters are the various rates with which the transitions occur. There are four rate parameter k_{req}, k_{thk}, k_{brk} and k_{fix}. We are going to assume that two of them, namely k_{thk}, k_{brk} are fixed at 0.1 and 0.2 respectively. In the following we use the methods previously described to fit the remaining two parameters.

Let us assume that the data available for parametrising the model are the time-series observations of the available servers. Furthermore, let us assume the following logical formula

$$G_{[0,10.0]}\{Client > ClientThink\}. \tag{13}$$

This means, in the time interval $[0, 10.0]$, we always have more clients ready to request data from the server than thinking. In this case again we have quantitative and a logical property about different aspects of the system dynamics.

The threshold for the discrepancy measure and MiTL formula construction parameter were again chosen by hand: they were fixed as $\epsilon = 3.0$ and $\{\delta = 2.05, \epsilon_t = 0.0\}$ respectively to give similar acceptance rates. The experiments were repeated for three parametrisations of the pCTMC model. Namely, $\{k_{req} = 0.4, k_{fix} = 0.3\}$, $\{k_{req} = 0.2, k_{fix} = 0.6\}$ and $\{k_{req} = 0.8, k_{fix} = 0.8\}$.

Figures 4, 5 and 6 show the distributions resulting from the rejection sampling based on combined quantitative data and the logical property as well as each separately. In this case the effect of taking the quantitative data and the logical property together has a stronger effect on the resulting posteriors than in the previous case-study. As discussed in Sect. 4.2 we assess the method by comparing the recovered posterior distribution when only quantitative, only the logical property and both sets of information are used. Similarly to the previous examples, Table 2 gives an overview of the trade-off in satisfaction relative to the quantitative data and the logical property when attempting to satisfy both.

(a) Quantitative.   (b) Logical property.   (c) Quantitative and logical property.

Fig. 4. Plot of the kernel density estimator based on accepted parameters for the client server model. The quantitative data was sampled from the model with parameters $k_{req} = 0.4$ and $k_{fix} = 0.3$. (a) shows the approximate posterior based on quantitative information only. (b) shows the posterior based on the logical property only. (c) shows the posterior for the combined information as found by method in Sect. 4.

(a) Quantitative.   (b) Logical property.   (c) Quantitative and logical property.

Fig. 5. Same as Fig. 4 with the quantitative data sampled from the model with parameters $k_{req} = 0.2$ and $k_{fix} = 0.6$.

(a) Quantitative.   (b) Logical property.   (c) Quantitative and logical property.

Fig. 6. Same as Fig. 4 with the quantitative data sampled from the model with parameters $k_{req} = 0.8$ and $k_{fix} = 0.8$.

Table 2. Expected satisfaction probabilities under different combinations of logical specifications.

Parameters	Formula	Expect. sat. w.r.t		
		$p(\theta|\varphi_D)$	$p(\theta|\varphi)$	$p(\theta|\varphi,\varphi_D)$
$(0.4, 0.3)$				
MiTL	φ	0.07	0.12	0.12
	φ_D	0.18	0.11	0.19
Discrepancy measure	φ	0.06	0.12	0.12
	φ_D	0.17	0.10	0.20
$(0.2, 0.6)$				
MiTL	φ	0.08	0.12	0.12
	φ_D	0.08	0.015	0.010
Discrepancy measure	φ	0.08	0.12	0.12
	φ_D	0.08	0.014	0.09
$(0.8, 0.8)$				
MiTL	φ	0.09	0.12	0.12
	φ_D	0.63	0.42	0.66
Discrepancy measure	φ	0.09	0.12	0.12
	φ_D	0.67	0.44	0.7

6   Conclusions

In this paper we presented a method for performing inference based on a combination of quantitative data and logical properties about a system's behaviour. Our approach was to construct a rejection sampling criterion such that the accepted samples correspond to trajectories that are close to the quantitative data and also satisfy the logical property. To achieve that, we provided a way of converting the quantitative data into a set of logical formulae. The benefit of this logic-based construction over standard approximate Bayesian rejection sampling acceptance criteria given in terms of discrepancy measures is that this construction can easily be interpreted in terms of measurement noise or uncertainty.

We studied the proposed method for two examples—a rumour spread model, which is based on the standard susceptible-infected-recovered model, and a simple client-server model. In both case we supplemented the quantitative data which gave information about one aspect of the model with quantitative data given as a logic specification. We saw that the logic-based specification successfully supplements the quantitative information. It allows us to refine the posterior compared to the rejection sampling ABC with only quantitative data.

Further work can be done to investigate the effects of attributing weight to different sources of information. For example, more reliable pieces can be given more weight during the parameter fitting process. This can improve accuracy of the model and allow information with different certainties to be used more effectively. Even in the case of information defined in a logic specification we may want to assign an uncertainty to the specification. In addition we are looking to provide more rigorous justification for the method used in this paper. Finally, further work can be done to improve the accuracy and robustness of the results.

References

1. Anderson, D.F., Kurtz, T.G.: Continuous Time Markov Chain Models for Chemical Reaction Networks, pp. 3–42. Springer, New York (2011). https://doi.org/10.1007/978-1-4419-6766-4_1
2. Aziz, A., Sanwal, K., Singhal, V., Brayton, R.: Verifying continuous time Markov chains. In: Alur, R., Henzinger, T.A. (eds.) CAV 1996. LNCS, vol. 1102, pp. 269–276. Springer, Heidelberg (1996). https://doi.org/10.1007/3-540-61474-5_75
3. Balbo, G.: Introduction to generalized stochastic petri nets. In: Bernardo, M., Hillston, J. (eds.) SFM 2007. LNCS, vol. 4486, pp. 83–131. Springer, Heidelberg (2007). https://doi.org/10.1007/978-3-540-72522-0_3
4. Bortolussi, L., Sanguinetti, G.: Learning and designing stochastic processes from logical constraints. Log. Methods Comput. Sci. **11**, 2 (2015)
5. Češka, M., Dannenberg, F., Paoletti, N., Kwiatkowska, M., Brim, L.: Precise parameter synthesis for stochastic biochemical systems. Acta Informatica **54**(6), 589–623 (2016). https://doi.org/10.1007/s00236-016-0265-2
6. Chen, T., Diciolla, M., Kwiatkowska, M., Mereacre, A.: Time-bounded verification of CTMCs against Real-time specifications. In: Fahrenberg, U., Tripakis, S. (eds.) FORMATS 2011. LNCS, vol. 6919, pp. 26–42. Springer, Heidelberg (2011). https://doi.org/10.1007/978-3-642-24310-3_4
7. Georgoulas, A., Hillston, J., Sanguinetti, G. Proppa: probabilistic programming for stochastic dynamical systems. ACM Trans. Model. Comput. Simul. **28**(1), 3:1–3:23 (2018)
8. Gillespie, D.T.: Exact stochastic simulation of coupled chemical reactions. J. Phys. Chem. **81**(25), 2340–2361 (1977)
9. Hillston, J. A compositional approach to performance modelling. PhD thesis, University of Edinburgh, UK (1994)
10. Legay, A., Lukina, A., Traonouez, L.M., Yang, J., Smolka, S.A., Grosu, R.: Statistical model checking. In: Steffen, B., Woeginger, G. (eds.) Computing and Software Science. LNCS, vol. 10000, pp. 478–504. Springer, Cham (2019). https://doi.org/10.1007/978-3-319-91908-9_23
11. Maler, O., Nickovic, D.: Monitoring temporal properties of continuous signals. In: Lakhnech, Y., Yovine, S. (eds.) FORMATS/FTRTFT -2004. LNCS, vol. 3253, pp. 152–166. Springer, Heidelberg (2004). https://doi.org/10.1007/978-3-540-30206-3_12
12. Mitra, E.D., Dias, R., Posner, R.G., Hlavacek, W.S.: Using both qualitative and quantitative data in parameter identification for systems biology models. Nat. Commun. **9**, 1 (2018)
13. Mitra, E.D., Hlavacek, W.S.: Bayesian inference using qualitative observations of underlying continuous variables. Bioinformatics **36**(10), 3177–3184 (2020)
14. Schmiester, L., Weindl, D., Hasenauer, J.: Statistical inference of mechanistic models from qualitative data using an efficient optimal scaling approach. bioRxiv (2019)

15. Toni, T., Welch, D., Strelkowa, N., Ipsen, A., Stumpf, M.P.: Approximate Bayesian computation scheme for parameter inference and model selection in dynamical systems. J. R. Soc. Interface **6**(31), 187–202 (2009)
16. Wood, S.N.: Statistical inference for noisy nonlinear ecological dynamic systems. Nature **466**(7310), 1102–1104 (2010)
17. Xu, Z., Wu, B., Topcu, U.: Control strategies for covid-19 epidemic with vaccination, shield immunity and quarantine: a metric temporal logic approach. PLoS ONE **16**(3), 1–20 (2021)

A Refinement Based Algorithm
for Learning Program Input Grammars

Hannes Sochor[✉] and Flavio Ferrarotti

Software Competence Center Hagenberg, Hagenberg, Austria
{hannes.sochor,flavio.ferrarotti}@scch.at

Abstract. We propose and discuss a new algorithm for learning (or equivalently synthesizing) grammars. The algorithm provides good approximations to the set of valid inputs accepted by computer programs. Different to previous works, our algorithm assumes a seed grammar whose language grossly overestimates the target program input language, in the sense that it ideally constitutes a super-set of that. It works by reducing the set of productions from the seed grammar through a heuristically guided process of step-by-step refinement, until a good approximation of the target language is achieved. Evaluation results presented in this paper show that the algorithm can work well in practice, despite the fact that its theoretical complexity is high. We present the algorithm in the context of a use-case and consider possible forms of seed grammar extraction from program abstract syntax trees.

Keywords: Program input · Grammar · Learning · Synthesis · Fuzzing

1 Introduction

We propose a new algorithm for learning (or equivalently synthesizing) grammars that provide good approximations to the set of valid inputs accepted by computer programs. Our algorithm makes use of information extracted from the source code of the targeted program via standard multi-language reverse engineering tools, as provided by the eKnows platform developed in our research institute Software Competence Center Hagenberg (SCCH) [13]. More concretely, we assume that the input to the algorithm is a generic abstract syntax tree (AST). The ASTs are extracted by a fully-automated tool which works with diverse programming languages, including COBOL, Java and C among others. In this sense, we can say that our approach is generic, i.e., not tied to a specific programming language. Our main motivation is the possibility of using the resulting grammars together with grammar-based fuzzers for automated testing (see e.g. [3, 4, 8, 12]).

The research reported in this paper was supported by the Austrian Research Promotion Agency (FFG) through the COMET funding for the Software Competence Center Hagenberg.

© Springer Nature Switzerland AG 2022
J. Bowles et al. (Eds.): DataMod 2021, LNCS 13268, pp. 138–156, 2022.
https://doi.org/10.1007/978-3-031-16011-0_10

Different algorithms have been proposed in the literature for learning grammars. Some prominent examples can be found in [1, 2, 7, 10, 14]. What all of them seem to have in common is the fact that they all start from a seed grammar (obtained by diverse methods) which only covers a small subset of the targeted language. The grammar is then successively expanded by new rules by using some inductive learning method, so that it covers an increasing number of valid words. We follow a different approach. We start from a seed grammar that over-approximates the targeted language, ideally one that produces a super-set of the input language recognised by the program. This grammar is then refined in successive steps by methodically eliminating rules (of the grammar) responsible for producing invalid words.

In order to learn program input grammars, one needs to examine a finite number of executions of the program with different inputs, and then generalize these observations to a representation of valid inputs. Typical approaches are either white-box or black-box. In the former case, the learning algorithm needs full access to the source code of the program as well as to that of its associated libraries for examination during the learning process. See for instance the approach based in dynamic taint analysis implemented in [11]. By contrast, the black-box approaches do not require the source code of the program, only relying on the ability to execute the program for a given input to determine whether this input is valid or not. Common black-box approaches (see e.g. [2]) take as input a small, finite set of examples of valid inputs, and then incrementally generalize this language. Sometimes negative examples are also considered, so that gross over-generalizations can be avoided.

In this paper we are interested in what we could call a "grey-box" approach, since it sits somehow in between the white- and black-box approaches. As we have mentioned before, we do not allow direct access to the source code of the program during the learning process, only to its AST. This has the advantage that our approach is not tied to a specific programming language and particular libraries. That is, we can apply our approach without the need for time consuming re-configurations and tuning. The open question is whether we can still hope to achieve results that are comparable to state-of-the-art white-box approaches such as [11]. Different to pure black-box approaches, we can still access some generic information extracted from the source code. In a related work [16], the black-box approach have been combined with a symbolic execution engine to generate an initial set of inputs for the given target program. The question here is whether the access to the AST of the program in our approach results in an actual advantage with respect to (only) relying on symbolic execution for the initial examples in an otherwise full black-box approach.

Since it is not decidable in general to determine whether the language of a grammar G corresponds to a program input language $\mathcal{L}_p$, it is usual in this area to consider appropriate measures of precision and recall of G w.r.t. $\mathcal{L}_p$. High precision (i.e. close to 1) means in this context that most of the words in the language $\mathcal{L}(G)$ of G are also in $\mathcal{L}_p$. Conversely, high recall means that most of the words in $\mathcal{L}_p$ are also in $\mathcal{L}(G)$. The new approach to learning program input grammars proposed in this paper can be roughly described by the following two-step process:

1. *Seed grammar extraction*: Consists on extracting an initial grammar using the AST of the program source code. Here the focus is on obtaining a seed grammar that has a high recall, even at the expense of precision.
2. *Grammar refinement*: Consists on increasing the precision of the seed grammar by means of successive refinement steps of the set of productions.

Our main contribution in this paper concerns Step 2 above. This is presented in Sects. 4 and evaluated in Sect. 6. We also provide some initial ideas regarding Step 1 in Sect. 3. Although this part is still a work in progress, we think it is important to discuss that in this paper, so that the reader can have a better idea of the possibilities and limitations of the proposed approach. The necessary background and formal definitions of the key measures of precision and recall are introduced in the next section. The last section of the paper includes the conclusions and discusses future steps.

2   Preliminaries

In this section we fix the notation used through the paper. We assume basic knowledge of language theory as presented in the classic book by Hopcroft and Ullman [9].

Let Σ be an *alphabet*, i.e., a finite set of symbols. A finite sequence of symbols taken from Σ is called a *word* or *string* over Σ. The free monoid of Σ, i.e., the set of all (finite) strings over Σ plus the empty string λ, is denoted as Σ^* and known as the *Kleene star* of Σ. If $v, w \in \Sigma^*$, then $vw \in \Sigma^*$ is the *concatenation* of v and w and $|vw| = |v| + |w|$ is its length. If $u = vw$, then v is a *prefix* of u and w is a *suffix*. A *language* is any subset of Σ^*.

A grammar is formally defined as a 4-tuple $G = (N, \Sigma, P, S)$, where N and Σ are finite disjoint sets of *nonterminal* and *terminal symbols* respectively, $S \in N$ is the *start symbol* and P is a finite set of *production rules*, each of the form:

$$(\Sigma \cup N)^* N (\Sigma \cup N)^* \to (\Sigma \cup N)^*.$$

G *derives* (or equivalently *produces*) in one step a string y from a string x, denoted $x \Rightarrow y$, iff there are $u, v, p, q \in (\Sigma \cup N)^*$ such that $x = upv$, $p \to q \in P$ and $y = uqv$. We write $x \Rightarrow^* y$ if y can be derived in zero or more steps from x, i.e., $\Rightarrow^*$ denotes the reflexive and transitive closure of the relation $\Rightarrow$. The language of G, denoted as $\mathcal{L}(G)$, is the set of all strings in Σ^* that can be derived in a finite number of steps from the start symbol S. In symbols,

$$\mathcal{L}(G) = \{w \in \Sigma^* \mid S \to^* w\}$$

In this work, Σ always denotes the "input" alphabet (e.g., the set of ASCII characters) of a given executable (binary) program p. The set of *valid inputs* *of* p is defined as the subset of Σ^* formed by all well formed inputs for p. In symbols:

$$validInputs(p) = \{w \in \Sigma^* \mid w \text{ is a well formed input for } p\}$$

The definition of well formed input for a given program p depends on the application at hand. Here we only need to assume that it is possible to determine weather a given input string w is well formed or not for a program p by simply running p with input w.

As usual in this setting, we assume that $validInputs(p)$ is a context-free language. Consequently, there must be a context-free grammar G_p such that $\mathcal{L}(G_p) = validInputs(p)$. Recall that a grammar is context-free if its production rules are of the form $A \to \alpha$ with A a single nonterminal symbol and α a possibly empty string of terminals and/or nonterminals.

Let s_p be the source code of a binary program p, we denote as $T(s_p)$ the standard AST model of s_p that complies with the AST metamodel specifications of the OMG[1]. In this paper we present an algorithm that, given p and $T(s_p)$ as input, returns a grammar G_p. Ideally, $\mathcal{L}(G_p)$ should coincide with $validInputs(p)$. However, this is in general an undecidable problem [5]. A good alternative is to measure how well (or bad) $\mathcal{L}(G_p)$ approximates the input language of p in terms of precision and recall measures based in probability distributions over those languages, as proposed in [2].

The probability distribution of a language is calculated in [2] by using random sampling of strings from the corresponding grammar. We follow here the same approach. Let $G = (N, \Sigma, P, S)$ be a context-free grammar. As a first step, G is converted to a *probabilistic context-free grammar* by assigning a *discrete distribution* $\mathcal{D}_A$ to each nonterminal $A \in N$. As usual, $\mathcal{D}_A$ is of size $|P_A|$, where P_A is the subset of productions in P of the form $A \to \alpha$. Here, we assume that $\mathcal{D}_A$ is *uniform*. We can then *randomly sample a string* x *from the language* $\mathcal{L}(G, A) = \{w_i \in \Sigma \mid A \to^* w_i\}$, denoted $x \sim \mathcal{P}_{\mathcal{L}(G,A)}$, as follows:

- Using $\mathcal{D}_A$ select randomly a production $A \to A_1 \cdots A_k \in P_A$.
- For $i = 1, \ldots, k$, recursively sample $x_i \sim \mathcal{P}_{\mathcal{L}(G,A_i)}$ if $A_i \in N$; otherwise let $x_i = A_i$.
- Return $x = x_1 \cdots x_k$.

The *probability distribution* $\mathcal{P}_{\mathcal{L}(G)}$ *of the language* $\mathcal{L}(G)$ is simply defined as the probability $\mathcal{P}_{\mathcal{L}(G,S)}$ induced by sampling strings in the probabilistic version of G defined above.

Again following [2], we now measure the quality of a learned (or induced) language $\mathcal{L}'$ with respect to the target language $\mathcal{L}$ in terms of precision and recall.

- The *precision* of $\mathcal{L}'$ w.r.t. $\mathcal{L}$, denoted $precision(\mathcal{L}', \mathcal{L})$, is defined as the probability that a randomly sampled string $w \sim \mathcal{P}_{\mathcal{L}'}$ belongs to $\mathcal{L}$. In symbols, $\Pr_{w \sim \mathcal{P}_{\mathcal{L}'}}[w \in \mathcal{L}]$.

---

[1] https://www.omg.org/spec/ASTM/1.0/.

- Conversely, the *recall* of $\mathcal{L}'$ w.r.t. $\mathcal{L}$, denoted $recall(\mathcal{L}', \mathcal{L})$, is defined as $\mathrm{Pr}_{w \sim \mathcal{P}_\mathcal{L}}[w \in \mathcal{L}']$.

In order to be considered a good approximation to $\mathcal{L}$, the learned language $\mathcal{L}'$ needs to have both, high precision and high recall. Note that, a language $\mathcal{L}' = \{w\}$, where $w \in \mathcal{L}$, has prefect precision, but most likely has also very low recall. On the opposite end, $\mathcal{L}' = \Sigma^*$ has perfect recall, but most likely has low precision.

3 Seed Grammar Extraction

To be able to run our grammar refinement algorithm we first need to extract a seed grammar. In an optimal case, our seed grammar should have recall=1 regardless of precision. This means that every word in our target language is produced by our seed grammar. In addition, the seed grammar should contain information on the basic structure of the target grammar (e.g. Nonterminals, number of rules etc.). To extract a seed grammar we take the following steps:

1. Learn tokens of a program p.
2. Extract the basic structure of the seed grammar from the AST model $T(s_p)$.
3. Identify potential token positions.
4. Expand the seed grammar for all possible token combinations.

Token Learning: To be able to efficiently run our proposed algorithm we want to reduce the seed grammar to an absolute minimum. This can be achieved by reducing the amount of terminal symbols by summarizing them into tokens. For example a rule $S \to 1 \mid 2 \mid 3$ can be summarized to $S \to d$.

For our experiments we used a naive approach for token learning from a black-box given a set of known and valid words S of an unknown Language $L(G)$ as well as the alphabet Σ of G. We start by extracting potential token sets for each word $s \in S$. We do this by going through our alphabet and check if $a \in \Sigma$ is a substring of s. If yes we replace a in s with every other $a' \in \Sigma$ and then execute these new inputs. If the input is accepted, we add a' to the potential token set T_{as} of word s for symbol a. Note that T_{as} always contains a. If we continue to do this, we get a set of potential tokens for G. At the end we then check the set of potential tokens if one token T_{as} is a subset of another token $T_{a's'}$. If $T_{as} \subset T_{a's'}$, we remove $T_{a's'}$ from the potential tokens and add $T_{a''s''} = T_{a's'} \setminus T_{as}$. Finally we can be sure that every token left only contains symbols of A which are interchangeable in the context of the known words S.

Lets take a look at the parser source code given in listing 1.1 with alphabet $\Sigma = \{1, 2, 3, +, -, /, *, (,)\}$ and words $S = \{1 + 1/1, 1 + 1, (1)\}$. Following our simple approach for token learning we are able to extract the following tokens: $[1, 2, 3]$, $[+, -]$, $[*, /]$, $[(], [)]$. If we consider these tokens when constructing our seed grammar, we are able to reduce it from 454 rules to 170 rules in Chomsky normal form.

Extract Basic Structure: Next we take a close look at the AST of a given program p. We start by defining a nonterminal n for every function in p. Then we search for function calls to get insight on the control flow of p. With this information we are able to extract a basic structure for our seed grammar following some simple heuristics:

```java
public class ExprParser {
    public static int parse(char[] in) {
        int pos = expr(0, in);
        if (pos < in.length) {
            syntaxError("End of input", pos);
            pos = -1;}
        return pos;
    }
    public static int expr(int pos, char[] in) {
        pos = term(pos, in);
        if (pos == -1) return pos;
        if (pos == in.length) return pos;
        if (in[pos] == '+') {pos++; pos = term(pos, in);}
        else if (in[pos] == '-') {pos++; pos = term(pos, in);}
        return pos;
    }
    public static int term(int pos, char[] in) {
        pos = factor(pos, in);
        if (pos == -1) return pos;
        if (pos == in.length) return pos;
        if (in[pos] == '*') {pos++; pos = factor(pos, in);}
        else if (in[pos] == '/') {pos++; pos = factor(pos, in);}
        return pos;
    }
    public static int factor(int pos, char[] in) {
        if (pos == in.length) return -1;
        if (in[pos] == '1') return pos + 1;
        if (in[pos] == '2') return pos + 1;
        if (in[pos] == '3') return pos + 1;
        if (in[pos] == '(') {
            pos++; pos = expr(pos, in);
            if (pos == -1) return pos;
            if (pos == in.length) return -1;
            if (in[pos] == ')') {pos++; return pos;}
            else {syntaxError("invalid factor ", pos);}}
        return -1;
    }
    public static void syntaxError(String msg, int pos) {
        final boolean log = false;
        if (log) {
            System.out.print("Syntax error ");
            System.out.print(msg);
            System.out.print(" col: ");
            System.out.println(pos);}}}
```

Listing 1.1. Java code.

- Add one rule to the seed grammar for every control flow path in the function where the left-hand side is the function and the right-hand side a sequence of functions which are called.
- If there exists a path without a function call, add ϵ.
- For every function in p, add potentially parsed terminals or tokens.

In the following example we assume that we know which tokens are parsed by which function of p. This gives us a more comprehensible example by reducing the amount of rules. For the example program given in Listing 1.1 this would lead to the following structure:

$$\text{parse} \rightarrow \text{expr} \qquad\qquad\qquad\qquad \epsilon$$
$$\text{expr} \rightarrow \text{term} \mid \text{term term} \qquad\qquad \{+, -\}, \epsilon$$
$$\text{term} \rightarrow \text{factor} \mid \text{factor factor} \qquad \{*, /\}, \epsilon$$
$$\text{factor} \rightarrow \text{expr} \mid \epsilon \qquad\qquad \{1, 2, 3\}, (,), \epsilon$$

Identification of Potential Token Positions: As a next step we identify positions for potential tokens in our grammar. We do this by adding a position marker before and after every nonterminal in our seed grammar, except it is the first or last statement in $T(s_p)$. E.g. the first statement in the function `parse` is a call to `expr`. As the call to `expr` is the first statement we know that it is not possible that there are some checks for tokens before that. If we apply this method we get the following seed grammar, where $\bigcirc$ denotes a potential token position:

$$
\begin{aligned}
&\texttt{parse} \rightarrow \texttt{expr}\ \bigcirc && \epsilon \\
&\quad \texttt{expr} \rightarrow \texttt{term}\ \bigcirc\ |\ \texttt{term}\ \bigcirc\ \texttt{term} && \{+,-\},\epsilon \\
&\quad \texttt{term} \rightarrow \texttt{factor}\ \bigcirc\ |\ \texttt{factor}\ \bigcirc\ \texttt{factor} && \{*,/\},\epsilon \\
&\texttt{factor} \rightarrow\ \bigcirc\ \texttt{expr}\ \bigcirc\ |\ \bigcirc && \{1,2,3\},(,),\epsilon
\end{aligned}
$$

Seed Grammar Expansion: As a final step we expand the grammar by adding a new rule for every token or terminal of p for every $\bigcirc$. The final seed grammar will look like this[2]:

$$
\begin{aligned}
&\texttt{parse} \rightarrow \texttt{expr} \\
&\quad \texttt{expr} \rightarrow \texttt{term}\ [+,-]\ |\ \texttt{term}\ [+,-]\ \texttt{term} \\
&\quad \texttt{term} \rightarrow \texttt{factor}\ [*,/]\ |\ \texttt{factor}\ [*,/]\ \texttt{factor} \\
&\texttt{factor} \rightarrow [1,2,3]\ |\ (\ |\ )\ |\ [1,2,3]\ \texttt{expr}\ [1,2,3]\ |\ [1,2,3]\ \texttt{expr}\ (\ |\ [1,2,3]\ \texttt{expr}\ ) \\
&\texttt{factor} \rightarrow (\ \texttt{expr}\ [1,2,3]\ |\ (\ \texttt{expr}\ (\ |\ (\ \texttt{expr}\ ) \\
&\texttt{factor} \rightarrow)\ \texttt{expr}\ [1,2,3]\ |\ )\ \texttt{expr}\ (\ |\ )\ \texttt{expr}\ )
\end{aligned}
$$

At this point we have to note that our approach to seed grammar extraction is limited on how a parser is implemented. Imagine a rule $S \rightarrow (\ S\ )$. This rule can be implemented in two ways: By means of recursive calls or by counting and remembering the amount of opening brackets and then checking if the same amount of closing brackets is present. As the latter case does not make use of a call to itself, we are not able to extract a correct seed grammar. This means that our approach to seed grammar extraction is limited to recursive descending parsers. However our approach to grammar refinement is not limited to such parsers if a correct seed grammar can be provided by other means.

4   Grammar Refinement Algorithm

The central grammar refinement task in our approach is described in Algorithm 1.

We illustrate how the algorithm works by means of a simple example. Let us assume an executable program p with valid inputs $validInputs(p) = \mathcal{L}(G_p)$, where G_p is the context-free grammar with start symbol S, set of terminal and non terminal symbols $\Sigma = \{+,*\}$ and $N = \{S\}$, respectively, and production rules:

$$
S \rightarrow +*\ |\ +S*
$$

---

[2] The expression [...] is used to denote optional parts in our grammar.

Algorithm 1. Grammar Refinement Algorithm
___
Input: Seed context-free grammar G and program p.
Output: Refined grammar G' in Chomsky normal form.
Ensure: $precision(\mathcal{L}(G'), validInputs(p)) \geq precision(\mathcal{L}(G), validInputs(p))$.

```
 1: G' ← G.to_normal_form()
 2: countEmpty ← 0
 3: length ← 1
 4: while G'.getWords(length) = ∅ do
 5:     countEmpty ← countEmpty + 1;
 6:     length ← length + 1;
 7: end while
 8: refinedProductions ← G'.productions();
 9: safeProductions ← {A → t ∈ refinedProductions | A ∉ G.non_terminals()};
10: seenProductions ← ∅;
11: l ← 1
12: while (refinedProductions ∩ safeProductions) ≠ refinedProductions do
13:     repeat
14:         words ← G'.getWords(length);
15:         deleteCandidates ← ∅;
16:         for w ∈ words do
17:             parseTree ← G'.getParseTree(w);
18:             seenProductions ← seenProductions ∪ parseTree.getProductions();
19:             evalProductions ← parseTree.getProductionsUpToLevel(l);
20:             if w ∈ validInputs(p) then
21:                 safeProductions ← safeProuctions ∪ evalProductions;
22:             else
23:                 deleteCandidates ← deleteCandidates ∪ evalProductions;
24:             end if
25:         end for
26:         deleteProductions ← deleteCandidates \ safeProductions;
27:         if deleteProductions ≠ ∅ then
28:             refinedProductions ← refinedProductions \ deleteProductions;
29:             refinedProductions ← reachable(refinedProductions);
30:             G'.update(refinedProductions);
31:         end if
32:     until deleteProductions = ∅
33:     if refinedProductions ⊆ seenProductions then
34:         l ← length
35:     else
36:         if length − countEmpty > 1 ∧ isInteger(log₂(length − countEmpty)) then
37:             l ← log₂(length − countEmpty)
38:         end if
39:     end if
40:     length ← length + 1;
41: end while
```

Let us further assume that the input seed grammar G in Algorithm 1 has, respectively, the same sets Σ and N of terminal and non terminal symbols than G_p, and that it has also S as its start symbol. The set of seed productions of G, i.e., the set of productions that we want to refine with our algorithm to increase the precision of G, is formed by the following rules:

$$S \rightarrow + \mid * \mid ++ \mid +* \mid *+ \mid ** \mid +S \mid *S \mid S+ \mid S* \mid +S+ \mid +S* \mid *S+ \mid *S*$$

The first step in the algorithm (line 1) transforms the grammar G into an equivalent Chomsky normal form grammar $G' = (N', \Sigma, P', S)$, where $N' = \{S, N_+, N_*, A_1, A_2, A_3, A_4\}$ and P' is formed by the following productions:

$$S \rightarrow + \mid * \mid N_+N_+ \mid N_+N_* \mid N_*N_+ \mid N_*N_*$$
$$S \rightarrow N_+S \mid N_*S \mid SN_+ \mid SN_* \mid N_+A_1 \mid N_+A_2 \mid N_*A_1 \mid N_*A_2$$
$$A_1 \rightarrow SN_*$$
$$A_2 \rightarrow SN_+$$
$$N_+ \rightarrow +$$
$$N_* \rightarrow *$$

Lines 2–11 of the algorithm simply initialise the required variables. Note that $countEmpty + 1$ is the minimum word length among all words in $\mathcal{L}(G')$. This means that in our example we need to start by inspecting words of $length = countEmpty + 1 = 1$. Further, we assign to $refinedProductions$ the set of production in G', and initialize the sets of $safeProductions$ and $seenProductions$. In $safeProductions$ we initially include those productions in G' of the form $A \rightarrow t$, where A is a non terminal symbol added by the transformation to Chomsky normal form and $t \in \Sigma$. These rules are then safe from elimination during the whole refinement process, unless they become unreachable from S. Thus, after executing these steps, we get the following values:

$$length = 1$$
$$refinedProductions = P'$$
$$safeProductions = \{N_+ \rightarrow +, N_* \rightarrow *\}$$
$$seenProductions = \emptyset$$

At this point the algorithm is ready to start the refinement process, i.e., to step-by-step eliminate rules from the grammar that are responsible for producing words which do not belong to the input language of p. This has to be done as careful as possible, trying not to adversely affect the recovery rate of the candidate grammar. We have found out during the experiment reported in the paper, that a good rule of thumb is to only eliminate rules used in the corresponding parsing tree up to level denoted by the parameter l in the algorithm. Notice that to set the parameter l we use the fact that the minimum possible depth of the parse tree of a word of length n (if the grammar in Chomsky normal form) is $\lceil \log_2 n \rceil + 1$. A more aggressive approach to refinement, i.e., an approach that increases the value of l faster, has the advantage of reducing the computation time considerably. However, as witnessed by our experiments, if the approach is too aggressive in this regard, then it considerably reduces the recall rate of the obtained grammar. The while-loop in Line 12 defines the termination condition, which is met when there is no further rule among *refinedProductions* that can be disposed of. If the termination condition has not been meet, then the algorithm continues by repeating the procedure defined in Lines 13–32 until no production can be further deleted from the set of refined productions by examination of parse trees of words of the current length.

This repeat-until loop accounts for the fact that the seed grammar will most probably be ambiguous, i.e., there will be words in its language which can be derived using different parse trees. Since the number of parse trees grows too fast, we cannot look at all parse trees for each inspected word. Instead, we just take the first parse tree returned by the parsing algorithm (in our case CYK). The intuitive idea is that by repeating the process for the same length of word after each refinement of the grammar, we can still examine the relevant parse tree that were missed in the previous round.

Following with our example, at this point line 14 assigns to the variable *words*, all words of length 1 that can be produced by G' (i.e., $+$ and $*$). Clearly, after the for loop in Lines 16–25 is executed, the variable *deleteCandidates* contains the set $\{S \rightarrow +, S \rightarrow *\}$ of productions. Since none of these productions is among those in *safeProductions*, both are deleted from *refinedProductions* and the set of productions of the grammar G' is updated accordingly (Lines 28–30). Since the updated grammar G' does no longer produces any word of length 1, no refinement take place in the next iteration of the repeat-until loop. Then the value of *length* is incremented by 1 and the process repeats itself, with the following outcomes for each subsequent step:

- For $length = 2$,
    - G' produces the words: $+*, *+, ++$ and $**$.
    - Since $*+, ++, ** \notin validInputs(p)$ and $l = 1$, *deleteCandidates* takes the value $\{S \rightarrow N_*N_+, S \rightarrow N_+N_+, S \rightarrow N_*N_*\}$.
    - Since $+* \in validInputs(p)$, $S \rightarrow N_+N_*$ is added to *safeProductions*.
    - Thus *refinedProductions* reduces to

$$S \rightarrow N_+N_* \mid N_+S \mid N_*S \mid SN_+ \mid SN_* \mid N_+A_1 \mid N_+A_2 \mid N_*A_1 \mid N_*A_2$$
$$A_1 \rightarrow SN_* \qquad A_2 \rightarrow SN_+ \qquad N_+ \rightarrow + \qquad N_* \rightarrow *$$

- For $length = 3$,
    - G' produces the words: $++*, *+*, +*+$ and $+**$.
    - Since none of the word of length 3 produced by G' is in $validInputs(p)$ and $l = 1$, then *deleteCandidates* takes the value $\{S \rightarrow N_+S, S \rightarrow N_*S, S \rightarrow SN_+, S \rightarrow SN_*\}$ and *safeProductions* reminds unchanged.
    - At the end of this step, *refinedProductions* further reduces to

$$S \rightarrow N_+N_* \mid N_+A_1 \mid N_+A_2 \mid N_*A_1 \mid N_*A_2$$
$$A_1 \rightarrow SN_* \qquad A_2 \rightarrow SN_+ \qquad N_+ \rightarrow + \qquad N_* \rightarrow *$$

- For *length* = 4,
  - G' produces the words: $++**, +++*, *+**$ and $*+*+$ with the corresponding parse trees shown in Fig. 1.
  - Since $+++*, *+*+, *+** \notin validInputs(p)$ and $l = 1$, *deleteCandidates* takes the value $\{S \to N_+A_2, S \to N_*A_1, S \to N_*A_2\}$.
  - Since $++** \in validInputs(p)$, $S \to N_+A_1$ is added to *safeProductions*.
  - Thus, the content of *refinedProductions* further reduces to (notice that $A_2 \to SN_+$ is no longer reachable and therefore also eliminated)

$$S \to N_+N_* \mid N_+A_1 \qquad A_1 \to SN_* \qquad N_+ \to + \qquad N_* \to *$$

- For *length* = 5, The value of l is set to 2 and nothing else changes since the grammar obtained in the previous step does not produce words of length 5.
- Finally, for *length* = 5, the grammar only produces words that belong to *validInputs(p)* and, since $l = 2$, the rule $A_1 \to SN_*$ is added to the *safeProductions*. By now all productions in *refinedProductions* belong to *safeProductions* and thus the termination condition is met.

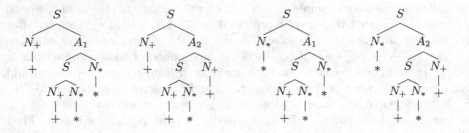

Fig. 1. Parse trees

Notice that the language of G' returned by the algorithm corresponds exactly to *validInputs(p)*. Of course, given the heuristic nature of our algorithm, this satisfactory result cannot be guaranteed. Even when we are certain that the language recognized by the seed grammar G includes the input language of p, an exact solution would need to take into account all possible derivations trees for each word generated by the grammar, which would make the approach unfeasible. A non ambiguous seed grammar would solve this problem, but this cannot be realistically ensured for the targeted use cases of our algorithm.

5   Running Time Analysis

Since G' is in Chomsky normal form (see Line 1 in Algorithm 1), we get that every parsing tree of G' is a binary tree. Therefore, the main while loop from Lines 12–41 in Algorithm 1 will be repeated at most $p = 2^m$ times, where $m = |N'|$ is the number of non-terminals in the initial G'. Notice that by the pumping lemma for context-free languages, every word z in $\mathcal{L}(G)$ such that $|z| \geq p$ can be written as $z = uvwxy$ with the following conditions:

- $|vwx| \leq p$
- $vx \neq \lambda$
- For $i \geq 0$, the word uv^iwx^iy is also in $\mathcal{L}(G)$.

Therefore, when *length* in the algorithm reaches the value p, then $l = length$ and all remaining productions are added to *seenProductions*. Thus each production in the initial G' is at this point no longer in *refinedProductions* or is in *safeProductions*, and the termination condition is meet.

Our algorithm examines in the first step all words of length 1 produced by the grammar, then all words of length 2 produced by the refined grammar in the previous step, and so on. As seen before, this can go on up to words of length p. If there are $|\Sigma| = n$ terminals in the grammar G', then the number of different words that we will have to examine is bounded by $\mathcal{O}(n^p)$, i.e., $\mathcal{O}(n^{2^m})$. This complexity bound, makes our algorithm intractable in theory. In practice however, the values for the exponent p are in our experience usually somewhere between 3 and 8, since it corresponds to the nesting depth of the production rules in the grammar. The higher this value however, the more important it is to keep the number of symbols in Σ in check, using tokens to represent sets of symbols. For instance, replacing symbols $0, 1, \ldots, 9$ in Σ by a token d.

As shown in our evaluation section, another point that allows the algorithm to perform reasonably well in practice, is the fact that each time we eliminate a production rule from the grammar, the number of words that needs to be checked in the next round reduces considerably.

Regarding the production of the words ordered by length for a given grammar $G = (N, \Sigma, P, S)$ in Chomsky normal form, we notice that one can do that quite efficiently. First, we fix a total order $<$ of $N \cup \Sigma$, where the symbols in N precede those in Σ. Then using a priority queue Q defined in terms of $<$, the words belonging to $\mathcal{L}(G)$ can be generated without repetitions and ordered by length then lexicographical as follows:

1. Add S to Q.
2. Remove the first element w from Q (i.e., the one with higher priority).
3. If w contains only terminals, output w.
4. If w contains a non-terminal, for each production α for the first non-terminal in w, append the results of expanding α to Q.
5. Repeat step 2–4 until either Q is empty, or all the required words have been produced.

Finally, we note that for each word w generated by the previous procedure, we can in parallel keep an associated parsing tree. Thus, it is relatively inexpensive in terms of computational time to produce the necessary parsing tree. In our prototype implementation of the algorithm, we use instead a less efficient approach consisting on applying the well known CYK parsing algorithm for retrieving the parsing tree for each examined word. Even this less efficient approach, still works reasonably well in practice, as shown by our experiments.

Table 1. Precision improvement over time, final recall and running time

	$\mathcal{L}(G_p)$	MathExpr	MathExpr2	Mail	JSON	JSON opt.
Seed G.	0.0702	0.129	0.058	0.0025	0.3841	0.3841
Word length 1	0.1517	0.3792	0.3751	0.0025	0.3841	0.3841
Word length 2	0.5904	0.5914	0.5817	0.0025	0.3841	0.3841
Word length 3	0.6401	0.6486	0.584	0.0025	0.3841	0.3841
Word length 4	1.0	0.8974	0.5919	0.0025	0.3841	0.3841
Word length 5		1.0	1.0	0.0025	0.3841	0.3841
Word length 6				0.0025	0.3841	0.3841
Word length 7				0.0025	0.3841	0.3841
Word length 8				0.0032	0.3841	0.3841
Word length 9				0.0107	0.3841	0.3841
Word length 10				0.1808	0.3841	0.3841
Word length 11				0.1808	0.9	0.8983
Word length 12				0.1808	0.9	0.8983
Word length 13				0.1808	0.9	0.8983
Word length 14				0.59	0.9148	0.9038
Word length 15				0.59	0.964	0.9142
Word length 16				1.0	0.964	0.9142
Word length 17					1.0	0.9142
Word length 18						0.9142
Word length 19						1.0
Final Recall	1.0	1.0	1.0	1.0	0.9265	0.9604
Running time	0.4 s	2.7 s	2.6 s	34.7 s	30 m 18.8 s	260 m 2.2 s

6   Experiments and Evaluation

We conducted a series of test runs to evaluate the performance in terms of precision and recall of Algorithm 1 for grammar learning through refinement. The precision and recall was measured as described in the preliminaries, random sampling 10,000 words from each grammar. The results of those experiments are summarised in Table 1. Each column represents a different input language which we detail next. The first line with label "Seed G." shows the initial precision of each of the seed grammars w.r.t. its corresponding target language. Each subsequent line labeled as "Word length X" shows the evolution of the precision value after the algorithm has refined the grammar based on the examination of words of length X. The second-to-last line shows the recall of each of the refined grammars at the end of the process. At the beginning of the process, all the seed grammars have perfect recall 1. The final line is self explanatory and shows the running time for each of the experiments.

First, we should note that the running times could be improved substantially, by simply making use of the fact that the examination of words of a given length can clearly be done in parallel. Furthermore, these running times correspond to a prototype implementation of the algorithm in Python, using an educational library for formal language manipulation (Pyformlang) [15], which is simple to use but not the most efficient for the task. The experiments were run in a Linux installation in a modest virtual machine with 16 GB of RAM and an Intel(R) Core(TM) i7-8665U CPU at 1.90 GHz. In any case, even the worst case running time shown in the table is still somehow acceptable for the envisaged applications of our algorithm.

The column labeled as "$\mathcal{L}(G_p)$" shows the results corresponding to the execution of the algorithm with $validInputs(p) = \mathcal{L}(G_p)$, where G_p is the simple grammar used as example in Sect. 4. The seed grammar provided as input for this experiment corresponds to the seed grammar G, also given as example in Sect. 4. With this simple example, it only takes our implementation 0.4 s to return a grammar with perfect precision and recall.

The columns labeled as "MathExpr" and "MathExpr2" show the results corresponding to the execution of the algorithm with $validInputs(p) = \mathcal{L}(G)$, where G is the following grammar for mathematical expressions:

$$S \rightarrow S + S \mid S - S \mid S * S \mid S/S \mid (S) \mid d$$

In the first case, i.e. in the MathExpr experiment, the seed grammar given as input was formed by all 100 rules obtained from the expansion (as described in detail in Sect. 3) of the following skeletal rules:

$$S \rightarrow \bigcirc T \bigcirc T \bigcirc \mid \bigcirc T \bigcirc \qquad\qquad +, -, \epsilon$$
$$T \rightarrow \bigcirc F \bigcirc F \bigcirc \mid \bigcirc F \bigcirc \qquad\qquad *, /, \epsilon$$
$$F \rightarrow \bigcirc S \bigcirc \mid \bigcirc \qquad\qquad d, (,), \epsilon$$

In turn, in the MathExpr2 experiment we used an alternative seed grammar with 630 initial rules. This corresponds to the expansion of the following skeletal rules:

$$S \rightarrow \bigcirc S \bigcirc S \bigcirc \mid \bigcirc S \bigcirc \mid \bigcirc \qquad\qquad +, -, *, /, (,), d, \epsilon$$

In both cases, the algorithm returned a grammar with perfect recall and precision in less than 3 s. In the case of MathExpr2, this is rather surprising given the high number of initial rules in the grammar. This is explained by the fact that the nesting depth of the rules in the seed grammar used in MathExpr2 is 0, while the corresponding nesting depth of the rules in the seed grammar used in MathExpr is 3.

In the experiment labeled "Mail", we used $validInputs(p) = \mathcal{L}(G)$, where G is the grammar that recognizes valid e-mail addresses defined by the following productions:

$$S \rightarrow Body\ @\ Head\ .\ Tag$$
$$Body \rightarrow Char\ Chars$$
$$Head \rightarrow Char\ Chars$$
$$Tag \rightarrow Char\ Char \mid Char\ Char\ Char$$
$$Chars \rightarrow Char\ Chars \mid \epsilon$$
$$Char \rightarrow t \qquad\qquad being\ t\ a\ token\ for\ \{a, b, \ldots, z\}.$$

The corresponding seed grammar used in this experiment has the following skeletal rules, which generated a total of 96 actual rules:

$$S \rightarrow \bigcirc\ Body\ \bigcirc\ Head\ \bigcirc\ Tag\ \bigcirc \qquad @, ., \epsilon$$
$$Body \rightarrow Char\ Chars$$
$$Head \rightarrow Char\ Chars$$
$$Tag \rightarrow Char\ Char \mid Char\ Char\ Char$$
$$Chars \rightarrow \bigcirc\ Char\ \bigcirc\ Chars \bigcirc \mid \bigcirc \qquad\qquad \epsilon$$
$$Char \rightarrow \bigcirc \qquad\qquad t$$

Since our approach does not work well when the empty symbol is part of the seed grammar, mostly due to the fact that it is based in inspecting increasing word lengths, we treat ϵ in the seed grammar as a non-empty standard symbol. Thus, the resulting seed grammar contains rules such as $Chars \rightarrow \epsilon\ Char\ Chars$, where ϵ is simply a non-terminal symbols of length 1. After the learning process is concluded, we simply eliminate all ϵ symbols from the refined grammar except for those which appear in rules of the form $A \rightarrow \epsilon$. This trick works well in our experiments. Indeed, in this case we were able to again learn a grammar with precision 1 and without degrading the perfect initial recall. The increase in running time w.r.t. the previous experiments is due mostly to the fact that the algorithm can only start to eliminate rules from the seed grammar after it has considered words of length at least 8. Notice that this seed grammar does not produce any word of length smaller than 8, and that the number of words that need to be examined grows exponentially on the length, unless some rules are eliminated from the grammar.

Our final experiment concerns learning a grammar that can recognize well formed JSON files. The set *validInputs*(*p*) is defined as the language recognized by the JSON grammar with the following rules.

$$S \to Element$$
$$Element \to Ws\ Value\ Ws$$
$$Value \to Object \mid String \mid Number \mid Array \mid false \mid true \mid null$$
$$Object \to \{\ Ws\ \} \mid \{\ Members\ \}$$
$$String \to "\ Characters\ "$$
$$Number \to Digit \mid Digit\ Number$$
$$Digit \to d \qquad\qquad\qquad\qquad beingd\text{a token for}\{0,\dots,9\}$$
$$Array \to [\ Elements\ ] \mid [\ Ws\ ]$$
$$Members \to Member \mid Member\ ,\ Members$$
$$Member \to Ws\ String\ Ws : Element$$
$$Elements \to Element \mid Element\ ,\ Elements$$
$$Characters \to Character\ Characters \mid \epsilon$$
$$Character \to t \qquad\qquad\qquad beingt\text{a token for}\{a,\dots,z\}$$
$$Ws \to \_ \mid \epsilon$$

In this case the seed grammar has the following skeletal rules and 70 actual rules:

$$S \to Element$$
$$Element \to Ws\ Value\ Ws$$
$$Value \to \bigcirc Object \bigcirc \mid \bigcirc String \bigcirc \qquad\qquad false, true, null, \epsilon$$
$$Value \to \mid \bigcirc Number \bigcirc \mid \bigcirc Array \bigcirc \mid \bigcirc \qquad\qquad false, true, null, \epsilon$$
$$Object \to \bigcirc Ws \bigcirc \mid \bigcirc Members \bigcirc \qquad\qquad \{,\},\epsilon$$
$$String \to \bigcirc Characters \bigcirc \qquad\qquad ","，\epsilon$$
$$Number \to Digit \mid Digit\ Number$$
$$Digit \to d$$
$$Array \to \bigcirc Elements \bigcirc \mid \bigcirc Ws \bigcirc \qquad\qquad [,],\epsilon$$
$$Members \to \bigcirc Member \bigcirc \mid Member \bigcirc Members \qquad\qquad ,;\epsilon$$
$$Member \to Ws \bigcirc String \bigcirc Ws \bigcirc Element \qquad\qquad :,\epsilon$$
$$Elements \to Element \mid Element\ ,\ Elements$$
$$Character \to a\dots z$$
$$Characters \to Character \bigcirc Characters \mid \bigcirc \qquad\qquad \epsilon$$
$$Ws \to \bigcirc \qquad\qquad \_,\epsilon$$

As before, ϵ is considered in the last two rules not only as the empty symbol, but also as a terminal symbol of length 1.

The experiment with JSON is divided in two parts and the results shown in the last two columns of Table 1. In the column labeled "JSON" we show the result of the standard run of our algorithm. The seed grammar starts to produce words that allow the algorithm to increase the precision of the refined grammar after it has examined words of length 11. At that point the grammar is able to produce 9432 words which are used to eliminate most of the incorrect productions with *Value* in its left-hand side. Unfortunately, at this point the algorithm also eliminates a production, namely *Value* → {#CNF# C#CNF#33, which decreases the recall of the refined grammar from 1 to 0.9265. Note that this rule belongs to the Chomsky normal form version of the seed grammar described above. Given the high number of words examined of length 11 (after this step less than 5000 in total are produced by the grammar for lengths 12 − 17) and our inefficient prototype, the running time for learning these grammar increases considerably w.r.t. the previous experiments. Nevertheless, this is still acceptable for the use cases described in this paper.

Finally, in the column labeled "JSON opt." we show the results of running the same JSON experiment, but including the rule *Value* → {#CNF# C#CNF#33 among the set of safe from the start productions (see *safeProductions* in Algorithm 1). This allowed us to increase the recall of the resulting grammar to 0.9604 without decreasing its precision. The only downside is a considerable increase in the running time, from half an hour to more than 4 hours. Again, this shows that the running time is highly influenced by the number of words of each given length that the algorithm needs to evaluate.

7   Conclusion

The main contribution of this paper is a novel algorithm for program input grammar learning. Different to previous work, our algorithm starts from a seed grammar with high recall and low precision. Then, through a process of step-by-step refinements of the seed grammar, which considers sets of words of increasing length, our heuristic algorithm tries to increase the precision of the grammar without decreasing its initial recall. While the theoretical complexity of the algorithm is high in theory, we show through a running time analysis and also through empirical experiments that the algorithm can be successfully used in practice for learning program input grammars of reasonable large size such as JSON. The initial results obtained in this paper are indeed very encouraging, achieving in all evaluated cases a perfect precision as well as a perfect or close to perfect recall.

As future work, we plan to study possible improvements to our grammar refinement algorithm, considering for instance how the measures of recall and precision can be included in the refinement process to improve the applied heuristics. Our last experiment with the JSON language offers a hint in this direction.

In this paper we only touched the problem of how to come up with appropriate seed grammars for our novel algorithm. Given the positive results obtained so far, we believe this area also warrants future research. Once these hurdles have been cleared, we plan to perform a though and fair comparison with state of the art grammar miners such as autogram [11] and its successor mimid [6].

References

1. Angluin, D.: Learning regular sets from queries and counterexamples. Inf. Comput. **75**(2), 87–106 (1987). https://doi.org/10.1016/0890-5401(87)90052-6
2. Bastani, O., Sharma, R., Aiken, A., Liang, P.: Synthesizing program input grammars. In: Cohen, A., Vechev, M.T. (eds.) Proceedings of the 38th ACM SIGPLAN Conference on Programming Language Design and Implementation, PLDI 2017, pp. 95–110. ACM (2017). https://doi.org/10.1145/3062341.3062349
3. Eberlein, M., Noller, Y., Vogel, T., Grunske, L.: Evolutionary grammar-based fuzzing. In: Aleti, A., Panichella, A. (eds.) SSBSE 2020. LNCS, vol. 12420, pp. 105–120. Springer, Cham (2020). https://doi.org/10.1007/978-3-030-59762-7_8
4. Godefroid, P., Kiezun, A., Levin, M.Y.: Grammar-based whitebox fuzzing. In: SIGPLAN Not, vol. 43, pp. 206–215, June 2008. https://doi.org/10.1145/1379022.1375607
5. Gold, E.M.: Language identification in the limit. Inf. Control **10**(5), 447–474 (1967). https://doi.org/10.1016/S0019-9958(67)91165-5
6. Gopinath, R., Mathis, B., Zeller, A.: Inferring input grammars from dynamic control flow. CoRR abs/1912.05937 (2019). arxiv.org/abs/1912.05937
7. De la Higuera, C.: Grammatical Inference: Learning Automata and Grammars. Cambridge University Press, New York (2010)
8. Hodován, R., Kiss, A., Gyimóthy, T.: Grammarinator: a grammar-based open source fuzzer. In: Proceedings of the 9th ACM SIGSOFT International Workshop on Automating TEST Case Design, Selection, and Evaluation, pp. 45–48. A-TEST 2018, Association for Computing Machinery, New York, NY, USA (2018). DOIurl10.1145/3278186.3278193
9. Hopcroft, J.E., Ullman, J.D.: Introduction to Automata Theory. Languages and Computation. Addison-Wesley, Boston (1979)
10. Höschele, M., Zeller, A.: Mining input grammars from dynamic taints. In: Lo, D., Apel, S., Khurshid, S. (eds.) Proceedings of the 31st IEEE/ACM International Conference on Automated Software Engineering, ASE 2016, pp. 720–725. ACM (2016). https://doi.org/10.1145/2970276.2970321
11. Höschele, M., Zeller, A.: Mining input grammars with AUTOGRAM. In: Uchitel, S., Orso, A., Robillard, M.P. (eds.) Proceedings of the 39th International Conference on Software Engineering, ICSE 2017, pp. 31–34. IEEE Computer Society (2017). https://doi.org/10.1109/ICSE-C.2017.14
12. Le, X.B.D., Pasareanu, C., Padhye, R., Lo, D., Visser, W., Sen, K.: Saffron: adaptive grammar-based fuzzing for worst-case analysis. SIGSOFT Softw. Eng. Notes **44**(4), 14 (2021). https://doi.org/10.1145/3364452.3364455
13. Moser, M., Pichler, J.: eKnows: platform for multi-language reverse engineering and documentation generation. In: IEEE International Conference on Software Maintenance and Evolution, ICSME 2021, pp. 559–568. IEEE (2021). https://doi.org/10.1109/ICSME52107.2021.00057
14. Oncina, J., García, P.: Identifying regular languages in polynomial time. In: Advances in Structural and Syntactic Pattern Recognition, pp. 99–108 (1992). https://doi.org/10.1142/9789812797919_0007

15. Romero, J.: Pyformlang: an educational library for formal language manipulation. In: Sherriff, M., Merkle, L.D., Cutter, P.A., Monge, A.E., Sheard, J. (eds.) SIGCSE 2021: The 52nd ACM Technical Symposium on Computer Science Education, pp. 576–582. ACM (2021). https://doi.org/10.1145/3408877.3432464
16. Wu, Z., et al.: REINAM: reinforcement learning for input-grammar inference. In: Dumas, M., Pfahl, D., Apel, S., Russo, A. (eds.) Proceedings of the ACM Joint Meeting on European Software Engineering Conference and Symposium on the Foundations of Software Engineering, ESEC/SIGSOFT FSE 2019, pp. 488–498. ACM (2019). https://doi.org/10.1145/3338906.3338958

Spatio-temporal Model Checking for 3D Individual-Based Biofilm Simulations

Bowen Li[1,2], Jayathilake Pahala Gedara[3], Yuqing Xia[4],
Thomas P. Curtis[4], and Paolo Zuliani[1,2(✉)]

[1] School of Computing, Newcastle University, Newcastle upon Tyne, UK
[2] Interdisciplinary Computing and Complex bioSystems (ICOS) Research Group,
Newcastle University, Newcastle upon Tyne, UK
{bowen.li2,paolo.zuliani}@newcastle.ac.uk
[3] Department of Oncology, University of Oxford, Oxford, UK
jayathilake.pahalagedara@oncology.ox.ac.uk
[4] School of Engineering, Newcastle University, Newcastle upon Tyne, UK
{yuqing.xia,tom.curtis}@newcastle.ac.uk

Abstract. Individual-based microbial modelling (IbM) is a bottom-up
approach to study how the heterogeneity of individual microorganisms
and their local interactions influence the behaviour of microbial communities. In IbM, microbes are represented as particles endowed with
a set of biological and physical attributes. These attributes are affected
by both intra- and extra-cellular processes resulting in the emergence
of complex spatial and temporal behaviours, such as the morphology
of microbial colonies. However, the quantitative and qualitative analysis of such behaviours is difficult and often relies on visual inspection of
large quantities of simulation data or on the implementation of sophisticated algorithms for data analysis. In this work, we aim to alleviate
the problem by applying SSTL (Signal Spatio-Temporal Logic) model
checking to formally analyse the spatial and temporal properties of 3D
microbial simulations (so-called traces). Complex behaviours can be then
described by simple logical formulas and automatically verified by a
model checker. We apply SSTL to analyse several outstanding spatio-
temporal behaviours regarding biofilm systems, including biofilm surface
dynamics, their detachment and deformation under fluid conditions.

Keywords: Spatio-temporal model checking · Individual-based
modelling · SSTL · NUFEB · Biofilm

1   Introduction

Spatial bio-modelling and simulation are powerful methods for understanding complex structural characteristics of biological systems. The approach uses
mathematical equations and computers to mimic, simulate, and predict the system behaviour in an explicit and efficient way. In the realm of microbial ecology,
spatial modelling of microbial communities is typically constructed in two ways.

© Springer Nature Switzerland AG 2022
J. Bowles et al. (Eds.): DataMod 2021, LNCS 13268, pp. 157–174, 2022.
https://doi.org/10.1007/978-3-031-16011-0_11

Population-based Models (PbMs) use partial differential equations to directly describe population changes over time and space [11]. They are continuum models where time, space, and microbial density are continuous variables (based on a mesh-represented structure) rather than discrete variables. An alternative to PbMs are *Individual-based Models* (IbMs) [10,12] which have gathered considerable attention due to their ability to precisely capture how the heterogeneity of individual organisms and local interactions influence emergent behaviour of microbial communities. Unlike PbMs, conventional IbMs combines both continuum and discrete methods by representing environmental conditions such as soluble nutrients as continuum fields, and individual microbes as discrete particles. In addition, each microbe has its own set of biological and physical attributes, such as growth rate, mass, position, and diameter. The collective action of each individual allows one to explore hypotheses relating local changes to attributes at the population or community level. As an example, changing the amount of nutrients in a growth environment can significantly affect both the thickness and surface area of the resulting microbial colony due to the heterogeneity of microbial metabolism [2].

While IbMs and PbMs offer powerful frameworks to facilitate bio-modelling in space and time, the post-hoc analysis of spatio-temporal properties of simulations can be challenging. Such analysis is often achieved by either manual (visual or textual) inspection of simulation traces, or by developing sophisticated bespoke algorithms for data processing. For example, to quantify the geometrical characteristics of a simulated 3D biofilm colony (surface area, roughness, average height, *etc.*), one may have to implement a set of analysis algorithms based on discrete approximations of specific simulation domains, as third-party functions of existing software [10]. This becomes one of the major barriers preventing scientists to gain a rigorous understanding of complex behaviours from model simulations.

To alleviate the problem, we propose the use of *spatio-temporal model checking* to specify and formally verify biological characteristics in space and time. Unlike traditional model checking where the analysis focuses on temporal evolution of system, spatio-temporal model checking allows reasoning about both time and space, with topology as a mathematical framework. In our case, spatio-temporal properties such as biofilm surface structure over time, are expressed by *Signal Spatio-Temporal Logic* (SSTL) [7,18,19]. SSTL is a linear-time temporal logic to describe behaviours of traces generated from simulations (or even measured from real systems). The logic integrates the temporal modalities of STL (*Signal Temporal Logic*) [15] with two spatial operators: *somewhere* and *surrounded* which enable specifying properties over discrete space models. Given a SSTL property, SSTL model checking automatically checks its satisfaction by exhaustively exploring all the data points (w.r.t, space and time) in the simulated trace, in order to identify spatial patterns and structures of interest over a time series. To date, spatial and spatio-temporal logics have been successfully applied to various systems, examples include identifying vehicular movement in public transport systems [6], monitoring mobile ad-hoc sensor network [3], identifying diffusion pattern [19], and specifying spatio-temporal patters in particle-based simulation [22].

In this paper, we apply SSTL model checking to analyse the dynamics of 3D individual-based biofilm simulations. Biofilms are communities of microorganisms encased in a self-produced extracellular matrix where microbes stick to each other or to a surface. This structural complexity provides both biological and mechanical stability for the biofilms against environmental stress such as nutrient limitation or shear forces due to fluid flow [16]. Understanding the change of biofilm structural characteristics in response to changing environments can therefore yield essential information to design and maintain biofilm-related applications, such as waster water treatment or bioremediation where the spatial dynamics of biofilms dramatically affects their ability to remove toxic pollutants [23,24]. In this work, we first use an IbM solver to model and simulate two biofilm systems: biofilm growth in quiescent environment, and biofilm deformation and detachment under fluid force. Then we show how to use SSTL model checking to analyse various spatial and temporal aspects of the biofilm systems. In particular, we evaluate the effect of nutrient availability on biofilm surface structure, and the effect of fluid strength (shear rate) on biofilm streamer formation and detachment.

2   Methods

This section gives a brief overview of the computational methods as well as the software that we used for the modelling, simulation and model checking of biofilm systems – more details can be found in [10,14,19,20].

2.1   Individual-based Model

A mechanical individual-based model developed in our previous work is applied for modelling biofilm systems [10]. The model combines fundamental biological processes and physical interactions to simulate the growth of microbes and their response to fluid flow at the micro-scale.

Figure 1 gives an overview of the model framework. Individual microbes are represented as rigid spheres, with each microbe having a set of attributes, including position, diameter, outer-diameter, biomass, outer-mass, velocity, force, growth rate, yield coefficient, and genotype. Some of the attributes vary among individuals and can change through time, others are constant throughout a simulation (e.g.,yield coefficient and genotype). Outer-diameter and outer-mass represent an EPS (Extracellular Polymeric Substances) shell. EPS are biopolymers that play a major role in keeping the mechanical stability of biofilms. They are initially accumulated as an extra shell around the microbes before being excreted to the environment. Microbial functional classes (or genotypes, such as heterotrophs, ammonia oxidizing bacteria, nitrifying oxidizing bacteria, *etc.*) are groups of one or more individual microbes that share the same characteristics

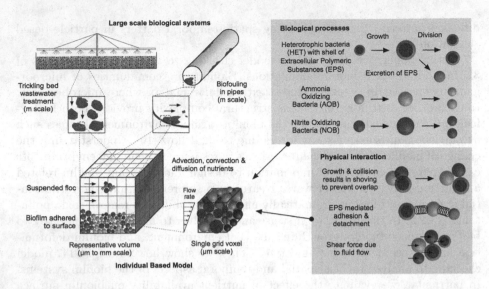

Fig. 1. Overview of the individual-based biofilm model. The micro-scale computational domain represents a small volume of the large-scale biological systems. The attributes of the microbes in the domain are govern by biological, chemical, and physical processes. Figure adopted from [10]

or parameters. For the sake of simplification, a mono-species biofilm is considered in this work that consists of heterotrophic bacteria (HET) and their EPS production. Moreover, the excreted EPS are represented as spheres rather than a continuum matrix structure.

The computational domain is the environment where microbes reside and the biological, physical and chemical processes take place. It is defined as a micro-scale 3D rectangular box. Within the domain, chemical properties such as nutrient concentration or nutrient consumption rate are represented as continuous fields. To resolve their dynamics over time and space, the domain is discretised into Cartesian grid elements so that the values can be calculated at each discrete grid on the meshed geometry. The style of domain boundary can be defined as either periodic or fixed. The former allows microbes to cross the boundary, and re-appear on the opposite side of the domain, while a fixed wall prevents microbes to interact across the boundary or move from one side of the domain to the other. Microbial attributes are governed by both inter-cellular and intra-cellular processes. We consider the following processes that capture the essential behaviours of biofilms and their response to fluid flow.

Microbial Growth. An individual microbe grows and its mass and outer-mass increase by consuming nutrients in the grid where the microbe resides. The growth of heterotrophic bacteria is calculated based on the Monod equation described in [21]. The new mass and outer mass are then used to update diameter and outer-diameter of the microbe, respectively.

Microbial Division. Cell division is the result of microbial growth and is considered as an instantaneous process. Division occurs if the diameter of a microbe reaches $1.35\,\mu m$; the cell then divides into two daughter cells. The total mass of the two daughter cells is always conserved from the parent cell. One daughter cell is (uniformly) randomly assigned between 40% and 60% of the parent cell's mass, and the remaining mass is assigned to the other daughter cell. Moreover, one daughter cell takes the position of the parent cell while the other daughter cell is randomly placed next to the first one.

EPS Production. Heterotrophs can secrete EPS into their neighbouring environment. Initially, EPS is accumulated as an extra shell around the secreting microbe. When the relative thickness of the EPS shell of the microbe exceeds a certain threshold value (outer-diameter/diameter >1.3), around half (uniformly random ratio between 0.4–0.6) of the EPS mass excretes as a separate EPS particle and is (uniformly) randomly placed next to the microbe.

Mechanical Relaxation. When microbes grow and divide, the system may deviate from mechanical equilibrium (*i.e.*, non-zero net force on microbes) due to microbe overlap or collision. Hence, mechanical relaxation is required to update the location of the microbes and minimise the stored mechanical energy of the system. Mechanical relaxation is carried out using the discrete element method, and the Newtonian equations of motion are solved for each microbe in a Lagrangian framework [9]. The model considers three forces: 1) The contact force is a pair-wise force exerted on the microbes to resolve the overlap problem at the individual level. The force equation is solved based on Hooke's law, as described in [5]; 2) The EPS adhesive force is also a pair-wise interaction imposed by EPS to attract nearby microbes. The force is modelled as a spring, with the spring coefficient being proportional to the combined EPS mass of the two individuals [10]; 3) The drag force is the interaction of fluid and particulate microbes, which is simplified by modelling one way coupling, *i.e.*, only the effect of the fluid on the microbes is considered, the flow field is not affected by the movement of microbes. In this work, the force is based on Stokes flow past a sphere [10].

Nutrient Mass Balance. Nutrient distribution within the 3D computational domain is calculated by solving the advection-diffusion-reaction equation for soluble substrates. The transport equation is discretised on a Marker-And-Cell (MAC) uniform grid and the scalar is defined at the centres of the grid (cubic element). The temporal and spatial derivatives of the transport equation are discretised by Forward Euler and Central Finite Differences, respectively. The equation is solved for the steady state solution of the concentration fields.

2.2 Signal Spatio-Temporal Logic

The *Signal Spatio-Temporal Logic* (SSTL) is a spatial extension of the Signal Temporal Logic (STL) [15]. The logic allows specifying spatio-temporal properties over discrete space and continuous time series generated during the simulation of a (stochastic) complex system.

Discrete Space Model. In SSTL, the discrete space representation is modelled as a weighted undirected graph. Formally, a weighted undirected graph is a tuple $G = (L, E, w)$ where L is a finite set of nodes (locations), $E \subseteq L \times L$ is a finite set of edges (connections between nodes), and $w : E \rightarrow R_{>0}$ is a function that returns the positive weight of each edge. In addition, the discrete space is also equipped with a metric, which is a function that gives the shortest weighted path distance between each pair of element in L, *i.e.*, the shortest path between any two different locations.

Signal and Trace. A *spatio-temporal signal* is a function $\vec{s} : \mathbb{T} \times L \rightarrow \mathbb{E}$ where $\mathbb{T}$ is a dense real interval representing time, L is the set of locations, and the domain of evaluation $\mathbb{E}$ is a subset of $\mathbb{R}^* = R \cup \{+\infty, -\infty\}$. Signals can be described in either a qualitative or a quantitative way: those with $\mathbb{E} = \mathbb{B} = \{0, 1\}$ are qualitative Boolean signals, whereas signals with $\mathbb{E} = \mathbb{R}^*$ are quantitative real signals. A *spatio-temporal trace* is a function $\mathbf{x} : \mathbb{T} \times L \rightarrow \mathbb{R}^n$, s.t. $\mathbf{x}(t, \ell) := (\mathbf{x}_1(t, \ell)), ..., \mathbf{x}_n(t, \ell) \in \mathbb{D} \subseteq \mathbb{R}^n$ where each $\mathbf{x}_i : \mathbb{T} \times L \rightarrow \mathbb{D}_i \subseteq \mathbb{R}$, for $i = 1, ..., n$ is the projection on the ith coordinate/variable. Intuitively, each trace is a unique simulation trajectory containing both temporal and spatial information of the simulated system.

SSTL. The syntax of SSTL is given by:

$$\varphi := \mu \mid \neg\varphi \mid \varphi_1 \wedge \varphi_2 \mid \varphi_1 \mathcal{U}_{[t_1,t_2]}\varphi_2 \mid \Diamond_{[d_1,d_2]}\varphi \mid \varphi_1 \mathcal{S}_{[d1,d2]}\varphi_2$$

where μ is an atomic predicate, negation and conjunction are the standard Boolean connectives, and $\mathcal{U}_{[t_1,t_2]}$ is the temporal *until* operator, where $[t_1, t_2]$ is a real positive closed interval with $t_1 < t_2$ representing time. A trace satisfies the until formula if φ_2 is satisfied at some time point within the interval $[t_1, t_2]$ and φ_1 is true up until that point. Additional temporal operators can be derived as syntactic sugar:

- the *eventually* operator $\mathcal{F}$ where $\mathcal{F}_{[t_1,t_2]}\varphi := true\ U_{[t_1,t_2]}\varphi$, and
- the *always* operator $\mathcal{G}$ where $\mathcal{G}_{[t_1,t_2]}\varphi := \neg\mathcal{F}_{[t_1,t_2]}\neg\varphi$.

Intuitively, $\mathcal{F}_{[t_1,t_2]}\varphi$ expresses that φ is eventually satisfied at some time point in the $[t_1, t_2]$ interval, whereas a trace satisfies $\mathcal{G}_{[t_1,t_2]}\varphi$ if φ is true for every time point in $[t_1, t_2]$.

The spatial operators $\Diamond_{[d_1,d_2]}$ and $\mathcal{S}_{[d1,d2]}$ are *somewhere* and *surrounded*, respectively. The former means that φ holds in a location reachable from the current one with a distance between d_1 and d_2, whereas the latter is satisfied by locations in a φ_1-region, and surrounded by φ_2-region at a distance between d_1 and d_2. SSTL has both classical Boolean semantics and quantitative semantics. The former returns true or false depending on the satisfaction of a SSTL formula, whereas the quantitative semantics returns a real value that 'measures' how robustly a formula is satisfied (or not). The formal SSTL semantics and the algorithms are detailed in [19].

2.3 Software

We use the NUFEB[1] software [14] for the modelling and simulation of (individual-based) biofilm system, and the jSSTL[2] library [20] for the specification and verification of SSTL properties of simulation traces produced by NUFEB.

NUFEB [14] (Newcastle University Frontiers in Engineering Biology) is a 3D, open-source, massively parallel simulator for individual-based modelling of microbial communities. The tool is built on top of the state-of-the-art software LAMMPS (Large-scale Atomic Molecular Massively Parallel Simulator) [26] extended with IbM features. NUFEB allows flexible microbial model development from a wide range of biological, chemical and physical processes, as well as individual microbes types via an input script. The tool supports parallel computing on both CPU and GPU facilities based on domain decomposition, which enables simulating large number of microbes (beyond millions of individuals). During a simulation, NUFEB can output any state variable of microbes or grids. The output results can be stored into various formats for visualisation or analysis.

In this work, we extend NUFEB with new functions for coupling with SSTL. In particular, the SSTL space model is based on the existing NUFEB mesh structure. SSTL-based attributes such as volume fraction will be calculated at each discrete cubic grid (so-called *SSTL grid*). A new output format is implemented for dumping the space model as well as simulation traces during simulation. A new post-processing routine is also implemented to read and visualise model checking results from the SSTL model checker.

jSSTL [20] is a Java-based tool for SSTL property specification and model checking. The tool takes three types of input written in CSV or tabular based ASCII files: a SSTL formula file, a SSTL space model file, and a spatio-temporal trace file. The latter two are obtained from (NUFEB) simulations, while the formula file is specified by the user. jSSTL can compute both the Boolean and the quantitative spatio-temporal semantics of a SSTL formula at each time point and in each location. The tool also provides a simple user interface as an Eclipse plug-in to specify and verify SSTL properties.

jSSTL utilises the Floyd-Warshall algorithm to compute the shortest path for each location pair in a weighted directed space model. The space model in NUFEB is a simple lattice-like mesh structure restricted to orthogonal box (see, for example, the computational box in Fig. 1). We therefore extend jSSTL with a new algorithm specifically for computing the distance matrix of our NUFEB space model. The algorithm takes the indexes of each node pair and directly compute the distance (*i.e.*, the number of SSTL grids between the two nodes) based on a 3D box. Our algorithm takes less than three seconds to build the distance matrix of a $30 \times 12 \times 24$ mesh – the default algorithm takes instead

---

[1] https://github.com/nufeb.
[2] https://github.com/Quanticol/jsstl.

more than 20 min. All the codes used and developed in this work are publicly available[3].

3   Results

In this section, we address SSTL model checking on spatio-temporal emergent properties of biofilm systems. We first apply the technique to study the surface morphology of a biofilm growing in a quiescent medium. Then we use SSTL to analyse biofilm streamer formation and detachment in a fluid environment.

3.1   Biofilm Surface Morphology

Biofilms can sense nutrient concentration gradients by adjusting their surface structure. Understanding biofilm morphology in relevant environmental conditions is therefore essential to predict biofilm effects in many practical applications. For example, biofilm morphology is thought to be crucial for the emergence of mutations conferring antimicrobial resistance. Again, biofilms with irregular surface (thus large surface area) can significantly improve their performance in wastewater treatment processes. In this section, we use SSTL to evaluate the influence of nutrient gradients on biofilm structure in a quiescent growth medium.

Table 1. Key parameters and IbM processes used in the biofilm growth model

Parameters and settings	Value	Unit
Parameters		
Dimensions	$100 \times 40 \times 80$	μm
Cartesian grid elements	$30 \times 12 \times 24$	Grids
SSTL grid elements (Property 1)	$30 \times 12 \times 24$	Grids
Initial microbes	40	
SSTL time point (dt)	1000	Seconds
Simulation time	9.5	Days
Substrate bulk concentration	0.1–0.3	g/m^3
IbM processes		
Biology: Microbial growth, division, EPS production		
Chemistry: nutrient mass balance		
Physics: contact force, EPS adhesion		

Biofilm Growth Model. A mono-species biofilm model (HETs and their EPS production) is developed for modelling biofilm formation and its spatial

---

[3] https://github.com/shelllbw/NUFEB-sstl.

dynamics. Table 1 highlights the key parameters and the IbM processes used in the model. Initially, 40 heterotrophs are inoculated on the substratum of a $100 \times 40 \times 80\,\mu\text{m}$ computational domain. We assume that the bulk environment is situated at the top and supplies a constant bulk nutrient concentration to the computational domain. A nutrient concentration gradient can be therefore formed due to the diffusion as well as the consumption by microbes. Two independent simulations are then carried out to simulate biofilm growth in different bulk nutrient concentrations ($0.1\,\text{g/m}^3$ and $0.3\,\text{g/m}^3$). In the nutrient-limited environment, a mushroom-shaped biofilm structure results from the competition between microbes at the biofilm surface (Fig. 2(a)). Biofilms growing in a nutrient-rich environment form instead a smooth surface (Fig. 2(b)).

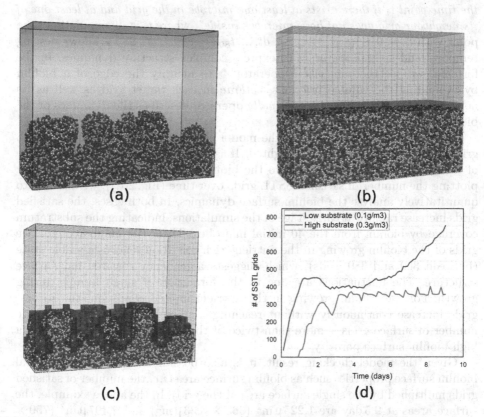

(a)   (b)

(c)   (d)

Fig. 2. Simulation and model checking results of biofilm formation at 9.5 days: (a) biofilm growing in nutrient-limited condition (max number of microbes = 4.2×10^4; CPU time = 4 mins (four cores)), (b) biofilm growing in nutrient-rich condition (max number of microbes = 8.1×10^4; CPU time = 11 mins (four cores)) with the SSTL grids satisfying Property 1 highlighted, (c) satisfaction of Property 1 for the biofilm simulation in nutrient-limited condition, and (d) number of SSTL grids satisfying Property 1 under different growth conditions and over time.

Model checking. The SSTL space model is generated at the beginning of each simulation, and its structure is same as the NUFEB mesh structure ($30 \times 12 \times 24$ grids), *i.e.*, 24 layers with 360 grids in each layer. The spatio-temporal trace **x**, generated during the simulation, consists of a set of signals of microbial volume fraction *VolFrac* at each SSTL grid and at each time point ($1,000\,\mathrm{s}$), where *VolFrac* is defined as the total volume of microbes in the SSTL grid divided by the volume of the grid. The following SSTL formula characterises biofilm surface structure:

Property 1 (surface structure):

$$\mathcal{F}_{[t_i,t_i]}[VolFrac > 0 \wedge \diamondsuit_{[0,1]}(VolFrac = 0)]. \tag{1}$$

The above formula states that *"an SSTL grid is considered biofilm surface at the time point t_i if there exists at least one microbe in the grid and at least one of its neighbour grid does not have microbes inside"*, where t_i is i^{th} simulation time point with $t_0 = 0, t_1 = dt, t_2 = 2 \times dt, ..., t_{800} = 800 \times dt$. SSTL allows nesting temporal and spatial operators to express complex structure dynamics. In the formula, we use the *somewhere* operator $\diamondsuit$ to identify the edge of a biofilm by evaluating the volume fractions *VolFrac* in each target grid as well as its neighbouring grids, while the *eventually* operator describes the dynamics of the biofilm surface *over time*.

Figures 2(b) and (c) illustrate the model checking result with all the SSTL grids satisfying the formula highlighted. It is clear that the formula is capable of identifying which grids belong to the biofilm surface and which do not. By plotting the number of satisfied SSTL grids over time (Fig. 2(d)), we are able to quantitatively analyse the biofilm surface dynamics. In both cases, the satisfied grids increase rapidly at early stage of the simulations, indicating the substratum coverage by biofilm from the 40 initial microbes. Then, the number of surface grids of the biofilm growing in the nutrient-rich condition reaches a stable state (between 360 and 380 grids), which suggests a tendency towards flat surface structure. The fluctuations are due to the formation of small bumps during growth. For the biofilm growing in the nutrient-limited condition, the surface grids increase continuously without reaching a stable state. At 9.5 days, the number of surface grids is more than twice of the layer grids (360) indicating a high biofilm surface porosity.

Given the model checking result, it is also possible to estimate additional biofilm surface properties such as biofilm surface area (*i.e.*, the number of satisfied grids multiplied by the single surface area of the grid). In the above example, the surface areas at 9.5 day are $1,225\,\mu\mathrm{m}^2$ ($368 \times 3.33\,\mu\mathrm{m}^2$) and $2,497\,\mu\mathrm{m}^2$ ($750 \times 3.33\,\mu\mathrm{m}^2$) in the two systems, respectively.

3.2   Biofilm Deformation and Detachment

Biofilms attached to surfaces under fluid flow behave in a complex way due to fluid-microbe and microbe-microbe interactions. Understanding how biofilms interact with the fluid can help unravel their survival mechanisms, which is essential for biofilm removal or preservation in practical applications. For example, the accumulation of biofilms in industrial pipelines may lead to biocorrosion, while their removal can be achieved by the application of hydrodynamic shear forces [1,8]. Here we apply IbM and SSTL to model and analyse two important spatial emergent behaviours of hydrodynamic biofilms: streamer formation and detachment. A biofilm streamer is a filament-like biofilm structure that can cause rapid and catastrophic clogging in biomedical systems. Biofilm detachment, on the other hand, is essential for removing biofilms.

Table 2. Key parameters and IbM processes used in the hydrodynamic biofilm model

Parameters and settings	Value	Unit
Parameters		
Dimensions	$200 \times 40 \times 100$	µm
Cartesian grid elements	$24 \times 8 \times 20$	Grids
SSTL grid elements (Property 2 & 4)	$15 \times 8 \times 20$	Grids
SSTL grid elements (Property 3)	$1 \times 8 \times 20$	Grids
Simulation time	4×10^5	Seconds
SSTL time point	1800	Seconds
Shear rate	$0.15 - 0.3$	s^{-1}
IbM processes		
Physics: contact force, EPS adhesion, shear force		

Biofilm Hydrodynamic Model. To model hydrodynamic biofilms, we apply shear force to a pre-grown biofilm that consists of heterotrophs and their EPS production. For the sake of simplification, the model does not consider biological activities during the fluid stage. The presence of EPS imposes adhesion to the microbes whereas the shear force drives microbe motion along the flow direction (+x). We simulate the model with various shear rates γ in order to study the effect of shear rate on the biofilm structure (Table 2). Figures 3(a)-(c) illustrate the biofilm dynamics at the rate $\gamma = 0.2\,s^{-1}$. In the early stage, the biofilm forms short streamers, and small microbial clusters detach from the head of the streamer due to cohesive failures. As the fluid continues to flow, the top of the biofilm is highly elongated. Although large chunks of detached microbes can be observed at this stage, the streamer continuously grows to a significant length and maintains a stable condition.

Model Checking. We now show how to use SSTL model checking to analyse the formation of biofilm streamers and to quantify their spatial properties. The space model is defined as a $15 \times 8 \times 20$ mesh structure which covers the downstream area and excludes the biofilm body, as shown in Fig. 3. The following formula is used to evaluate whether a SSTL grid is part of a biofilm streamer:

Property 2 (Streamer Formation):

$$\mathcal{F}_{[t_i,t_i]}\mathbf{G}_{[0,t_{\max}]}(\mathit{VolFrac} > 0). \tag{2}$$

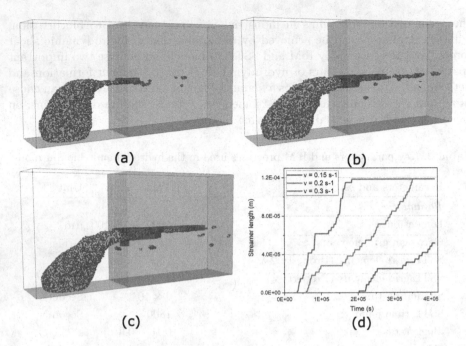

Fig. 3. Simulation of biofilm under shear force and satisfaction of Property 2 with $\gamma = 0.2\,\mathrm{s}^{-1}$ and $t_{\max} = 36{,}000$, at (a) $t_i = 1 \times 10^5$ s, (b) $t_i = 2 \times 10^5$ s, and (c) $t_i = 3 \times 10^5$ s; (d) Streamer length temporal dynamics under different shear rates. Max number of microbes $= 4.6 \times 10^4$ (simulation start); min number of microbes $= 3.2 \times 10^4$ (simulation end); CPU time $= 32$ mins (four cores)

The formula intuitively means that *"an SSTL grid is considered biofilm streamer at time point t_i if the grid is occupied by microbes continuously for the next $t_{\max}$ time units"*. The formula is checked at each SSTL grid over a series of simulation time points t_i, with $t_{\max} = 36{,}000$ (*i.e.*,10 h to ensure the continuity of microbes passing grids). Figures 3 (a)-(c) visualise the model checking results for the simulation trace $\mathbf{x}$ generated for the $\gamma = 0.2\,\mathrm{s}^{-1}$ case. It can be seen that the satisfied grids (highlighted) are in agreement with the streamer structure. The grids occupied by the detached clusters do not satisfy the property as there will be a time point when the clusters leave such grids. In Fig. 3(d), we evaluate the effect of shear rates on streamer formation by plotting the satisfied grid with largest coordinate in x direction over time. As expected, when the shear rate increases the streamer formation rate also increases. For example, when $\gamma = 0.3\,\mathrm{s}^{-1}$ the streamer length reaches 120 μm after 1.6×10^5 s, whereas the streamer takes twice of the time to reach the same length when $\gamma = 0.2\,\mathrm{s}^{-1}$.

Property 2 combines the temporal operator *always* and the geometry of SSTL grids to identify the spatial structure of streamers. This expression is different from Property 1 where the biofilm surface structure is described by a spatial operator. A similar idea can be also applied to detect biofilm detachment events.

In such case, we define the space model as a single layer wall located at the downstream side as shown in Fig. 4(a). We use the following SSTL (temporal) formula to check whether SSTL grids are occupied by detached clusters.

Property 3 (Biofilm Detachment):

$$\mathcal{F}_{[t_i,t_i]}[\textit{VolFrac} > 0 \wedge \mathcal{F}_{[0,t_{\max}]}(\textit{VolFrac} = 0)]. \tag{3}$$

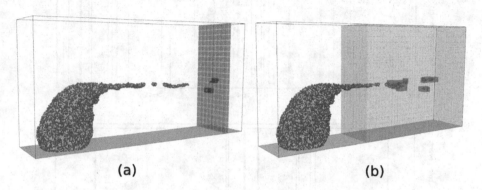

(a)   (b)

Fig. 4. (a) Satisfaction of Property 3 with $\gamma = 0.2\,\mathrm{s}^{-1}$, $t_i = 1.5\times10^5$ s, and $t_{\max} = 3{,}600$ (b) Satisfaction of Property 4 with $t_i = 1.5 \times 10^5$ s, $[\mathrm{d_1, d_2}] = [0,3]$

The formula states that *"an SSTL grid is considered detached cluster at time point t_i if the grid is occupied by microbes, but it will become free in the next $t_{\max}$ time units"*. Figure 4(a) illustrates an example of the model checking result. At each time point t_i, the formula is satisfied at any grid in the wall if its volume fraction is greater than zero but will become zero in the future. The second argument makes sure microbes crossing the grid are (part of) detached clusters rather than continuous streamer. The use of wall-like grid structures allows us to analyse the frequency of detachment events over time. In Fig. 5, we show the effect of shear rates on detachment frequency by plotting the Boolean satisfaction of Property 3 with respect to all grids at each time point (*i.e.,* for each time point in **x**, record true if there exists at least one grid satisfying the formula, otherwise record false). The result shows that the detachment frequency increases as the shear increases, thus indicating a positive correlation between biofilm cohesive failure and fluid strength. This is in agreement with both experimental observations [25] and simulations using other approaches [27]. Moreover, by recalling the streamer length result shown in Fig. 3 (d), we can conclude that biofilm deformation and detachment are closely related, as the occurrence of detachment is consistent with the appearance of streamers.

The above property can identify whether incoming microbes are (or are part of) a detached cluster, but it is unable to accurately quantify physical attributes of clusters, such as volume or shape. Inspired by [19] where the authors use the

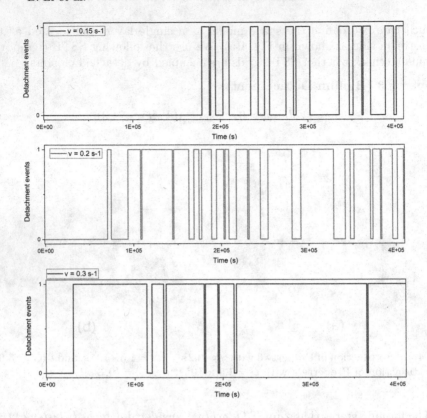

Fig. 5. Boolean evaluation of Property 3: detachment under different shear rates

surrounded operator $\mathcal{S}$ to characterise diffusion pattern in 2D, we introduce the following SSTL formula to identify the geometry of any detached cluster.

Property 4 (Detached Cluster):

$$\mathcal{F}_{[t_i, t_i]}[(\mathit{VolFrac} > 0)\mathcal{S}_{[d_1, d_2]}(\mathit{VolFrac} = 0)]. \tag{4}$$

Informally, the formula checks *"whether there exists a sub-region of the grids such that all the grids of the sub-region are occupied by microbes (i.e., VolFrac > 0). Furthermore, the sub-region is surrounded by grids without microbes inside (i.e., VolFrac = 0)"*. Note that the use of distance bounds $[d_1, d_2]$ in the surrounded operator allows us to constrain the cluster size. For example, Fig. 4 (b) reports the Boolean satisfaction of the formula in each grid for the $\gamma = 0.2\,\mathrm{s}^{-1}$ simulation, with $[d_1, d_2] = [0, 3]$. As shown in the figure, only the grids containing detached clusters satisfy the formula, whereas those containing continuous streamers do not. It is worth to note that the granularity of the SSTL mesh structure is important in spatial model checking. In this case, for example, a more precise cluster structure can be captured when a fine mesh is used. Such accuracy, however, can be significantly offset by the *state space explosion prob-*

lem when handling large 3D space models, and it is therefore beyond the scope of the current work.

3.3 Performance

Several performance statistics of the SSTL model checking are given in Table 3. As previously mentioned, the SSTL distance matrix needs to be built just once and takes a few seconds only. The verification of properties involving spatial operators, in particular the *surrounded* operator in Property 4, can be computationally more expensive compared to properties with temporal operators only (Property 2 and 3). All the simulations and model checking analyses reported in this paper were carried out on a Linux system with a 3.4 GHz Intel Core i5 processor and 12 GB RAM.

Table 3. CPU time and memory usage for building distance matrices and model checking Properties 1–4 (single core)

	Property 1	Property 2	Property 3	Property 4
Distance matrix (s)	2.1	N/A	N/A	2.8
Memory usage (MB)	789	N/A	N/A	823
Model checking (s)	18.5	35.3	47.1	1,161
Memory usage (MB)	1,357	1,430	1,329	2,513

4 Conclusion

In this paper we utilised SSTL model checking to identify dynamic spatio-temporal behaviours arising from individual-based simulations. We first extended our previous developed IbM (Individual-based Model) solver NUFEB to support additional output data for SSTL (Spatio-Temporal Logic) model checking. We added a new, more efficient algorithm in the SSTL model checker jSSTL specifically for computing the distance matrix of the NUFEB mesh structure. Then we used SSTL to specify complex properties of two biofilm systems including dynamics of biofilm surface morphology, biofilm streamer formation and biofilm detachment under shear force. The model checking results demonstrated that SSTL can capture and analyse such behaviours.

The advantages of using SSTL for post-hoc analysis of 3D IbM simulations are two-fold. First, the approach is capable of expressing complex spatio-temporal properties in a relatively simple and succinct logic language that can be model checked in a robust and automatic way. Such a formal verification is not only more reliable than manual inspection of simulation traces, but it can also greatly reduce the complexity of post-processing simulation data. Second, while in this work we integrated the NUFEB solver with jSSTL, the model checker could be combined with minor modifications with other IbM tools such as iDy-noMiCS [13], Simbiotics [17], and BioDynaMo [4], since they are all equipped with a Cartesian grid mesh structure which can be directly used with SSTL.

In the current work, we focused on off-line (post-hoc) verification of SSTL properties. In the future, it would be interesting to explore the use of real-time SSTL verification, where SSTL can be interfaced with NUFEB or other IbM simulators and alert the user if a SSTL property is violated (or satisfied) during a simulation. Such runtime verification is particularly important for monitoring large individual-based simulations (which can run for days or weeks on high-performance systems) by providing instant feedback on the correctness of the model. Moreover, SSTL can quantify the degree with which a simulation trace satisfies or violates a property. Such "robustness" information could be useful to assess quantitatively the severity of unexpected behaviour in a simulation, thereby increasing the confidence in the analysis of the simulation traces.

Acknowledgements. This work was supported by the Impact Acceleration Account award 'BioHPC: Simulating Microbial Communities on High-Performance Computers' to Newcastle University, funded by the EPSRC (UK).

References

1. Abe, Y., Skali-Lami, S., Block, J.C., Francius, G.: Cohesiveness and hydrodynamic properties of young drinking water biofilms. Water Res. **46**(4), 1155–1166 (2012)
2. Allan, V., Callow, M., Macaskie, L., Paterson-Beedle, M.: Effect of nutrient limitation on biofilm formation and phosphatase activity of a citrobacter sp. Microbiology. **148**, 277–288 (2002). https://doi.org/10.1099/00221287-148-1-277
3. Bartocci, E., Bortolussi, L., Loreti, M., Nenzi, L.: Monitoring mobile and spatially distributed cyber-physical systems, pp. 146–155 (2017). https://doi.org/10.1145/3127041.3127050
4. Breitwieser, L., et al.: BioDynaMo: an agent-based simulation platform for scalable computational biology research (2020). https://doi.org/10.1101/2020.06.08.139949
5. Brilliantov, N., Spahn, F., Hertzsch, J.M., Poschel, T.: Model for collisions in granular gases. Phys. Rev. E. **53**, 5382 (2002). https://doi.org/10.1103/PhysRevE.53.5382
6. Ciancia, V., Gilmore, S., Grilletti, G., Latella, D., Loreti, M., Massink, M.: Spatio-temporal model checking of vehicular movement in public transport systems. Int. J. Softw. Tools Technol. Transfer **20**(3), 289–311 (2018). https://doi.org/10.1007/s10009-018-0483-8
7. Ciancia, V., Latella, D., Loreti, M., Massink, M.: Specifying and verifying properties of space. In: Diaz, J., Lanese, I., Sangiorgi, D. (eds.) TCS 2014. LNCS, vol. 8705, pp. 222–235. Springer, Heidelberg (2014). https://doi.org/10.1007/978-3-662-44602-7_18
8. Donlan, R.: Biofilms: microbial life on surfaces. Emerg. Infect. Dis. **8**, 881–90 (2002). https://doi.org/10.3201/eid0809.020063
9. Ghaboussi, J., Barbosa, R.: Three-dimensional discrete element method for granular materials. Int. J. Numer. Anal. Meth. Geomech. **14**(7), 451–472 (1990). https://doi.org/10.1002/nag.1610140702

10. Jayathilake, P.G., et al.: A mechanistic individual-based model of microbial communities. PLoS ONE **12**(8), 1–26 (2017). https://doi.org/10.1371/journal.pone.0181965

11. Klapper, I., Dockery, J.: Mathematical description of microbial biofilms. SIAM Rev. **52**, 221–265 (2010). https://doi.org/10.1137/080739720

12. Kreft, J.U., Picioreanu, C., Wimpenny, J.W.T., van Loosdrecht, M.C.M.: Individual-based modelling of biofilms. Microbiology **147**(11), 2897–2912 (2001). https://doi.org/10.1099/00221287-147-11-2897

13. Lardon, L., et al.: iDynoMiCS: next-generation individual-based modelling of biofilms. Environ. Microbiol. **13**, 2416–34 (2011). https://doi.org/10.1111/j.1462-2920.2011.02414.x

14. Li, B., et al.: NUFEB: a massively parallel simulator for individual-based modelling of microbial communities. PLoS Comput. Biol. **15**, e1007125 (2019). https://doi.org/10.1371/journal.pcbi.1007125

15. Maler, O., Nickovic, D.: Monitoring temporal properties of continuous signals. In: Lakhnech, Y., Yovine, S. (eds.) FORMATS/FTRTFT -2004. LNCS, vol. 3253, pp. 152–166. Springer, Heidelberg (2004). https://doi.org/10.1007/978-3-540-30206-3_12

16. Nadell, C., Drescher, K., Wingreen, N., Bassler, B.: Extracellular matrix structure governs invasion resistance in bacterial biofilms. ISME J. **9**, 1700–1709 (2015). https://doi.org/10.1038/ismej.2014.246

17. Naylor, J., et al.: Simbiotics: a multiscale integrative platform for 3D modeling of bacterial populations. ACS Synth. Biol. **6**, 11941–120 (2017). https://doi.org/10.1021/acssynbio.6b00315

18. Nenzi, L., Bortolussi, L.: Specifying and monitoring properties of stochastic spatio-temporal systems in signal temporal logic. EAN Endors. Trans. Cloud Syst. **19**, e4 (2015). https://doi.org/10.4108/icst.valuetools.2014.258183

19. Nenzi, L., Bortolussi, L., Ciancia, V., Loreti, M., Massink, M.: Qualitative and quantitative monitoring of spatio-temporal properties with SSTL. Log. Methods Comput. Sci. **14**(4) (2018). https://doi.org/10.23638/LMCS-14(4:2)2018

20. Nenzi, L., Bortolussi, L., Loreti, M.: jSSTL - A Tool to Monitor Spatio-Temporal Properties (2017). https://doi.org/10.4108/eai.25-10-2016.2266978

21. Ofiţeru, I., Bellucci, M., Picioreanu, C., Lavric, V., Curtis, T.: Multi-scale modelling of bioreactor-separator system for wastewater treatment with two-dimensional activated sludge floc dynamics. Water Res. **50**, 382–395 (2013). https://doi.org/10.1016/j.watres.2013.10.053

22. Ruscheinski, A., Wolpers, A., Henning, P., Warnke, T., Haack, F., Uhrmacher, A.: Pragmatic logic-based spatio-temporal pattern checking in particle-based models, pp. 2245–2256 (2020). https://doi.org/10.1109/WSC48552.2020.9383908

23. Sehar, S., Naz, I.: Role of the biofilms in wastewater treatment. In: Dhanasekaran, D., Thajuddin, N. (eds.) Microbial Biofilms, IntechOpen, Rijeka (2016). https://doi.org/10.5772/63499

24. Singh, R., Paul, D., Jain, R.: Biofilms: Implications in bioremediation. Trends Microbiol. **14**, 389–397 (2006). https://doi.org/10.1016/j.tim.2006.07.001

25. Stoodley, P., Wilson, S., Hall-Stoodley, L., Boyle, J.D., Lappin-Scott, H.M., Costerton, J.W.: Growth and detachment of cell clusters from mature mixed-species biofilms. Appl. Environ. Microbiol. **67**(12), 5608–5613 (2001). https://doi.org/10.1128/AEM.67.12.5608-5613.2001

26. Thompson, A.P., et al.: LAMMPS - a flexible simulation tool for particle-based materials modeling at the atomic, Meso, and continuum scales. Comp. Phys. Comm. **271**, 108171 (2022). https://doi.org/10.1016/j.cpc.2021.108171

27. Xia, Y., Jayathilake, P.G., Li, B., Zuliani, P., Chen, J.: CFD-DEM modelling of biofilm streamer oscillations and their cohesive failure in fluid flow. Biotechnol. Bioeng. **118**, 918–929 (2020). https://doi.org/10.1002/bit.27619

A Web-Based Tool for Collaborative Modelling and Analysis in Human-Computer Interaction and Cognitive Science

Antonio Cerone(✉) [ID], Anel Mengdigali, Nuray Nabiyeva, and Temirlan Nurbay

Department of Computer Science, School of Engineering and Digital Sciences, Nazarbayev University, Astana, Kazakhstan
{antonio.cerone,anel.mengdigali,nuray.nabiyeva,temirlan.nurbay}@nu.edu.kz

Abstract. Human-computer interaction and cognitive science are interdisciplinary areas in which computer scientists and mathematicians often work together with social scientists, such as psychologists and sociologists, as well as with more focussed practitioners such as usability experts and system analysts. In order to work effectively, interdisciplinary teams need to agree on a common communication language as a compromise between the computer scientists and mathematicians' formal modelling approach and the conceptual models normally used by social scientists for describing their domain-related theories and frameworks. Moreover, even when proper communication is established within a specific research team, the next challenge is the presentation of the result to a heterogeneous international community, to allow for cross-fertilisation, exchanges of ideas, sharing of models, results and data, work replication and review. This tool paper presents ColMASC, a web-based tool and portal for the collaborative modelling and analysis of human cognition and behaviour as well as interactive systems. ColMASC aim is for researchers in human-computer interaction and cognitive science to freely use the tool provided by the web portal in order to collaborate in the development of models of computer/physical systems as well as human behaviour, run in silico experiments, compare the results of in silico experiments and experiments with human beings, perform simulations, analyse systems consisting of computer/physical components and human components, as well as download and upload datasets and models. Domain oriented modelling and visualisation interfaces ease the modelling and analysis processes by hiding the simulation and formal analysis engines.

Keywords: Tool development · Formal methods · Collaborative research · Human-computer interaction · Cognitive science

Work partly funded by Project SEDS2020004 "Analysis of cognitive properties of interactive systems using model checking", Nazarbayev University, Kazakhstan (Award number: 240919FD3916).

J. Bowles et al. (Eds.): DataMod 2021, LNCS 13268, pp. 175–192, 2022.
https://doi.org/10.1007/978-3-031-16011-0_12

1   Introduction

Research in cognitive science has resulted in the development of a large number of *cognitive architectures* over the last decades [6,11]. Cognitive architectures are based on three different modelling approaches, *symbolic* (or *cognitivist*), such as Soar [7], which are based on a set of predefined general rules to manipulate symbols, *connectionist* (or *emergent*), such as DAC [13], which count on emergent properties of connected processing components (e.g. nodes of a neural network), and *hybrid*, such as CLARION [12], which combine the two previous approaches.

However, the complexity of these cognitive architectures makes it difficult to fully understand their semantics and requires high expertise in programming them. Moreover, Kotseruba and Tsotsos [6] note that most cognitive architectures have been developed for research purposes rather than for real-life usage. They are actually very specialised tools, each of them only usable within focussed research communities and normally capable to address only one of the following categories of application [6]: psychological experiments, robotics, human performance modelling, human-robot interaction, human-computer interaction, natural language processing, categorisation and clustering, computer vision, games and puzzles, and virtual agents. Finally, although cognitive architectures can mimic many aspects of human behaviour and learning, they never really managed to be easily incorporated in the system and software verification process.

In our previous work, we proposed a notation, the *Behaviour and Reasoning Description Language (BRDL)* [1], for describing human behaviour and reasoning. The semantics of the language is based on a basic model of human memory and memory processes and is adaptable to different cognitive theories. This allows us, on the one hand, to keep the syntax of the language to a minimum, thus making it easy to learn and understand and, on the other hand, to use alternative semantic variations to compare alternative theories of memory and cognition. In our previous work we have implemented parts of BRDL [2–4] using the Maude rewrite language and system [8,9]. The automatic translation from BRDL to Maude facilitates modelling, but the results are still the formal textual output from Maude, which is difficult to interpret.

This paper describes ColMASC (Collaborative Modelling and Analysis of Systems and Cognition), a web-based tool and portal[1] that we are developing to address the widespread and heterogenous scientific community that is interested in the modelling and analysis of cognitive systems and interactive systems. The current version of the tool allows researchers to collaborate in modelling systems consisting of cognitive components (cognitive models), which describe human thinking and behaviour, and physical components (system models), which describe computer systems, electronic/mechanical devices, as well as any components without cognition or whose cognition is not relevant to the modelling context (e.g. animals or other humans, whose behaviour is observed or expected to occur in a specific way). Users can perform experiments on an overall model consisting of the composition of a cognitive component and a system component.

---

[1] colmasc.herokuapp.com/.

The tool is structured in terms of projects and enables model reuse within and between projects, thus fostering collaboration. Modelling is based on a linguistic approach [5,10]. The *basic entities* of the model are combined to define syntactic structures that formally describe linguistic phrases. Phrase construction is driven by one of the tool interfaces by allowing the user to appropriately choose and correctly and unambiguously combine the syntactic elements of the phrase. Other interfaces support the guided creation of rules by filling their structural templates with the appropriate entities. Rules are then used to define cognitive and system models. The simulation of an overall model, given by combining a cognitive and a system model, can be carried out in steps and the output may be presented as a global state, as specific component states and even in natural language.

This approach make the tool usable by researchers working in different areas, from social scientists to computer scientists. In fact, the implicit linguistic knowledge of an average user is sufficient for creating meaningful basic entities and use them to create the rules defining the models, while the correctness of the syntax is guaranteed by the tool interfaces. Moreover, the alternative views for the presentation of the simulation results address different categories of users. For example, computer scientists would be interested in seeing the entire global state or just the system state, cognitive scientists would be interested in seeing the cognitive components, and psychologists and other social scientists would be interested in a presentation in natural language.

The paper is structured as follows. Section 2 presents our BRDL-based modelling approach and illustrates it informally using phrases in natural language as elements of the rule templates. Section 3 describes the formal construction of such elements using a linguistic approach. Section 4 describes the tool, the database, the web portal and the project management, using an example to illustrate how simulation is carried out. Finally, Sect. 5 summarises the current implementation of ColMASC and plan and discusses current and future development.

2   The Modelling Approach

In this section, we present our modelling approach in a top-down way, starting from cognitive and system models down to basic and structured entities.

2.1   Cognitive Model

A cognitive model consists of human memory components, in particular *long-term memory* (LTM), which has a virtually unlimited capacity and permanently stores the acquired knowledge, and *short-term memory* (STM), which has a small capacity and temporarily stores the information needed for cognitive processing. STM plays an important role in cognitive processing, since information must be normally transferred to STM in order to be processed. The STM temporary store is often called *Working Memory* (WM) when it is considered together with all its information processing functionalities.

Long-Term Memory (LTM) Model. Any piece of knowledge stored in LTM may be either a *fact*, which we can retrieve and transfer to STM in order to answer *questions* that we are processing in STM, or a rule, which is enabled by information in STM and/or by a perception in the environment and drives human thinking and behaviour. In this section we consider rules, whose definition and usage are already implemented in ColMASC. In Sect. 3.3 we will discuss facts and questions, which can currently be defined by the tool, but whose usage is still under development. ColMASC models LTM using six kinds of BRDL rules, which we call *LTM rules*. Each LTM rule has a general structure

$$g : info_1 \uparrow perc \implies act \downarrow info_2$$

where

- g is a goal
- $perc$ is a perception;
- act is an action;
- $info_1$ information to be removed from STM;
- $info_2$ information to be stored in STM.

Symbol $\uparrow$ suggests removal from STM whereas symbol $\downarrow$ suggests storage in STM. We call *enabling* the part of the rule on the left of $\implies$ and *performing* the part of the rule on the right of $\implies$. Depending on which components are present an LTM rule models distinct cognitive activities as explained below and summarised in Table 1.

Table 1. Structure of LTM rules

Rule	Goal	STM removal	Perception	Action	STM storage
Automatic behaviour	Absent	Only one mandatory		Mandatory	Optional
Deliberate behaviour	Present	Only one mandatory		Mandatory	Optional
Implicit attention	Absent	Optional	Mandatory	Absent	Mandatory
Explicit attention	Present	Optional	Mandatory	Absent	Mandatory
Inference	absent	Mandatory	Absent	Absent	Mandatory
Planning	Present	Mandatory	Absent	Absent	Mandatory

Automatic Behaviour Rule: $info_1 \uparrow perc \implies act \downarrow info_2$

This rule models a basic activity of human automatic behaviour, that is, the performance of an action act as a response to the presence of some information $info_1$ (which is not a goal) in STM and/or a perception $perc$ from the environment, and may result in further information $info_2$, which may be a goal, stored in STM. Only act and one between $info_1$ and $perc$ are necessary, the other rule elements are optional. For example, an adult who is a dog lover, is perceiving a dog close enough to be touched and knows that the dog is friendly, will be automatically driven to perform the action of patting the dog and will know that the dog is happy about it. Using natural language phrases as the BRDL rule elements, we can semi-formally describe this human basic activity as follows:

$$\text{the dog is friendly} \uparrow \text{the dog is close enough}$$
$$\Longrightarrow \text{pat the dog} \downarrow \text{the dog is happy} \qquad (1)$$

Deliberate Behaviour rule: $g : info_1 \uparrow perc \Longrightarrow act \downarrow info_2$

This rule models a basic activity of human deliberate behaviour, that is, the performance of an action act that is also driven by a goal g in STM. For example, a child who is not familiar with dogs and may also be scared by them will not be automatically driven to pat the dog, but may be willing to do so by setting the goal of patting in STM. Using natural language phrases as the BRDL rule elements, we can semi-formally describe this human basic activity as follows:

$$\text{I want to pat the dog: the dog is friendly} \uparrow \text{the dog is close enough}$$
$$\Longrightarrow \text{pat the dog} \downarrow \text{the dog is happy} \qquad (2)$$

Implicit Attention rule: $info_1 \uparrow perc \Longrightarrow \downarrow info_2$

This rule models a basic activity of human implicit attention, that is, the implicit selection of focusing on a specific perception $perc$ from the environment and transfer such a perception to STM by representing it as information $info_2$. Such information may be a direct representation of the perception or include some form of processing. Only $perc$ and $info_2$ are necessary, whereas $info_1$ is optional. For example, an adult who is a dog lover may be focussing on a wagging dog without any explicit will and without any goal. Using natural language phrases as the BRDL rule elements, we can semi-formally describe this human basic activity as follows:

$$\uparrow \text{the dog is wagging} \Longrightarrow \downarrow \text{the dog is wagging} \qquad (3)$$

Some form of implicit processing of the wagging perception could be carried out to directly acquire the knowledge that the dog is friendly:

$$\uparrow \text{the dog is wagging} \Longrightarrow \downarrow \text{the dog is friendly} \qquad (4)$$

It is also possible that the attention is driven by some information $info_1$ already present in STM. For example, the presence of the dog may have been noticed earlier and the information concerning it be already in STM:

$$\text{there is a dog} \uparrow \text{the dog is wagging} \Longrightarrow \downarrow \text{the dog is wagging} \qquad (5)$$

Explicit Attention rule: $g : info_1 \uparrow perc \Longrightarrow \downarrow info_2$

This rule models a basic activity of human explicit attention, that is, the explicit selection, driven by goal g, of focusing on a specific perception $perc$ from the environment. For example, a child who is not familiar with dogs may focus on the dog's behaviour only after setting the intention to pat it as a goal. Using natural language phrases as the BRDL rule elements, we can semi-formally describe this human basic activity as follows:

$$\text{I want to pat the dog:} \uparrow \text{the dog is wagging} \implies \downarrow \text{the dog is wagging} \qquad (6)$$

Inference rule $info_1 \uparrow \implies \downarrow info_2$

This rule models the inference of information $info_2$ from information $info_1$. It is based on logic, which may be deductive logic but also other forms of logic, such as inductive logic and abductive logic. It is pure reasoning independent of possible established goals, so that it can be used in any context. Moreover, neither $info_1$ nor $info_2$ may be a goal. For example, although an adult who sees a dog wagging may automatically internalise this perception by knowing that the dog is friendly, as we have seen in rule 4, a child who knows about dog behaviour but seldom interacts with dogs will need to explicitly apply the learned inference rule that a wagging dog is friendly:

$$\text{the dog is wagging} \uparrow \implies \downarrow \text{the dog is friendly} \qquad (7)$$

Planning rule $g : info_1 \uparrow \implies \downarrow info_2$

This rule models the mental planning defined by information $info_2$, which may be a goal, whereas, obviously, $info_1$ cannot be a goal. The planning is driven by goal g and depends on $info_1$. For example, a child who wants to pat the dog may establish the goal of following the dog if this leaves:

$$\text{I want to pat the dog: the dog leaves} \uparrow \implies \downarrow \text{I want to follow the dog} \qquad (8)$$

Short-Term Memory (STM) Model and Cognitive Processing. STM is modelled as a set of pieces of information. A piece of information may be

- a goal, which may be established initially or be produced by the application of an LTM rule, normally a planning rule;
- an element produced by the application of a LTM rule;
- a fact retrieved from LTM or observed in the environment;
- a question observed in the environment.

The content of STM provides the state of the cognitive model in terms of the information and goals that contribute to enable rules stored in LTM. Normally the initial state is either the empty STM or one or more goals, though some additional information may be added to set the context provided by a previous, non-modelled behaviour. Cognitive processing is carried out in two possible ways:

- by applying an LTM rule whose enabling part matches the content of STM and storing the information or goal from the performing part of the rule (which may be a representation of a perception from the environment) in STM;
- by retrieving, driven by a question in STM, a fact from LTM and storing a copy of it in STM.

The retrieval part is currently under implementation.

2.2   System Model and Interaction

A system that provides an environment for a given human behaviour is modelled as a transition system.

Transition rule $state_1 \xrightarrow{act} state_2$

This rule models the transition from state $state_1$ to state $state_2$ triggered by action act, which is the action performed by the user on the environment (interface, device, human/animal, etc.). The interaction between the human and the system is given through the synchronisation between an LTM rule and a transition rule, which share the same action, and by identifying $state_2$ of the transition rule with a new perception available for the user. For example, a dog who enjoys being patted will not go away

$$\text{the dog is close enough} \xrightarrow{\text{pat the dog}} \text{the dog is close enough} \qquad (9)$$

whereas a dog who does not enjoy being patted will go away

$$\text{the dog is close enough} \xrightarrow{\text{pat the dog}} \text{the dog is far away} \qquad (10)$$

Either transition rules may synchronise with one of the LTM rules 1 (automatic behaviour) or 2 (deliberate behaviour). Autonomous system behaviour with no interaction is also possible. In such a case, there is no action in the transition. For example, the dog may autonomously decide to go away:

$$\text{the dog is close enough} \longrightarrow \text{the dog is far away} \qquad (11)$$

Autonomous behaviour can be observed by the user in terms of the target state ('far away' in LTM rule 11).

3   The Linguistic Approach

In Sect. 2 we have focussed on our modelling approach and used informal phrases as elements of LTM rules and transition rules. This allowed us to illustrate the modelling approach in a simple, understandable way. However, in order to allow cognitive and system models to be executable and be able to synchronise, it is necessary to structure the LTM rule and transition rule elements and associate them with semantics.

To this purpose, we exploit BRDL flexibility and extensibility and we use a linguistic approach to define the building blocks of our models, starting from *basic entities*, which are basically names associated with (linguistic) syntactic categories. Based on Chomsky's concept of *universal grammar* [5], we then combine basic entities using *deep structure* to produce *phrases* [10]. The resultant *structured entities* are then equipped with semantics that becomes operational when such *semantic entities* are used as components of *dynamic entities*, which are the rules, facts and questions we introduced in Sect. 2. Models are basically sets of dynamic entities. The semantics embedded in the dynamic entities is reflected in the Java functions that define the simulation engine and, in future versions of the tool will be also reflected in the Maude rewrite rules that will define the analysis engine.

3.1   Basic Entities

A *basic entity* consists of three components:

name chosen by the user to provide a concise but meaningful characterisation of the entity linguistic and semantic role in modelling;

kind which characterises the entity syntactic role as a word;

definition a string of characters that is not as general as a dictionary definition but is specific to the abstraction level of the system under analysis and to the world of entities considered.

We can denote basic entities by their names. The *kind* of a basic entity may be one of the following:

Noun such as *child*, *lover* and *dog*;
Verb such as *leave*, *pat*;
Participle such as *wagging* (present participle) and *inserted* (past participle);
Adjective such as *friendly*, *happy* and *close*;
Adverb such as *enough*, *fast* and *slow*;
Auxiliary such as *can*, *has* and *is*;
Preposition such as *to*, *from*, *in*, *at* and *on*.

3.2   Structured Entities

A *structured entity* consists of the same type of components as a basic entity. However,

name may be structured and its purpose is to be used as an element in rule, fact and question definitions.

kind characterises the entity syntactic role as a phrase;

Structured entities are recursively defined on basic entities as follows:

- Any basic entity whose kind k is not Auxiliary or Preposition is a structured entity with kind k Phrase.
- Given a structured entity whose name is h and whose kind is k Phrase and a structured entity whose name is a and whose kind is compatible with k according to Table 2, we define a new structured entity with name $h(a)$, kind k Phrase and a new description that characterises $h(a)$

Table 2. Possible argument kinds for each kind of head in structured entitites

Head Kind	Possible Phrase Kinds as Argument
Noun	Noun, Participle, Adjective, Preposition
Verb	Noun, Participle, Adverb, Preposition
Participle	Noun, Adverb, Preposition
Adjective	Noun, Adjective, Adverb, Preposition
Adverbs	Adverb
Auxiliary	Noun, Verb, Adjective, Preposition
Preposition	Noun

Therefore the name $h(s)$ of a structured entity consists of a part h called *head* and a possible part s called *argument*. It follows from the definition that the argument is mandatory when the head is the name of a basic entity of kind Auxiliary or Preposition, it is optional otherwise.

We can denote structured entities by their names. A structured entity may be of one of the following *kinds*:

Noun Phrase such as *child, lover, lover(dog)*, dog(friendly), child (running), child(at(school));

Verb Phrase such as *leave, pat(dog), go(shopping), drive(fast),* *go(to(school))*;

Participle Phrase such as *wagging, inserted(bankcard), inserted(completely), coming(from(school))*;

Adjective Phrase such as *happy, slow(car), high(fat)), close(enough)* *(dog), happy(at(school))*));

Adverb Phrase such as *enough, slowly(enough), enough(slowly)*;

Auxiliary Phrase such as *has(legs), can(move), is(black), is(on(table))*;

Preposition Phrase such as *in(box), on(table)*.

3.3   Semantic and Dynamic Entities

A *positive declarative semantic entity* is a structured entity with the additional component:

semantics which characterises the set of its possible semantic roles.

Table 3 maps the kind of a semantic entity to its possible semantics.

Table 3. Possible semantics for each kind of semantic entity

Kind	Possible Semantics
Noun Phrase	Identifier, State, Information, Goal
Verb Phrase	Action, Goal
Participle Phrase	State, Information, Goal
Adjective Phrase	State, Information, Goal
Adverbs Phrase	State, Information, Goal
Auxiliary Phrase	Fact, Question, Goal
Preposition Phrase	State, Information, Goal

Any positive declarative semantic entity e may be turned into a *negative declarative semantic entity* by changing its name to $not(e)$. Any positive or negative declarative semantic entity e may be turned respectively into a *positive* or *negative interrogative semantic entity* by changing its name to $?(e)$. Any positive or negative declarative semantic entity e may be turned respectively into a *goal* by changing its name to $goal(e)$. Note that the application of $goal$, not or $?$ does not change the kind of the semantic entity. Therefore, we can now formally define STM as a set of semantic entities.

As an example of semantic entity consider the phrase "the dog is close enough" from LTM rule 1 in Sect. 2.1. The most important part in the context of the rule is "close enough". In fact, regardless of whether the animal is a cat or a dog, the human can only pat it if the animal is close enough. Therefore, $close(enough)$ must be the head of the semantic entity and the phrase is formalised as $close(enough)(dog)$. This is a correct formalisation because, according to the compatibility in Table 2, Adjective *close* as head can have Adjective *enough* as an argument and Adjective Phrase $close(enough)$ as head can have Noun *dog* as an argument.

A *dynamic entity* is of one of the following three kinds:

> **fact** which is a (positive or negative) declarative semantic entity;
> **question** which is a (positive or negative) interrogative semantic entity;
> **activity** which is the instantiation of a rule with names of semantic entities.

The instantiation of the rules should match the following instantiation for the semantics of the rule elements:

> **LTM rules** Information $\uparrow$ State $\Longrightarrow$ Action $\downarrow$ Information
> **transition rules** State $\xrightarrow{\text{Action}}$ State

As an example, State is one possible semantics for an Adjective Phrase, as shown in Table 3. Thus Adjective Phrase $close(enough)(dog)$ can instantiate the State element of a cognitive rule, as in the formalisation below of rule 1 from Sect. 2.1. In fact, rules 1–8 from Sect. 2.1 can be rewritten as dynamic entities (activities) as follows:

1. friendly(dog) ↑ close(enough)(dog) ⟹ pat(dog) ↓ happy(dog)
2. goal(pat(dog)): friendly(dog) ↑ close(enough)(dog) ⟹ pat(dog) ↓ happy(dog)
3. ↑ wagging(dog) ⟹ ↓ wagging(dog)
4. ↑ wagging(dog) ⟹ ↓ friendly(dog)
5. present(dog) ↑ wagging(dog) ⟹ ↓ wagging(dog)
6. goal(pat(dog)): ↑wagging(dog) ⟹ ↓ wagging(dog)
7. wagging(dog) ↑ ⟹ ↓ friendly(dog)
8. goal(pat(dog)): dog(left) ↑ ⟹ ↓ goal(follow(dog))

Our notation is obviously not as expressive as natural languages. In fact, as
shown in Table 3, its aim is to express, in a meaningful, unambiguous way:
names of components (Identifier), system states (State), information in STM
(Information) including goals (Goal), actions performed by the human (Action),
facts that are part of the human knowledge or are perceived and possibly learned
by the human (Fact) and questions that are perceived from the environment or
internally elaborated through self-reflection (Question).

The fact "A dog is an animal" is formally modelled as

– $is(dog)(animal)$

Its negation is

– $not(is(dog)(animal))$

and the corresponding questions are

– $?(is(dog)(animal))$
– $?(not(is(dog)(animal)))$

4   Tool and Web Portal

A high-level visual description of the ColMASC tool and web portal is provided
in Fig. 1. The thick boxes with names in bold represent components already
developed and included in the current release (Version 1.0). The other components are still under development.

The purpose of ColMASC is to allow an interdisciplinary community of scientists and practitioners to model cognitive and interactive systems, share their
models and collaborate with each other, both within the modelling process itself
and by providing feedback and reviews. The ColMASC modelling approach aims
at addressing the knowledge domain of a variety of modellers, including computer
scientists, interaction designers, usability analysts, cognitive scientists, psychologists and linguists. The current version features a Java-based engine, which is
described in Sect. 4.1. A Maude-based Analysis Engine is currently under development.

4.1   Java-based Simulation Engine

Purpose of the Java-based engine is to provide system simulation and presentation of the results. This simulation engine has been integrated into the server-side, which is a Spring Boot project using Java 11 and the Maven framework.

Since an overall system produces, in general, a non-deterministic behaviour, it could be possible to run the simulation in several modes, depending on how non-determinism is resolved. In the current implementation, choices are deterministically made by the simulation engine, consistently with the way simulation is carried out in the Maude system. The user can choose, instead,

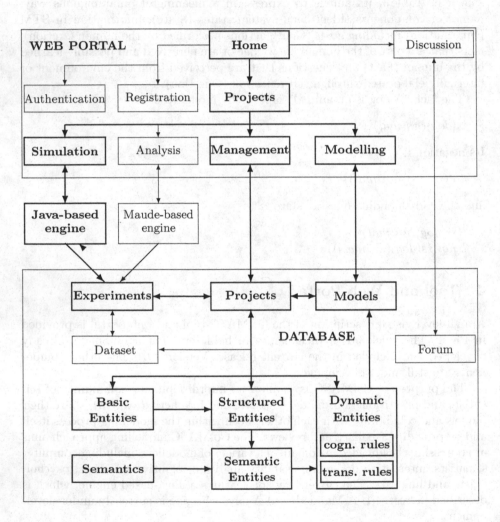

Fig. 1. High-level description of the tool architecture

- either a *stepwise* simulation, in which the system state is presented after each rule application and the user may move forward and backward through the steps,
- or an *all steps* simulation, which shows all steps in one screen.

Furthermore, the user may select which of the following information to include in the presentations:

System State which only presents applied transition rules and resultant system states;

STM Content which only presents applied LTM rules and resultant STM contents;

Natural Language which use natural language to informally describe the application of the rules and their effects.

Two further simulation modes are currently under development:

- making the choices *randomly*
- making the choices *interactively* (stepwise simulation only), whereby the user resolves non-determinism.

Finally, the storage of the results of the simulation in the CoIMASC database is also under development.

As an example of simulation, consider the following cognitive model *Child* of a child who is willing to pat a dog, but has not developed any automatic behaviour for this task. This may be modelled by the following LTM rules

1. $goal(pat(dog)): \uparrow wagging(dog) \implies \downarrow wagging(dog)$
2. $goal(pat(dog)): wagging(dog) \uparrow \implies \downarrow friendly(dog)$
3. $goal(pat(dog)): friendly(dog) \uparrow far(dog) \implies approach(dog) \downarrow friendly(dog)$
4. $goal(pat(dog)): friendly(dog) \uparrow close(enough)(dog) \implies pat(dog) \downarrow happy(dog)$

The dog is actually the 'system' and may be modelled by the cognitive model *Dog* consisting of the following transition rules:

1. $far(dog) \xrightarrow{approach(dog)} close(enough)(dog)$
2. $close(enough)(dog) \longrightarrow far(dog)$
3. $sleepy(dog) \longrightarrow wagging(dog)$
4. $wagging(dog) \longrightarrow sleepy(dog)$
5. $sleepy(dog) \xrightarrow{pat(dog)} wagging(dog)$
6. $wagging(dog) \xrightarrow{pat(dog)} wagging(dog)$

Note that the dog is modelled from the human perspective. Transition rule 1 of *Dog* models that if the dog is far from the child, the child can approach it and the dog will be close enough to the child (in order to be patted). Transition rule 2 of *Dog* models that if the dog is close enough to the child (in order to be patted), the dog may autonomously decide to get far away from the child.

If the goal $goal(pat(dog))$ is the initial STM content and $far(dog)$ and $sleepy(dog)$ make up the initial system state, none of the LTM rules 1–4 of

Child is enabled. Only transition rule 3 of *Dog* is enabled and its occurrence changes the system state to *far*(*dog*) and *wagging*(*dog*). Note that, although the 'system dog' may be approached when the system state contains *far*(*dog*) (transition rule 1 of *Dog*), the cognitive model *Child* enables approaching only after the dog has been assessed as friendly (LTM rule 3 of *Child*).

Once the system state has been changed to *far*(*dog*) and *wagging*(*dog*) there is a non-deterministic choice between the autonomous transition rule 4, which sets the dog back in a sleepy state, and the human explicit attention modelled by LTM rule 1, which may only be followed by the human inference modelled by LTM rule 2 (assuming that the dog is not getting sleepy). If the non-determinism is resolved by applying LTM rules 1 and 2 in sequence, *friendly*(*dog*) is added to the goal in STM (*wagging*(*dog*) is added by LTM rule 1 and then removed by LTM rule 2) while the system state is unchanged.

Now LTM rule 2 can synchronize with transition rule 1 and the system state changes to *close*(*enough*)(*dog*) and *wagging*(*dog*) while STM is unchanged. Figure 2 shows a screenshot of the presentation of this step in ColMASC. This presentation includes the applied LTM rule and/or transition rule, the natural language description and the formal description of STM content and system state. Note that in the step in Fig. 2 the dog is wagging, but LTM rule 3 is not dependent on this and can be applied also if the dog is no longer wagging and is sleepy instead.

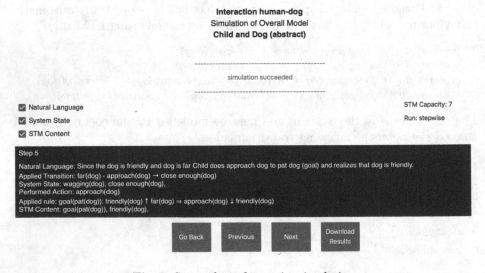

Fig. 2. Screenshot of stepwise simulation

Finally, LTM rule 4 can be applied, again independently on whether the dog is wagging or sleepy, establishing the knowledge that the dog is currently happy (*friendly*(*dog*) is replaced by *happy*(*dog*) in STM). However, the synchronisation of LTM rule 4 is with transition rule 5, if the dog is wagging, or with transition rule 6, if the dog is sleepy. But in both cases the dog will be wagging after being patted.

4.2   Database, Web Portal and Project Management

All defined entities and models are collected in a shared relational database. We have chosen PostgreSQL as the database management system for its power, high flexibility, and support for a wide range of data types and functions. The database is accessed with REST-controllers. The back-end, developed with Java 11 on Spring Boot, acts as middleware between the REST client and the database in order to validate the client input and format the output for presentation.

The portal allows researchers to access the database, create new entities and models as well as reuse existing entities and reuse and expand existing models, and use them to run experiments. We are currently developing a discussion forum which will support not just messaging and providing feedback, but also proposing features and reviewing models.

The current version of the *Projects* page is illustrated in Fig. 3. Each project is represented by a card showing title, development stage, an illustrative picture and a brief textual description. The card links to the *Specific Project Page*.

Projects are categorised according to their development stages, inspired by the development stages normally used for open source software products:

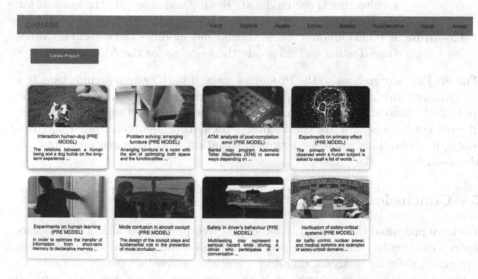

Fig. 3. Project main page

Pre-model It is a planning stage and comprises a description but no models, although models may be under construction at this stage.

Pre-alpha This stage is entered when at least one model is created. During this phase some tentative overall models may also be created and tested. Models are mostly unstable and subject to frequent changes. In general, models are tested using simple experiments and toy case studies.

Alpha Some models have reached a significant maturity level and may be used in real-world case studies with real datasets. The system architecture may still be changed and details and functionalities are added incrementally.

Beta The system architecture is now stable and includes all major functionalities. Most models are extensively used in real-world case studies with real datasets. The results of in silico experiments and simulations are compared with the results of real-world experiments and the outcome is used to calibrate component models and/or the overall model.

Stable All models are stable and can be now used as research tools to analyse cognitive science theories and to carry out system simulation.

Re-beta Stable overall models are reworked by changing the component models or starting the development or new models. The system architecture is not modified. Testing and usage are the same as for the Beta stage.

Re-alpha It builds up on a stable version but modifies the system architecture. Testing and usage are the same as for the Alpha stage.

The project may go back to the Pre-alpha stage if both system architecture and component models are heavily changed. Development stages are more dynamic and fluid than in software development. It is expected that for a number of projects their stages are continuously 'oscillating' between Stable and Re-alpha/Re-beta. This would be a typical situation when research outcomes are the main goals of the project.

5   Conclusion and Future Work

We have presented ColMASC 1.0, a tool and web portal that allows various categories of scientists and practitioners, including computer scientists, interaction designers, usability analysts, cognitive scientists, psychologists and linguists, to carry out collaborative research in human-computer interaction and cognitive science. Collaboration involves both the modelling process itself and testing and review activities. With the current version of the tool, cognitive scientists and psychologists may carry out in silico simulations to mimic and accelerate experiments with human subjects, aiming at testing theories in cognitive psychology, and computer scientists and usability experts may automatically generate formal models of computer interfaces and simulate their interaction with a human component. In fact, ColMASC 1.0 supports the composition of a cognitive model and a system model, and the untimed simulation of the resultant overall model. Additional features are currently under development:

- storage of the results of experiments as well as external datasets in the database and analytical features to compare results;
- extension of the simulation engine to fact retrieval from LTM and their processing aiming to both self-reflection and answering questions;
- development of an analysis engine by defining a translation to Maude and exploiting the Maude model-checking capabilities;
- development of a time extensions of the simulation and analysis engines.

These additional features will support cognitive scientists and psychologists in the modelling of long-term learning processes, linguists in performing in silico experiments to emulate human processing of texts and language learning processes and computer scientists in the formal verification of interactive systems. The tool is currently undergoing empirical evaluation with potential users from both the computer science and the cognitive science sides.

The current version of the tool features the automatic translation of the experiment outcomes into natural language. As part of our future work we aim at having various customised natural language translation that address the different domain expertises of users. We also will explore the possibility of considering task descriptions in natural language from which to extract structured entity definitions and infer their semantics, and then recombine these two kinds of information to build semantic and dynamic entities.

The Maude-based analysis engine will make use of Real-Time Maude [8,9], the real-time extension of Maude. The analysis engine will build on our previous work [2–4]. The Maude code will run in parallel to the backend code on a Linux virtual machine. In this way the web application will have access to the Maude system through bash scripts to ensure consistency of simulation results.

Although our web-based tool addresses research collaboration in human-computer interaction and cognitive science, the same approach may be used in other application domains. Other possible application domains are coordination model, socio-technical system, systems biology and ecology.

References

1. Cerone, A.: Behaviour and Reasoning Description Language (BRDL). In: Camara, J., Steffen, M. (eds.) SEFM 2019. LNCS, vol. 12226, pp. 137–153. Springer, Cham (2020). https://doi.org/10.1007/978-3-030-57506-9_11
2. Cerone, A., Murzagaliyeva, D.: Information retrieval from semantic memory: BRDL-based knowledge representation and Maude-based computer emulation. In: Cleophas, L., Massink, M. (eds.) SEFM 2020. LNCS, vol. 12524, pp. 159–175. Springer, Cham (2021). https://doi.org/10.1007/978-3-030-67220-1_13
3. Cerone, A., Ölveczky, P.C.: Modelling human reasoning in practical behavioural contexts using Real-Time Maude. In: Sekerinski, E., et al. (eds.) FM 2019. LNCS, vol. 12232, pp. 424–442. Springer, Cham (2020). https://doi.org/10.1007/978-3-030-54994-7_32

4. Cerone, A., Pluck, G.: A formal model for emulating the generation of human knowledge in semantic memory. In: Bowles, J., Broccia, G., Nanni, M. (eds.) Data-Mod 2020. LNCS, vol. 12611, pp. 104–122. Springer, Cham (2021). https://doi.org/10.1007/978-3-030-70650-0_7

5. Chomsky, N.: Language and Mind. Cambridge University Press, Cambridge (2006)

6. Kotseruba, I., Tsotsos, J.K.: 40 years of cognitive architectures: core cognitive abilities and practical applications. Artif. Intell. Rev. **53**(1), 17–94 (2018). https://doi.org/10.1007/s10462-018-9646-y

7. Laird, J.A.: The Soar Cognitive Architecture. MIT Press, Cambridge (2012)

8. Ölveczky, P.C.: Real-Time Maude and its applications. In: Escobar, S. (ed.) WRLA 2014. LNCS, vol. 8663, pp. 42–79. Springer, Cham (2014). https://doi.org/10.1007/978-3-319-12904-4_3

9. Ölveczky, P.C.: Designing Reliable Distributed Systems. UTCS, Springer, London (2017). https://doi.org/10.1007/978-1-4471-6687-0

10. Pinker, S.: The Language Instinct. William Morrow, New York (1994)

11. Samsonovich, A.V.: Towards a unified catalog of implemented cognitive architectures. In: Biologically Inspired Cognitive Architectures (BICA 2010), pp. 195–244. IOS Press (2010)

12. Sun, R., Slusarz, P., Terry, C.: The interaction of the explicit and implicit in skill learning: a dual-process approach. Psychol. Rev. **112**, 159–192 (2005)

13. Verschure, P.: Distributed adaptive control: a theory of the mind, brain, body nexus. Biol. Inspir. Cogn. Architect. **1**, 55–72 (2012)

Author Index

Printed in the United States
by Baker & Taylor Publisher Services

Printed in the United States
by Baker & Taylor Publisher Services